100 THINGS
STARS FANS
SHOULD KNOW & DO
BEFORE THEY DIE

100 THINGS STARS FANS SHOULD KNOW & DO BEFORE THEY DIE

Sean Shapiro

TRIUMPH
BOOKS

Library of Congress Cataloging-in-Publication Data

Names: Shapiro, Sean author.
Title: 100 things Stars fans should know & do before they die / Sean Shapiro.
Other titles: One hundred things Dallas Stars fans should know and do before they die | Hundred things Dallas Stars fans should know and do before they die
Description: Chicago, Illinois : Triumph Books LLC, [2018]
Identifiers: LCCN 2018012538 | ISBN 9781629375182
Subjects: LCSH: Dallas Stars (Hockey team)—History. | Minnesota North Stars (Hockey team)—History. | Dallas Stars (Hockey team)—Miscellanea. | Minnesota North Stars (Hockey team)—Miscellanea. | Hockey—Texas—Dallas—History. | Hockey—Minnesota—Minneapolis—History. | National Hockey League—History.
Classification: LCC GV848.D35 S53 2018 | DDC 796.9609764/2812—dc23 LC record available at https://lccn.loc.gov/2018012538

This book is available in quantity at special discounts for your group or organization. For further information, contact:
Triumph Books LLC
814 North Franklin Street
Chicago, Illinois 60610
(312) 337-0747
www.triumphbooks.com

Printed in U.S.A.
ISBN: 978-1-62937-518-2
Design by Patricia Frey
Photos courtesy of AP Images

For my wife, Christina, and daughter, Evangeline

Contents

Foreword *by Mike Modano* xi

1 Stars Win the Stanley Cup. 1

2 Stars Move to Dallas 2

3 Mike Modano 6

4 The Zubov Trade 13

5 Hitch. 17

6 Jere Lehtinen 24

7 Sergei Zubov 27

8 Jamie Benn 30

9 Bob Gainey 31

10 Why the Stars?. 33

11 Derian Hatcher 35

12 Ed Belfour. 36

13 Brett Hull 41

14 The Greatest American Scorer. 42

15 Drafting Jamie Benn 44

16 Art Ross Winner 47

17 The Seguin Trade 50

18 Marty Turco 52

19 Game 6 of the 1999 Stanley Cup Finals 57

20 Game 7 of the 1999 Western Conference Finals. 60

21 Game 5 of the 1999 Stanley Cup Finals 62

22 Why "No Goal" Counted 64

23 Joe Nieuwendyk 65

24 Brenden Morrow. 67

25 Stars' First Game in Texas. 68

26 Hullenium. 70

27 Modano, Lehtinen, and Turco Say Good-Bye. 71

28 2000 Stanley Cup Finals. 74

29 Roger Staubach. 77

30 Neal Broten. 78

31 Bill Masterton. 81

32 Bill Goldsworthy. 85

33 Iginla for Nieuwendyk. 88

34 Tyler Seguin. 91

35 Jim Nill. 92

36 Peverley Lives. 99

37 The "Turco Grip". 102

38 Strader Strong. 105

39 Craig Ludwig. 109

40 Pantera. 116

41 Shane Churla. 117

42 Guy Carbonneau. 120

43 Hockey Players Want to Come to Texas. 125

44 Dino Ciccarelli. 127

45 The Tent. 128

46 Hartsburg, Klingberg, and Hips. 130

47 Cinco de Morrow. 132

48 District 5. 136

49 Ralph and Razor. 138

50 Hockey History in Dallas. 139

51 Do the Stars Have a Rival?. 141

52 Dallas Stars All-Time Lineup 144

53 Minnesota North Stars All-Time Lineup. 146

54 The Frank Selke Trophy. 149

55 Video Clips and Rock Music. 151

56 Marketing Hockey to Texans 153

57 "Norm Greed" 155

58 Tom Hicks Saved the Stars. 156

59 Tom Gaglardi 159

60 Mr. Big Shot. 161

61 Richard Matvichuk 164

62 Darryl Sydor 165

63 Benn vs. Iginla. 167

64 Reunion Arena 170

65 Jokinen Masters the Shootout. 171

66 Youngest Captain in NHL History. 174

67 "Ambassador of Fun" in the GM Chair 176

68 Red, White, and Blue?. 178

69 Watch Practice 180

70 Les Jackson 180

71 1991 Stanley Cup Finals 186

72 1981 Stanley Cup Finals 190

73 2007 NHL All-Star Game. 193

74 Trevor Daley. 199

75 Kari Lehtonen. 200

76 "Never Leave a Hockey Game". 202

77 Growing the Game 204

78 The Stretcher Drop. 205

79 Barons and Golden Seals. 206

80 Fabian Brunnstrom. 209

81 The Texas Stars. 210

82 Drink Modano's Beer 213

83 Fight Night. 215

84 Mark Parrish Hat Trick 217

85 Boucher Plays Big for Parents 218

86 Stefan's Slipup. 221

87 Gagner Gets Caught in the Snow 223

88 Lucky Lotto. 224

89 The Wrong Lundqvist. 227

90 Visit the Hockey Hall of Fame 229

91 Jordie Benn. 230

92 15 Goals in One Game. 233

93 The 2016 Hall of Fame Class 235

94 Guy Lafleur Was a North Star?. 238

95 Modano in Detroit 240

96 Jagr Comes to Dallas. 241

97 The Idaho Steelheads 244

98 North Stars End Flyers Streak. 246

99 One-Game Wonders. 247

100 The Mooterus. 252

Acknowledgments 255

Sources 257

Foreword

Before we moved to Dallas, I think we were all frustrated about moving the Minnesota North Stars to Texas. It was a frustrating time, and I think we all felt—and others across the country probably felt—that hockey in Minnesota is like football in Texas or anything else that belongs to an area. It's their religion or livelihood and to not have a pro team anymore...we were quite shocked, to say the least, about moving.

Minnesota felt like home, and I had some great years there. But then we moved to Dallas, and *it* started to feel like home. It didn't take very long, it was much quicker than I thought. Once I got down there, I realized what we could do. We went down to Dallas with clean heads and we saw the opportunity to grow our sport in a new home.

It was a clean slate, and we could see how it could happen, and the excitement started to build. Slowly at first, but then the fans really took it and ran with it. Their turnout was great. They really surprised us right away, and it slowly built from there. It turned into a really exciting place to play, and I'd say halfway through my first year in Dallas I found myself saying this was gonna be home for me for a long time.

People in Dallas have always been great sports fans, but they quickly became great hockey fans. We had to explain the knowledge of the game and the strategy that they didn't understand at first, but they started to really get it and become one of the best fanbases in the NHL.

We had some great memories and great teams in my time in Dallas. Personally, I had a lot of success, and we were winners and we brought a championship to Dallas in 1999. That meant a lot. To be in one place for so long and to win in that spot, that's something that's really special, and it's hard to explain. And I really think the fans had a lot to do with that. When we were in the championship run, Reunion Arena was one of the toughest places to play for people across the league. It really was a home-ice advantage and it's because of those fans who embraced us right away.

I never thought I'd spend so much time with one organization, but it ended up being really special closer to the end of my career. I didn't really think about it until my last two or three years with the Stars that I could play 20-plus seasons with one team and be in a category of guys, a very small handful, that has done the same in the NHL. That became a sense of pride for me, and I wanted to see how far we could take hockey in Texas.

Sean Shapiro has done his best to capture the history and stories of the franchise, including the highlights during my career and the moments both before and after I played for the North Stars and Stars. I'm very proud of my time with the Stars and what it meant to watch hockey grow, to be part of a winning franchise, and to be embraced by a fanbase in Dallas. Without the fans, none of this is possible, and this book helps capture some of those memories with the great people of Dallas.

—Mike Modano

1 Stars Win the Stanley Cup

It's a tie game, 1–1 in triple overtime.

The Dallas Stars have a 3–2 series lead on the Buffalo Sabres. The next goal either clinches the Stanley Cup or forces a decisive Game 7 back in Texas.

With 5:37 left in the third overtime, the Sabres won a clean faceoff in the neutral zone, but a pass to Miroslav Satan is intercepted by Brett Hull, who makes a pass to Jere Lehtinen as the Stars enter the zone.

It's been a long game, Lehtinen has already played more than 40 minutes, and is a step behind the pass, but still tracks it down on a forecheck, and the puck finds its way to Mike Modano. Modano can't control the puck, and as it skitters toward the Sabres net, Buffalo goalie Dominik Hasek spikes it toward the boards with a poke check.

Shawn Chambers keeps it at the boards and rims the puck around behind the net. Hull finds the puck in the left corner and leaves a backhand for Modano, who shakes off a check and leaves the puck for Lehtinen.

Lehtinen, who scored the only Stars goal so far in this game, hours ago, wins the battle for the puck and takes a sharp angle shot from above the faceoff dot.

Hasek makes the first save on a tip from Hull but can't control the rebound. It's sitting by Hull's left foot, and he kicks the puck to his blade and fires. "Stars just by Hull. Shot, Jere Lehtinen. Hull, loose puck. Hull shoots, scores! Scores! Scores! The Dallas Stars, Brett Hull, they've won the Stanley Cup! Deep in the heart of Texas the Stars are shining!"

Stars Move to Dallas

On March 10, 1993, Norm Green stood in the Dallas City Council chambers and announced he'd be bringing his NHL team to Texas.

It was a move that had been rumored for months, but it wasn't until that day and after final documents were reviewed by the city, that the Minnesota North Stars officially became the Dallas Stars.

While Texas had been home to hockey teams before and the NHL was expanding its sunbelt footprint the following season—introducing new expansion teams in California and Florida that would start play during the 1993-94 season—it was a bit of a head-scratching move.

The NHL in Texas? If it didn't work in Minnesota, the "State of Hockey" how could a team succeed in Dallas?

First you have to understand how things unraveled in Minnesota.

In the late 1980s, the North Stars were struggling financially. The North Stars' home at the time, the Met Center, was old and lacked modern conveniences that were generating profit. Suites weren't added to the Met Center until 1988, and the ownership group at the time, the Gund Brothers, wanted 45 more added at a cost of $15 million to their landlord: the Metropolitan Sports Facilities Commission. The proposal was voted down.

At the same time, the team was going through a bit of a public relations fiasco. Fans weren't happy when Herb Brooks, a Minnesota legend and the coach that led the Americans to the gold medal in the 1980 Winter Olympics, was fired. Trading away Bobby Smith didn't help either.

At the same time, the corporate support had dried up. When the North Stars first entered the NHL, they were neighbors with the Minnesota Vikings and Minnesota Twins in Bloomington.

Eventually, the Vikings and Twins moved to Minneapolis, taking much of the corporate sponsors and business with them.

By 1990 the Gunds, citing losses of more than $16 million, wanted to move the team to California. "Minnesota does not want the North Stars," Gordon Gund said at the time. "The only way you'll get Minnesota to want it is to let us leave. Then maybe two years later, they'll want an expansion franchise."

The Gunds put the team up for sale, but wouldn't sell for anything less than $50 million. It was a power play to dissuade any local investor from buying the team, which would clear the path for a move to the West Coast.

At the same time, Hollywood movie producer Howard Baldwin (well-known for *Mystery, Alaska*) was interested in applying for an expansion team in San Jose, California. The Gunds had San Francisco on their radar for relocation. Under league rules, NHL territorial rights were within a 50-mile radius, so there couldn't be a team in both San Francisco and San Jose.

The NHL was worried that allowing the Gunds to move their team would derail expansion plans. However, not approving the move could draw the league into a lengthy legal battle.

This is where Norm Green came into play, and actually saved the North Stars three years before he ultimately moved them. Green was a part owner of the Calgary Flames and suggested that the Gunds sell to a group run by Baldwin and Budget Rent-A-Car CEO Morris Belzberg, while the NHL would then grant an expansion franchise in San Jose to the Gunds.

That opened negotiations, and the Gunds almost got away with a laughable deal. The Baldwin-Belzberg group agreed to buy the team for $31 million but only have its players for one year. After one season the new expansion franchise would acquire all of the North Stars players—including those on minor league contracts—and the NHL Entry Draft picks for 1990 and 1991.

3

The NHL board of governors wouldn't approve the deal, and eventually an agreement was worked out where the new San Jose franchise would get to claim some of the North Stars players.

A deal was in place, but the Baldwin-Belzberg group struggled to come up with the money to finish the sale. Green stepped up to the plate, sold his ownership stake in the Flames, and bought a 51 percent controlling stake of the team. Not long after the initial sale, Green bought out both Baldwin and Belzberg for full control.

Green thought his past success and experience in Calgary would help him rekindle fan support in Minnesota. He worked to renovate the Met Center, which was a battle every step of the way, and the team made a run to the Stanley Cup Finals in 1991.

Even with those efforts fans weren't showing up and attendance was frequently below 60 percent capacity. "We were probably two or three thousand shy of capacity most of the time," North Stars center Dave Gagner later remembered in the book *Frozen in Time: A Minnesota North Stars History.* "It wasn't a huge rink. One thing that really bothered us as players was that the year after we went to the Finals, we only had 8,000 or 9,000 for opening night the next season. Opening night is usually a big kickoff when tickets sell out pretty fast. After the playoff run we had the year before, we were all really shocked at that. That was probably the day Norm Green said, 'I'm taking this team out of here.'"

Gagner wasn't far off.

Three months later, in December of 1992, the board of governors granted Green permission to move the team within a year. Green hadn't ruled out staying in Minnesota, but stated he would need a commitment from the community for 10,000 season tickets.

Green also considered moving into Minneapolis' Target Center, home of the NBA's Minnesota Timberwolves. That option was stalled when it would have required public money to bail out an NHL team, an NBA team, and an arena.

By midseason, Green announced the Minnesota-based options weren't sufficient and he would move the team. After being asked by the NHL not to move to California, he set his sights on Dallas and with the help of former Dallas Cowboys quarterback Roger Staubach, the wheels were put in motion.

By March, the team was officially moving to Dallas.

While he had ran into logistical issues every step of the way in Minnesota, Green was greeted with open arms in Dallas.

Dallas mayor Steve Bartlett was a big advocate of the move, and promised Green a new building would be built sooner than later. Through a mutual friend, former NFL star and commentator Frank Gifford, Green was introduced to Dallas Cowboys owner Jerry Jones.

Green said that the conversations with Jones gave him comfort that he'd chosen the right city. He also knew that Dallas loved a winner; with recent playoff success in Minnesota, the Stars were setup to succeed right away.

Green looked back fondly on the move and its impact in February 2016, when he wrote the following for *D Magazine*. "In 1993, there was only one poor sheet of ice at Valley Ranch. Now there are almost 30 in the area with tens of thousands of young people playing hockey and participating in skating programs. I look back with incredible pride at the decision to bring the NHL to Dallas."

3 Mike Modano

Mike Modano played 1,459 games in 20 seasons with the Minnesota North Stars and Dallas Stars. His 557 goals, 802 assists, and 1,359 points are franchise records that may never be broken and his iconic No. 9 hangs in the rafters at American Airlines Center. Modano looked back on his career with the franchise in an interview for this book in May of 2017:

Q: What do you remember about the move from Minnesota to Texas?
A: For a majority of the guys, I remember a lot of hesitation. We were going from what we thought was a cornerstone of hockey in the U.S., Minnesota, to Texas. A place where it hadn't been really well-received, there were a few minor league teams down there at the time. But ultimately moving a professional hockey franchise out of Minnesota, we thought it was like moving the Yankees out of New York or the Cowboys out of Dallas. We never figured it would work; we were kind of surprised and shocked about the location. Obviously, things changed for the better, but even for the initial first four or five years, there was a lot of transition, a lot of educational teaching going on about the game and trying to create a new fanbase. I think the first reaction from us was when we heard it of all places, was how did it become Dallas?

Q: So how long did it take to feel like home?
A: Not as long as I thought it would. For me, once I got there, it was kind of quick. I think I kind of loved the hospitality down there; I loved the southern mentality, I loved the location of it, I

love the way Texas people are. So I felt comfortable right off the start.

For my career it felt like a clean slate and a chance to start new. And I was excited to get people turned onto a sport. I was kind of into it right from the start. Business was business, and it was my job so I was going to go anywhere they told me to. I felt for me to do that I'd have to make it enjoyable from the start and accept it and fall in love from the start.

A holder of most franchise records, Mike Modano quickly became the face of the Stars when the team moved from Minnesota to Dallas.

Q: What was it like trying to have to educate a region about hockey?

A: The hardest part of it was even with the sports broadcasters and video shows, I don't think any of them were from the Midwest or out east originally. They were all southern guys; they did football, baseball, and basketball. For them to talk about hockey on the radio and TV, it just didn't make much sense. They didn't understand the ins and outs of the game, so it made it even more difficult since we didn't have those media people on board as far as helping educate. They announced the scores and a little bit of this or that on the radio, but they wouldn't go into the idiosyncrasies of the game, the strategies.

Even in the in-house, they would announce penalties and icings, and people were just cheering to cheer about anything. Guys' names would get announced for a penalty, and they would cheer. And we had a few real tough guys on the team, so they loved the fights, they loved the hitting, they loved that type of stuff. I think that kind of became the main selling point to get people to the game.

The game wasn't good on TV then. It was really hard to follow, and the quality of the television sets and broadcasts didn't really work for someone new to the game. So we just had to get them to Reunion (Arena), and then once they saw the speed and the nonstop action, the shift changing, that started to impress people.

Q: At what point did hockey grow to a spot where people would actually recognize you away from the rink?

A: I would say it kind of really happened kind of quick. I think we were marketing the game around a few of the names and I was one of them. And I was 23 at the time, so I was kind of bopping around doing every little thing for the team. For me personally, that was one of my best scoring years ever, so it came together real quick.

Q: How important was early success on the ice? Was that required for the market to work?

A: I don't know if it was the most important thing or one of the top two things. I think we knew were going to have a bit of a honeymoon phase and it would be a novelty for the first few years. I think once people kind of got through the learning process and started to hear about the playoffs and watched some playoffs, I think that's when the demand came in. Once there was a taste, we needed to keep going back to the playoffs because Reunion was always crazy at playoff time.

Q: What was Ken Hitchcock like?

A: I think he was "Hitch" from Day One. I think he knew what he needed to be and what needed to be addressed and knew how he was gonna coach. I think the biggest thing for him was he had the backing of (general manager) Bob Gainey and (owner) Tom Hicks. Especially Bob, because he was one of the smarter guys I've ever been around and he had Ken's back and allowed him to do whatever he wanted to do, however he wanted to do it. When that's the case, you've got the GM as you're No. 1 supporter, your freedom to be successful is easy to do.

He knew the biggest picture was to get the guys to play better hockey. We had the team to do it. We had the payroll, we had the money, we were starting to get some success, and free agents wanted to come to Dallas. So a lot of things were coming to fruition at the same time, and Hitch was Hitch from Day One. He had the pedal down, he went from zero to a hundred right away.

Q: How did your relationship with Hitch evolve? Did you realize his impact when you were playing?

A: I don't think you really understand the scheme of things or his plan when you're in the middle of it and I certainly didn't with Hitch. So I didn't really understand the whole playing a certain (way) or having to get certain parts of the game involved. But he made it real clear that in order for me to play and even be on the ice, I had to add these parts of my game fairly quick.

So when he kind of explained in that sense that if I want to keep playing and be part of the team I needed to find some things or add some things, it was a little kick and scratch and kind of biting stuff at the start. I was resentful and not really understanding the process, but once we started having success and I was doing well individually and playing his way, it was like "Wow, I guess this is the way he really envisioned things." And I think at that point it got better and better.

Certainly after I retired, I look back and appreciated him the way he was because I never really understood it when I was in it. But when you step back and think about it, I think about how thankful I was to have a guy really pushing me like that.

Q: What was the point you knew this could be a championship team?
A: When we played the (Detroit Red) Wings in the Conference Finals (in 1998). We all felt like we had been gaining on them and we all looked at them across the league as the No. 1 organization in the league. And the level of hockey they were playing at, that's what we aspired to be.

We had been building up since trading for Zubov and Nieuwendyk and in 1998 we were close to hitting on all cylinders, so we went into that 1999 season thinking it was a cup year or bust. It was kind of an autopilot; we went in every day to practice and games knowing what we needed to be.

Q: You mentioned Zubov. What did he bring to this franchise?
A: Just a patience and poise. He was never in a rush to do anything. One of the first good, solid puck movers and probably one of the

best I ever played with. He had all aspects of the game and was just fun to play with and fun to watch.

And then (Darryl) Sydor came in, and the two of them kind of really created a puck-moving tandem for us. Then we had (Derian) Hatcher and (Richard) Matvichuk that were our real shutdown pair. So we had a great mix of guys on the back end, and Zubie was the heartbeat of the defense. He was really calm, no panic in his game. Playing with him, you knew you were going to get the puck. It was fun to have him around for a long time.

Q: Assuming winning the Stanley Cup is No.1, what other memories are among your favorites from your time in Dallas?
A: Probably the first game down there. We started down there against the (Red) Wings in I think our home opener. And if I go back to a couple games, the two Game 7s against Colorado in the Western Conference Finals. I don't think I'll ever forgot how loud Reunion was for that two-and-a-half hours those games went on. Obviously the Stanley Cup was huge. Those four things really stand out for me.

Q: What about individually?
A: I think it was fun scoring 500 at home. That was the only real milestone or record I did at home. All the rest were really on the road. So it's kind of bittersweet, I wish some more of those events would be at home. The U.S. record, that was in San Jose. I would have loved to do that at home. Or the goal record, that was in Nashville. I would have loved to do that at home. One of those two at home would have been sweet to share with the fans, so I missed out on that. But scoring 500 at home at American Airlines Center was pretty special.

Q: Your No. 9 is arguably the most iconic in franchise history. Why did you wear No. 9?

A: My first year of mite hockey I was No. 10. And the second year of mite hockey, No. 10 was taken, and my dad was a big Boston fan so he mentioned Johnny Bucyk and then he mentioned Gordie (Howe); those guys wore No. 9. My dad was also a big Ted Williams fan. He wore No. 9, so there was a little Boston connection for my dad to the number.

But for me, being a young kid in Detroit and being such a young kid, Gordie was still the man when I was five, six, or seven, so everyone still talked about Gordie for years, and it was always that number. It just became available. And then after that, whenever I would come to a team, whoever had it before was leaving or didn't want it anymore. Then I went to juniors and McFee, who wore No. 9 in Prince Albert, he left. Then I got to Minnesota, and Dennis Maruk left. So it was a little bit of luck. Wherever I went it was a continuously open spot for No. 9 on the roster. Except for going back to the Wings. Gordie wouldn't let me take it down for at least one year.

Q: Speaking of numbers, your longtime linemate Jere Lehtinen was the next player to get his number retired. What are your memories of No. 26?

A: I could go on for hours about him. Sometimes you describe somebody with a lot of ability and tools as a Swiss Army knife. He had so many things and he did them all so well. And his work ethic...the way he prepared, the way he got ready for practice and got ready for games. It was a routine a lot of us had never seen before. He was so diligent and really I would just say disciplined; he had a routine and a program he stuck to.

He played that same way. He does so many things really well. For me, the time he came in, it couldn't have been a better time. I learned a lot playing with him; he was a really reliable guy. We could always kind of push each other. The way he got ready and prepared forced me to take a look at how I was doing things my way. So it forced me to raise my level. In a sense he was just as good for my game as Hitch and Bob Gainey. He's an A-1 typical type of guy that you wanted to emulate and you wanted to build a team around. He was Mr. Reliable.

Q: So, do you see Dallas as a hockey city now?
A: I think that's what is more gratifying than anything else: seeing kids getting excited about playing hockey. Parents are excited about getting their kids to the game. I think the growth of it has been more rewarding to me than a lot of things.

I think that kind of shows you are doing the right things and building the game as an enjoyable type sport. The kids have learned it and love it; it's a non-stop sport that gets out lots of energy. It's always going, there is no real downtime. It's really kind of neat to see the growth.

4 The Zubov Trade

A short conversation at the draft table helped the Dallas Stars pull off one of the biggest trades in franchise history on June 22, 1996. According to multiple accounts, the conversation went something like this between Stars general manager Bob Gainey and Pittsburgh Penguins general manager Craig Patrick.

Patrick: Would you be interested in Sergei Zubov?
Gainey: Yes.
Patrick: We'd want Hatcher.

Gainey: Derian?
Patrick: No, Kevin.

Gainey hung up the phone and asked the rest of the Stars representatives at the draft table, "Is there any reason we wouldn't trade Kevin Hatcher for Sergei Zubov?"

See, the Stars had been trying to get rid of Hatcher for a while. After arriving in a trade for Mark Tinordi and Rick Mrozik in 1995, the older Hatcher was a bad influence on his younger brother, who happened to be the Stars captain. "He had no character," Stars president Jim Lites said. "And all of a sudden, little brother fell right in step with him, and all of a sudden Derian wasn't a very good player."

The players had even given a mandate that Kevin Hatcher be traded. During a team party after the 1996 season, Guy Carbonneau told Lites and owner Tom Hicks that the Stars "would never win" with Kevin Hatcher on the team. "Carbo was a powerful person," Lites said. "And Bob loved Guy, since they had both been former captains of the Canadiens. And it led to the trade of Kevin Hatcher because we all wanted to get rid of him."

The Penguins were killing two birds with one stone for the Stars. They were taking a player Dallas wanted no part of, and offering back one of the NHL's better defenseman. Now all the Stars had to do was track down the owner. Hicks was a rather hands-off owner, but he had one rule: if you are going to trade an asset let me know beforehand.

None of the numbers worked, and Hicks was actually on the Black Sea with a client for another business venture. There was no way to get a hold of him. Lites and Gainey decided to make the deal. This was a trade worth breaking the rules for.

Later that day, a one-for-one trade was announced, sending Kevin Hatcher to the Penguins while Sergei Zubov was headed to Texas.

While it was an easy decision to make the trade, Gainey also had to sell the player on Texas. The Russian—who was 25 at the time—was hesitant about the deal. He didn't know anything about Dallas. Gainey said the trade wouldn't have gone smoothly if the Stars didn't immediately make contact with Zubov. "That was important," Gainey said. "It ended up being the right fit for both parties. But he was worried at first, and it was important for us to know what we were thinking as a franchise and as a team."

The trade worked out well for the Stars. In 12 seasons with Zubov, the Stars made the playoffs 10 times, won the Stanley Cup, and the defender became an iconic figure for the franchise. After a dozen years in Dallas, he had 549 points, 111 goals, and 438 assists in 839 games played—all franchise records for a defenseman.

But why was Zubov available on the trade market? Pittsburgh had recently acquired Zubov from the New York Rangers before the 1995–96 season. His vision and magic with the puck were obvious in Pittsburgh after he had 66 points in 64 regular season games.

During the playoffs Zubov had 15 points in 18 playoff games for the Penguins. That included a legendary performance in Game 4 against the Washington Capitals where Zubov played seemingly every other shift and assisted on the game-winning goal in quadruple overtime.

Certainly the Penguins wouldn't want to give up that type of player, right?

In Pittsburgh, blame has been spread to a couple camps. Some say Mario Lemieux ran Zubov out of town. There was only room for one power play wizard, and Zubov didn't shoot the puck enough to No. 66's liking. Others blame Zubov. Some say he asked for a trade since there weren't enough Russians in western Pennsylvania. Zubov had enjoyed the Russian community while playing in New York, and he wanted out.

Zubov later refuted both of those claims. "I would say that's all B.S., all that stuff about Mario not wanting me. I never had a problem with Mario. To me, it was very simple," Zubov told the *Pittsburgh Post-Gazette* in 2001. "One team was looking for one thing, and the other was looking for something else. That's all. That's all there is about the way it happened."

And on that Russian rumor? Also false. "I wasn't happy about the move, obviously, because that wasn't the place to go. The team pretty much sucked," Zubov said. "Plus, it was pretty far from New York. Just look at it from that point of view. How far are we here from New York? And how far is Dallas from New York? No, I didn't want to go there at all. I think, when I first heard about it, I would have been happier anywhere else."

The bottom line? The Penguins thought getting a more stable defensive player in Hatcher was worth parting with Zubov. "I guess management decided to get a more defensive player. That's the way it is," Zubov told the *Fort Worth Star-Telegram* in 2001. "Maybe they did want me to shoot more. I always want to make a play, maybe even a fancy play. I think that's the beauty of hockey."

While the trade was a beautiful thing for Dallas, it's a bit of a sore spot for Penguins fans. Hatcher played three solid seasons in Pittsburgh, but the hindsight of giving up on Zubov—especially after he won a Stanley Cup—still stings a bit in western Pennsylvania.

5 Hitch

Ken Hitchcock didn't play the game at a high level. While many NHL coaches eventually pivot to the coaching life after a playing career comes to an end, Hitchcock coached until he pivoted into more visible coaching roles.

With a gift for motivating players, Hitchcock spent 10 years coaching a Midget Triple A team named the Sherwood Park Chain Gang. The team went 575–69 during that time, an impressive enough mark for Hitchcock to get consideration from the Kamloops Blazers, who named him head coach before the 1984–85 season. In six seasons with Kamloops, Hitchcock had a 291–125–15 record, reached the Memorial Cup twice, and was named the WHL Coach of the Year twice.

He made the jump to the NHL in 1990 when the Philadelphia Flyers hired him as an assistant coach. After three seasons in Philadelphia, the Stars hired him to coach their minor league affiliate, the Kalamazoo Wings.

Hitchcock won 110 games in three seasons in Kalamazoo before getting a midseason call-up to the NHL team. Then Stars general manager Bob Gainey had decided to effectively fire himself as head coach to concentrate on management and he felt that he had the ideal coach in Hitchcock. "It was time to put the right people in the right places," Gainey said. "Ken was ready."

The Stars missed the playoffs in Hitchcock's first half season, but he quickly helped construct what became a championship team. The Stars reflected his defensive, disciplined style, and his tough, abrasive approach helped turn Mike Modano from a goal scorer into a complete player.

The Stars reached the playoffs in each of Hitchcock's five full seasons, and they won the Stanley Cup in 1999. His first run with the franchise came to an end midway through the 2001–02 season. It's often been said Hitchcock's style comes with a shelf life, which is probably an indicator of why he's coached four different franchises and hasn't ever stuck in one place for six full seasons.

But it worked for a long time, and the Stars turned back to Hitchcock before the 2017–18 season, bringing back the coach that won them a Stanley Cup. And early in his second stint with Dallas the longtime coach passed Al Arbour for third on the all-time win list with his 783rd career win. Hitchcock retired from coaching at the end of the 2017–18 season, and the Stars hired Jim Montgomery as his replacement. Prior to that, Hitchcock discussed his time with the Stars in an interview for this book:

Q: What was it like coming to Dallas the first time, taking over as the head coach for Bob Gainey?
A: Well it was a very fluid situation. When I came in January, Bob Gainey had decided to transfer the team into a younger group. So when I came in January, it was also in the middle of making a number of trades. They were moving on from some of the older players and incorporating some younger players in the team.

So it was exciting to coach in the NHL, but it was a team that was in the middle of transition. It was a different experience. It was a team that had gone as far as it could with the existing roster and Bob had made the decision to rebuild the franchise.

Q: What was it like to come to Texas? You had spent the first part of your career in Canada and Philadelphia.
A: I found on the day of the game, hockey is hockey. On the off days I found that we had to do a lot of patient educating. We had to work hard to get the people to understand the nuances of the

game, so they could appreciate the game the way we did. And I found a very eager fanbase and a very eager media, who wanted to learn about the nuances of our game.

I found myself spending a lot of time with the media to get them to understand why the end product looked like it did. We had long media sessions on the off days just to help people understand what coaching plan and being in the National Hockey League was right. Because it was a new experience for a lot of people. So you did a lot of communicating with people that later became good friends, but it started with an education base.

Q: Was it surprising that you had to do that?
A: It wasn't so much that. What surprised me was the football mentality of the way they watched the game. It took me a long time to understand. The fans at Reunion Arena never sat down for the third period, and then people told me, "Well they don't sit down in the fourth quarter." That was an eye opener for me; the way they watched the game and the way they approached watching the game was different for me. It was strange for me standing on the bench and looking across the stands and the whole stands are standing up.

Q: What was it like working with Bob Gainey?
A: Working for a guy like Bob is like working for a guy who has all the answers, but then lets you try to figure it out first. So I always felt like I had this security blanket; that if I didn't figure it out or couldn't figure it out, I could always go to him. He would always try to get me to sort it out myself, or solve it myself with my staff. You knew when you went to ask for Bob's help you would always get it. But you knew he wanted you to figure it out on your own.

Q: What was your evolution like as a head coach?
A: I had coached one way as a head coach. My background was watching the Edmonton Oilers play. There was a style of play the

Edmonton Oilers had and I believed in. I took that philosophy into the International Hockey League (with Kalamazoo) and I brought it to Dallas. And when I brought it to Dallas in January, it didn't work.

My style evolved that summer after the end of the 1996 season. I had to make changes. I had to understand that the way I wanted the team to play…we didn't have the personnel to play that way. We had to find a new and different way to play. So that summer I spent a lot of time with Rick Wilson and Doug Jarvis, and they really helped me understand the proper way to play based on the personnel you had. And that summer of '96 helped me become a National Hockey League coach because I completely changed the way I coached and the style of play based on personnel.

We didn't have the personnel to play that way and I was the guy that had to adjust, as opposed to trying to force the adjustment on the personnel, which I did when I first came here.

Q: How did players react to that change heading into the 1996–97 season?
A: I took a game plan from a baseball team. And that was that in spring training…I read some articles on one of the coaches on a Major League Baseball team who decided to go to his squad of 40 players on the second day. And he worked the 40 players hard to become the roster of 25 every day. So the first training camp in the 96–97 season, we went down to 30 players after the second day. And we ended up with two groups, two distinct groups: an A group and a B group. And you could tell the difference right away.

Then I worked really hard with that group of 30 to formulate the team of 23. And we added players into it. A couple guys in the group of 30 couldn't sustain it. But pretty much that 30 group of guys formed the team, and we spent the whole training camp with that group. So that we had a style of a play and a system of play integrated right away. And I learned from reading articles on a baseball team that did it.

Q: Which baseball team?
A: It was the St. Louis Cardinals, coached by Joe Torre.

Q: When did you know that this new style worked?
A: It was right after we had an early season road trip out east. We had three or four games out east, and we played very, very well against significant opponents. And I knew it would work after that road trip. So I knew very early in the season that all the work and discipline was going to pay dividends.

Q: Mike Modano credits you with changing his game. What was that like from your end?
A: I thought it was a difficult conversation to have, but the results were so immediate that it became easy. So the conversations leading up to Mike's participation on the ice were challenging and difficult at times, but then the success was so immediate that it became easy, to be honest with you.

Q: How important was his buy-in for the rest of the team?
A: He became the face of the team because the older players that were the image of the team—the Neal Brotens, the Shane Churlas, the Kevin Hatchers—they weren't there anymore. So Mike Modano became the face of the franchise.

He was the talent when I got here. But other people, because of their experience and their age and the way they played, they were more the face of the franchise. And then when the changes were made, Mike became the image of the franchise.

Q: You are getting ready for your second stint in Dallas. Anything from your first stop here that stands out?
A: To me the cup was just a result of being a committed, good team. That's what the cup is. It was the end result of this collective push by everybody.

But my memory of my first time in Dallas is this: we all talk about team and what it takes to be on a team. Well five of the six years I was here, I watched that in spades. I saw a team perform and act and behave as a team for five of six years. Which in this day and age of hockey is a very long stretch.

I watched a team act and behave in a proper fashion. I don't want to live in the past, but I sure as heck want to learn from it. That's what I learned. I learned what it took to observe a team and watch it come together very quickly and stay together for a long time. The one thing I wish is the key guys that made this team a team, that they were a little bit younger because this franchise could have gone on a very, very long run.

Q: Let's move to the present. You spent some time with Jim Nill and the Detroit Red Wings during the 2010–11 season when you weren't coaching. Did you realize that was a future stepping stone to returning to Dallas someday?
A: It was in 2011, I just observed full participation by everyone. Everyone was included, everyone was appreciated, everyone was involved. And that's what I learned. I saw recognition of everybody. I saw dinners that were huge—lots of people at them from every aspect of the team. I saw scouting meetings where everyone's opinion mattered. I saw coaching staffs that brought in coaching staffs from the American League and the East Coast Hockey League. I saw a lot of that. I saw a lot of inclusion and I saw something where there was no expense to include everybody, and it was impressive. A lot of that had to do with Jim, and when this opportunity was here, I remembered that about Jim.

Q: It meant a lot for you to return to Dallas, didn't it?
A: This place means a lot to me. A lot of people talk about Original Six franchises or places like that, but for me this was a special place.

I just felt this was a special place and I'm very emotionally connected to this.

Q: Do you ever take a look back and think about your spot in hockey history?
A: I don't. People give me a hard time because I don't. I love history, I love learning from history, I just don't like living it. I don't like coaching with a rearview mirror. I like learning about what life was like in the rearview mirror, I just don't like living in it is all. So I'm extremely uncomfortable on anything that goes down memory lane. I'm really uncomfortable about that.

I'll tell you what, this is the first time in 15 years where I hung pictures. Pictures of previous teams, pictures of the Olympics. They've all stayed in crates. And this is the first time in 15 years I've hung pictures.

Q: Why?
A: You're so quick to move on, you don't want to look back. That's just because I don't know and I'm not sure how long. I feel like as a coach, I can coach forever, but I also have high expectations of myself, and that's why I prefer to go at this year-to-year because I have very high standards, but I've also made the decision that this is my home now. And this will be my home for a very long time. Whether it's 100 percent I'll be coaching or doing something to help the franchise, this is the place I got off the stagecoach and this is it.

6 Jere Lehtinen

Jere Lehtinen was a lot of things during his NHL career. He was the best Finnish player in Dallas Stars history. He was the NHL's best defensive forward and won three Selke Trophies. While he spent most of his career playing on Mike Modano's wing, Lehtinen was dubbed "Mr. Fix-It" for his ability to get other lines going. "I think the fact that they would take him and put him on any line having trouble and it would automatically fix it says a lot about who he was," Craig Ludwig said. "He was one of the best players on those teams and he did things that nobody else could do."

He was also quiet, respectful, and never wanted the spotlight. Lehtinen did all the little things right and he was a winner. "He meant winning," Stars coach Ken Hitchcock said. "He was one of the only players in my career that I didn't have to coach. You would just check in and see how he was doing. He did everything right and not many bad things happened when he was on the ice."

The Stars drafted Lehtinen in the fourth round, 88th overall, in 1992. But they were patient with the Finn. He played three more years in Finland and helped his country win its first IIHF World Championship in 1995.

Lehtinen was part of the now-famed Finnish top line in that tournament with Saku Koivu and Ville Peltonen. Known as the "Ankkalinnan pojat"—the boys of Duckburg in English—each member of the Huey, Dewey, and Louie line were named tournament All-Stars and later had their numbers retired by the Finnish hockey federation.

After winning a gold medal at the World Championships, Lehtinen decided he was ready for the NHL before the 1995–96 season. "Jere was a player that wanted to be completely ready," Les

Considered one of the best defensive forwards in the league when he played, his teammates dubbed Jere Lehtinen "Mr. Fix-It" for his ability to make things happen on the ice.

Jackson said. "He wanted to be patient coming over to the NHL, and we were willing to let that happen. He proved to be more than worth the wait."

Lehtinen played one minor league game in the IHL with the Kalamazoo Wings and then became a fixture in Dallas for the next 14 years. He had 28 points (six goals, 22 assists) in 57 games as rookie and was named the team Rookie of the Year. By the end of his second season, he was on a wing with Mike Modano and during the 1998–99 season he was part of the best line in franchise history with Modano and Brett Hull.

When Hull scored the game-winning goal in Game 6 of the 1999 Stanley Cup Finals, it was Lehtinen who had the primary assist. "Jere made that line go," Modano said. "He was the one that put everything into motion. He was the one that made us successful in all situations. I don't think it needs to be said, but you don't win championships without a player like [Lehtinen]."

Lehtinen was the best defensive forward of his generation and won the Selke in 1998, 1999, and 2003. He is one of five players to win the trophy at least three times and frankly he likely would have won more if he had been listed as a center on the roster.

Throughout his career, there were opportunities where Lehtinen could have left Dallas and chased a more lucrative contract in free agency. But he never considered leaving the Stars. "I always looked at it this way," Lehtinen said. "I was happy, my family was happy, and the team always had a chance to win. What else could you ask for as a player?"

Lehtinen retired after the 2009–10 season, scoring a shootout goal in his dramatic final home game at American Airlines Center, and finished with 243 goals and 271 assists in 875 NHL games—all of them in a Stars jersey.

He still ranks among the Top 10 for goals, points, and his career plus-176 is far and away the highest in franchise history. "I never coached him once in six years," Hitchcock said. "I never told him how to kill a penalty, I never told him where to be, I just watched for six years and put him on the ice. Zero maintenance, zero instruction, and every day was like gold."

On November 24, 2017 the Stars retired Lehtinen's No. 26 in a pregame ceremony before a 6–4 win against the Calgary Flames. Lehtinen, much like his career, gave a simple yet effective speech and then watched the banner rise with his wife and three children. "That moment it hit me," Lehtinen said. "That's the moment when you really see it, it's true, it's happening."

Of the retired numbers in franchise history, Lehtinen is the only one to have played his entire career with the Dallas Stars. Pretty fitting for a player that ended his jersey retirement speech by saying, "I will forever be proud to call myself a Dallas Star."

7 Sergei Zubov

At some point the No. 56 will hang in the rafters at American Airlines Center. In fact, by the time you read this book, the Stars may have already made that decision and honored Sergei Zubov, permanently hanging his number alongside longtime teammates Mike Modano and Jere Lehtinen.

And hopefully by the time you've read this book, Zubov has been inducted into the Hockey Hall of Fame. As of 2018, Zubov had been snubbed five straight years by the hall. Every year since 2013, when the defender was first eligible for induction, Stars fans have rightfully complained about his lack of inclusion among hockey's all-time greats.

Zubov checks off all the boxes for enshrinement. He was a winner. He won the Stanley Cup with the New York Rangers in

1994 and had 19 points in 22 games during that championship season. Five years later he averaged more than 30 minutes per game and was plus-13 when the Stars won the Stanley Cup in 1999. His 771 career points are the 19th most among defenders in NHL history.

In 1,068 career regular season games, Zubov had 152 goals and 619 assists for 771 points. That's more points in fewer games than Scott Niedermayer (740 points in 1,263 games), who was deservedly inducted into the Hall of Fame in 2013. "Playing with him you knew you were going to get the puck," Modano said. "Just patient finding open guys, and he had a great shot. It was fun to have him around for a long time for sure."

Zubov even had international success and won the Olympic gold medal with the Unified Team in 1992 before starting his NHL career with the Rangers.

The case against Zubov is a shallow one.

Detractors point to the fact that Zubov never finished higher than third in Norris Trophy voting and that he only played in three NHL All-Star games (1998, 1999, and 2000). "If the coaches picked [the Norris], he'd be there every year because he does all the little things that you love as a coach," Ken Hitchcock said. "He makes all the little plays that get you out of all kinds of hot water, every game."

The lack of individual hardware is a side effect of the era Zubov played in. His career spanned the glory years of Chris Chelios, Niedermayer, and Niklas Lidstrom. That trio of players that was great and had a popular opinion advantage among media members as North Americans (Chelios and Niedermayer), or they were simply one of the best defenders in NHL history and played their entire career for one of hockey's beloved franchises (Lidstrom).

When you boil it down, the main reason Zubov isn't (or wasn't) in the Hall of Fame was because he wasn't better than arguably the greatest defender of all time. If that's the reason he's being kept out, more than half of the Hall of Famers should have their plaques taken down in Toronto.

While the rest of the hockey world may have missed out on his greatness, Zubov's place in Dallas Stars history is unquestioned. Modano may be the face of the franchise, but Zubov is arguably the most important player in Stars history. The Stars don't win the Stanley Cup without Zubov in 1999. They might not have even been a playoff team without the Russian.

Zubov's arrival in a trade with the Pittsburgh Penguins changed the franchise. His playmaking ability instantly improved what had been a lousy team the year prior, and he regularly churned out 50 points as a defender in the "dead puck era." "Just a poised player, real patient and poised and never in a rush," Modano said. "One of the best puck movers I've ever played with. He had all the aspects of the game that were fun to play with and fun to watch."

With Zubov the Stars became winners, and without him free agents Brett Hull and Ed Belfour—the final pieces of a championship—would have never considered signing in Dallas. "I'll publicly say he's probably the best player I ever played with," Marty Turco said. "And I played with some good ones. No. 9 was amazing, but just his competitiveness and his skillset, shooting and passing—I've just never seen anything like it. The guy was just so fricking good, could stay out there for two minutes, barely breathing hard. He probably could have scored more if he wanted to. But I think it was just more enjoyable for him to have the puck on his stick. He just wanted to pass it, sauce it around. He loved hockey and he's a great dude."

And with all of his success, Zubov was one of the heaviest smokers in the NHL, often putting away more than a pack a day. "Yeah, he was just a freak," Turco said. "He was just built for hockey."

8 Jamie Benn

On April 10, 2010, there was a passing of the guard that flew under the radar for the Dallas Stars. It was the final game of Mike Modano's career with Dallas and it was played in Minnesota. After serving as the face of the franchise for 20 years in two different states, Modano was done as a Star after a 4–3 shootout win in St. Paul.

Modano actually missed on his penalty shot in the second round, while Jere Lehtinen missed in the third round. But in the fourth round, a then 20-year-old Jamie Benn scored and delivered the win with a wrist shot past Niklas Backstrom. Whether fans knew it or not at the time, that was the play where Jamie Benn became the new face of the franchise.

Over the next four seasons, Benn's game took major strides. On a team that was struggling overall, Benn was the bright spot. He was quickly turning into a star in the league and, as a 24-year-old, he was named him captain on September 19, 2013. "He was ready to lead and be the cornerstone of a franchise already," Stars general manager Jim Nill said. "Jamie became a player that could define and lead a team; he was ready for that role."

In Benn's first season as captain, the Stars returned to the playoffs. In his second season, he won the Art Ross Trophy as the NHL's leading scorer. Not bad for a player that flew under the radar and wasn't drafted until the fifth round in 2007.

On July 15, 2016, the Stars signed Benn to the biggest contract in franchise history: an eight-year deal worth $76 million per season. And with a full no-movement clause, the captain is likely going to be a fixture in Dallas until at least 2025.

With that longevity and the first nine years of his career taken into account, Benn may be the only player in franchise history with a chance of catching Modano on top of the career leaderboard when it comes to games played, goals, or points in a Stars uniform.

9 Bob Gainey

The Dallas Stars wouldn't have been a successful franchise without Bob Gainey. The former Montreal Canadiens left wing, who was named one of the 100 best players in NHL history, joined the franchise and was named the Minnesota North Stars head coach before the 1990–91 season. In his first season as a head coach, he led the North Stars to the Stanley Cup Finals and he added general manager duties to his title before the 1992–93 season.

While Gainey coached the franchise for six seasons and posted a 165–190–60 record, he realized the Stars would be better served with him focusing on his duties as general manager and in the middle of the 1995–96 season he made the decision to remove himself as head coach and hired Ken Hitchcock. Gainey reflected on some of his moves as general manager in a Q&A for this book:

Q: What do you remember most about your time as general manager in Dallas?
A: In this job, over a 10-to-12-year period there were many highs and lows. The people I was involved with stand out. Norman Green, Tom Hicks in ownership, Jim Lites, Jeff Cogan in business management, Doug Armstrong and Les Jackson in hockey ops, Ken Hitchcock, Doug Jarvis, and Rick Wilson in coaching. There were so many committed people.

Q: You made the decision to step down from coaching in the middle of the season and hire Ken Hitchcock as your replacement. Why did that work out so well?
A: I felt I knew Ken very well from his IHL work for the Stars. We were in alignment on many aspects of directing a group of players to success. Our personalities and approach could be and often was different. But we had enough trust in each other that these differences were often an added strength rather than an area of discord.

Q: You coached and managed Mike Modano for more than half his career. What did you see with his growth over time?
A: Mike's development was based on a number of different things layered onto each other over time. For example, Mike Modano's maturity as a person. Mike Modano's maturity as a professional athlete and ice hockey player. The improvement of the team around him and the examples he received from experienced, successful, hardened teammates and those he encountered with Team USA. Ken Hitchcock was also so hands-on working to form Mike into an elite two-way player.

Q: One of your big moves was trading for Sergei Zubov in 1996. What are your memories of that move?
A: The acquisition of Sergei Zubov was based on my belief that the Stars would not progress with Kevin Hatcher as the foundation player of our defense group. The trade adage "you might know what you are getting, so be sure you know what you are giving," applied to this trade. Zubov was initially hesitant to join the Stars. But it became a great fit that benefited both parties short, medium, and long-term.

Q: How important were the additions of Brett Hull and Eddie Belfour in free agency?
A: Free agency was still new to the NHL at the time, and we used it as a way to enhance the roster. Brett and Eddie were both veteran elite players in their two separate disciplines; one stopping the puck from entering the Stars net, the other a goal-scoring phenom. Brett scores, Eddie saves, and the Stars became a threat that could challenge for the Stanley Cup.

Q: What was it like to watch both hockey and the team grow in Dallas after the move?
A: In my time with the Dallas Stars, we were rewarded with the acceptance of the community. Dallas fans came to love their team, and rightfully so. The players were a proud, talented group who made so many nights at Reunion Arena a happy, party-like experience for all of us, including a Stanley Cup Championship in the Spring of 1999 that was very special.

10 Why the Stars?

The Dallas Stars origins date back to March 1965, when NHL President Clarence Campbell announced that the league would double in size from six to 12 teams during the 1967–68 season. Dozens of cities and potential ownership groups sent applications for admission to the league, including the Minneapolis-St. Paul area in Minnesota.

While the Twin Cities may have been smaller than other applicants, the hockey history in the state and the success of the NFL's Minnesota Vikings and MLB's Minnesota Twins justified the area as a so-called "big league city." Walter Bush Jr., who had previously brought pro hockey to Minnesota with the Central Professional Hockey League's Minneapolis Bruins, brought credibility to one of two expansion bids from Minnesota. Bush joined a group led by construction mogul Bob McNulty and Gordon Ritz, a television executive who had also spent time as a publisher with *Sports Illustrated.*

Following the model the Vikings ownership used to lure an NFL expansion franchise, the group was careful to build an ownership group with representatives from both Minneapolis and St. Paul. The group was filled with former college hockey players, and their bid strengthened when the rival bid, headed up by a St. Paul lawyer named Joseph Maun, dropped out.

Over the next two years, there were back-and-forth conversations between the league and the potential Minnesota ownership group. Eventually, on February 9, 1966, Minnesota was part of the group of six teams officially accepted into the NHL alongside Los Angeles, San Francisco-Oakland, Philadelphia, Pittsburgh, and St. Louis.

Each team would pay a $2 million expansion fee with the existing team splitting the fee equally. The Twin Cities were the smallest market of the bunch, but the check cleared and the ownership group worked on finding an arena in which to play.

The best existing venue, the St. Paul Auditorium, was too small for the NHL's mandated minimum 12,500-seat capacity. So the group needed a new building built and worked with the Metropolitan Sports Commission to build a sports arena in Bloomington, a suburb that was also home to the Twins and Vikings.

With a venue and a spot in the league secured, it was time to pick a name and the ownership group held a fan contest to name the team.

Some of the suggestions that were actually considered:

- Blades
- Norsemen
- Lumberjacks
- Mallards
- Muskies
- Puckaroos
- Voyageurs

None of those names fit like North Stars, a name which was derived from the Minnesota state motto "L'Etoile du Nord," or "The Star of the North."

Three decades later it was an easy adjustment when the team moved to Texas, simply dropping the geographic disclaimer and calling the team the Stars.

Can you imagine if another team name had won? Dallas Puckaroos has a certain ring to it.

11 Derian Hatcher

Thanks to Mike Modano, this franchise has seen a large number of "firsts" or records set by an American player.

But Derian Hatcher may have the most important "first" by an American in team history after he became the first American captain to hoist the Stanley Cup in 1999.

In 12 years with the franchise, Hatcher was the muscle. He was the body-checking, hard-hitting monster that patrolled the blue line and played a shutdown role on the teams that competed for championships in the late 1990s.

He was drafted eighth overall by the Minnesota North Stars in 1990 and made the NHL team as a 19-year-old, scoring in his NHL debut on October 12, 1991.

When the Stars moved to Dallas in 1993, the six-foot-five, 235-pound defenseman was a fan favorite as the team sold the physical side of the game. His star only grew when he shared the captaincy with Neal Broten during the 1994–95 season and became the full-time captain the following season.

He held that role until 2003 and at this time is still the longest-serving captain in team history (a mark that will likely someday be passed by Jamie Benn). Hatcher finished his career with less-successful stints with the Detroit Red Wings and Philadelphia Flyers, before officially retiring in 2009. He was inducted into the United States Hockey Hall of Fame in 2010.

His 827 games with the Stars are second in franchise history among defensemen—Sergei Zubov played 839—and his 1,380 career penalty minutes rank third all-time.

12 Ed Belfour

The Dallas Stars needed Ed Belfour. At the same time, Ed Belfour needed the Dallas Stars. The Stars were a good franchise, a winning one, but they weren't elite and they were missing a reliable goalie that could deliver in the postseason.

In the 1997 Playoffs, the Stars were ousted in seven games by the Edmonton Oilers. Dallas was the better team, but Edmonton had Curtis Joseph. In three overtime games, the Oilers' goalie was the difference, and his performance effectively ended the Stars' season.

Dallas needed a goalie like that. And they found one in Ed Belfour. "We had planned to go into the next season with the goalies being Arturs Irbe and Andy Moog," Ken Hitchcock said. "Then on July 1, I got a call from Bob [Gainey], and he said, 'You won't believe this. But I just got a call from Eddie Belfour. He's a free agent and he wants to come to Dallas.'"

Belfour was already a two-time Vezina winner as the NHL's best goalie from his time with the Chicago Blackhawks. He had a history of delivering in the playoffs and had four separate playoff runs where he recorded a .915 save percentage or higher—an extreme rarity in the early 1990s.

But Belfour couldn't win the big one. That was the knock against the goalie. While he had come close with Chicago, he had been pulled, and the Blackhawks were swept out of the Finals by the Pittsburgh Penguins in 1992. Belfour started to fall out of favor in Chicago during the 1996–97 season and was traded midseason to the San Jose Sharks. After a lackluster 13-game stint in San Jose, Belfour decided to pursue his options in free agency, and Dallas seemed like the ideal fit.

The Stars were a playoff team, they played strong defensive hockey, and they had offensive weapons in Mike Modano and Joe Nieuwendyk. Belfour saw the only thing missing: a reliable goalie. He saw an opportunity to finally win his championship.

In his first season in Texas the goalie had a 37–12–10 record and 1.88 goals against average. The Stars won the Presidents' Trophy as the regular season champion and reached the Western Conference Finals, where Belfour once again came up just short of a Stanley Cup.

He and the Stars would make up for that the next season. Dallas repeated as the Presidents' Trophy Winner and Belfour was equally impressive in the regular season. Belfour had a 35–15–9 record, 1.99 goals against average, and .915 save percentage. The 1999 Playoffs were validation for Belfour. Winning the Stanley Cup would have been enough to cement his Hall of Fame legacy, but the competition he had to face made it even more impressive. "Going into the playoffs, we knew we had a real good team," Belfour said. "It was going to be a lot of bumps along the road, but guys were confident and knew what we could do for sure. But in no way did we think it was gonna be easy."

In the first round the Stars stormed past the Edmonton Oilers and Curtis Joseph, the goalie that had given Dallas a sobering message about goaltending just two years prior.

That set up a duel with future Hall of Famer and Belfour's idol Grant Fuhr, who was then playing for the St. Louis Blues. In a six-game series, Belfour got the best of Fuhr and made 28 saves in a series-clinching Game 6 that went to overtime. "Grant Fuhr was one of the goaltenders I looked up to when I was younger," Belfour said. "He was like one of my heroes. So looking down at the other end and knowing I was gonna play against Grant Fuhr, that was a huge challenge and great opportunity. And also a great feeling knowing that we did beat him."

In the Western Conference Finals, the Stars goalie dueled with Colorado Avalanche goalie Patrick Roy. Roy had what Belfour didn't; he was a Stanley Cup champion and had a reputation of being a big-game goalie. The Stars would have to go through him to help Belfour earn that reputation himself. "Patrick and I have always had real good competition playing against each other," Belfour said. "I think it brings the best out of both of us. Definitely a great feeling beating one of the best goaltenders ever to play. Knowing that we won gave me more confidence going into the final."

Dallas trailed 3–2 in the series heading into Game 6, but Belfour only allowed two goals on 46 shots in the final two games and the Stars advanced to the Stanley Cup Finals against the Buffalo Sabres.

The Sabres had reached the championship series on the back of their goaltender, Dominik Hasek. A two-time league MVP and Belfour's former backup in Chicago, Hasek was the talk of the hockey world. If there was an area where the Sabres had an edge in the series, it was in goal. "Him being the best goaltender in the world and anytime you see a team on a roll like that, you're like, 'geez, this is gonna be tough,'" Belfour said. "Whenever you hear

Already a superstar when he came to Dallas, Ed Belfour was often considered the difference maker in the Stars' postseason success, especially in the 1999 Stanley Cup Finals.

all that it, it motivates you, but you know it's going to be a huge challenge."

And Belfour answered the challenge. In a six-game series, Belfour posted a .941 save percentage and stopped 143 of 152 shots. In the cup-clinching game he dueled with Hasek one last time and made 53 saves to finally hoist his first Stanley Cup.

Throughout his time in Dallas, Belfour was an odd bird, but it was well worth it for the Stars. "Eddie was a unique teammate. Socially, he probably wasn't real tight with anybody, but we all admired the seriousness he took at this position. He prepared himself. He was the first guy there and the last guy to leave," Joe Nieuwendyk said before Belfour's Hall of Fame induction. "There were a lot of things that went with that. Eddie needed his certain type of groceries, he needed a skate sharpener and all that kind of stuff. But we accepted it because we knew the type of goalie that we had. We knew the competitor he was. He was maybe the best biggest game goaltender I ever played with. You think of the goalies he beat in '99 when we won the cup. He beat Grant Fuhr, Patrick Roy, and Dominik Hasek in the last three rounds. That's unreal. And he was better than all those guys."

Belfour spent three more seasons with Dallas and reached the Stanley Cup Finals again in 2000. In 2002, he was part of the Canadian team that won the Olympic Gold Medal and he finished his Stars career with a 160–95–44 record, 2.19 goals against average, and a .910 save percentage.

13 Brett Hull

Brett Hull was the final piece the Dallas Stars needed to win the Stanley Cup in 1999, so it's pretty fitting that he scored the game-winning goal in Game 6 against the Buffalo Sabres to clinch the first championship in franchise history.

After 11 seasons and more than 500 goals with the St. Louis Blues, Hull was one of the biggest names available in free agency after the 1997–98 season. Hull considered re-signing with St. Louis, and many thought he would sign with Chicago Blackhawks, the team his father Bobby Hull played for, but the opportunity to win right away by signing with Dallas outweighed sentimental value for the then 34-year-old. "Just because the media speculated on such things," Hull said at the time. "My standpoint was that I would listen to all the franchises that were interested. There was no frontrunner whatsoever."

On July 3, 1998, the Stars signed Hull to a three-year, $17.5 million contract, finding the final piece for a new top line with Mike Modano and Jere Lehtinen. The signing was a success right out of the gate. In his first season with Dallas, Hull scored 32 goals, including a franchise record 11 game winners. It was foreshadowing for a playoff run where Hull would score the biggest game-winning goal in franchise history.

Over three seasons Hull played 218 games with the Stars. He had 95 goals and 101 assists, won a Stanley Cup, and scored the final goal of the millennium on December 31, 1999. After his time in Dallas, Hull played three seasons with the Detroit Red Wings and won another Stanley Cup in 2002. The Stars thought he would return for a final swan song in Dallas, but the then 40-year-old

Hull picked the Phoenix Coyotes and played just five games with the franchise during the 2005–06 season.

14 The Greatest American Scorer

Mike Modano doesn't have many regrets from a career that lasted more than two decades and ended with induction in the Hockey Hall of Fame. But if Modano could change any detail, it might have been the location where some of his greatest achievements were accomplished. "A bunch of my milestone goals and points came on the road," Modano said. "If I could change one thing about that, I think it would have been nice to have some of those achievements at home in front of the fans in Dallas."

When Modano became the highest-scoring American-born goal scorer and the all-time points leader for Americans in 2007, both achievements came on the road in two-goal performances. On March 17, 2007 Modano scored twice in a 3–2 loss to the Nashville Predators, tying and passing Joe Mullen, who was the first American to score 500 goals and held the previous mark with 502 career goals.

Sitting at 501 goals entering the game, Modano scored 502 on a power play in the second period. He received a pass at the blue line, carried the puck in along the left side, and snapped home a wrist shot through the five-hole to tie Mullen. In the third period, Modano struck again on the power play—on a slap shot after a failed clearing attempt with 2:52 remaining in the game.

His 503rd career goal was a tough goal to celebrate. The Stars were losing at the time and ultimately lost the game 3–2. "I've been feeling good, I've been getting chances," Modano said after the game. "Tonight it just seemed like I only had a couple of shots and they seemed to go in."

Eight months later it was a bit easier to celebrate another milestone as Modano passed Phil Housley's record for all-time points by an American in a 3–1 win against the San Jose Sharks.

Modano entered that game stuck at 1,232 points, one behind Housley, and hadn't scored in three games. Earlier that week it had appeared he had tied the record, but reviews of the play confirmed that he didn't touch the puck despite what would have been an assist on a goal by Sergei Zubov.

But against San Jose, there wasn't much doubt as Modano scored twice within the first five minutes to officially become the greatest American scorer of all time. Just 2:19 into the game, Modano beat Sharks goalie Evgeni Nabokov with a long slap shot on a rush, tying Housley with 1,233 points.

He then set the record two minutes later, finishing off a short-handed breakaway for the 1,234th point. "I can finally take a deep breath and enjoy it a little bit," Modano said. "This is the last of the numbers situation, as far as records go. It was the last one of the bunch and it was something I was looking forward to at the start of the year to accomplish and get it over with. But it definitely means the most. You're thankful you've been in the game this long."

After each goal the San Jose crowd gave the Stars center a standing ovation—even if the second one was a bit more muted after Modano had put their team in an early 2–0 hole. "A lot of history here," Modano said after the game. "I've always enjoyed playing in San Jose, even back when they were in San Francisco. I've enjoyed it here. They've been a classy organization. It's a classy act on their part."

While the Stars celebrated a milestone that night, they wouldn't have been able to celebrate a victory without Marty Turco's superb play in net. Dallas was outshot 39–12 in a 3–1 victory, but Turco stole the game with 38 stops.

15 Drafting Jamie Benn

If you went back and re-drafted the 2007 NHL Draft, Jamie Benn would likely be the second overall pick after Patrick Kane, who was the first overall selection that year. Instead, 127 players were drafted between Kane and Benn, including four picks by the Stars before they took their future captain with the 129th overall pick in the fifth round.

The Stars players selected before Benn? Nico Sacchetti, Sergei Korostin, Colton Sceviour, and Austin Smith. Of those players, only Sceviour played in the NHL. "We were lucky," said Les Jackson, who was the Stars director of player personnel at the time. "If we were so smart, we would have had him earlier. If we knew he was going to be this good, he would have been a first-round pick."

So how did Benn end up on the Stars radar? You can thank a scout by the name of Dennis Holland. The brother of Detroit Red Wings general manager Ken Holland, he was the Stars scout in western Canada responsible for scouting the British Columbia Hockey League, where Benn played for his hometown Victoria Grizzlies.

Holland was one of the first NHL scouts to watch Benn play, from any NHL team. "He was a player with outstanding stick skills and an NHL shot back when he was 17. He had real good vision," Holland said. "What I noticed about him was his improvement potential. He was just a raw, raw kid. When talking to the coaches and talking to people, he was an outstanding baseball player and really never physically trained for hockey. You could tell his strength and conditioning wasn't there."

A number of factors limited Benn's profile heading into the draft. He wasn't playing in a top-end league, he didn't have

Re-Drafting the 2007 NHL Draft

Hindsight is 20-20, so if you have a chance to re-draft the 2007 NHL Draft, this would be the first round.

Patrick Kane (originally 1st overall)
Jamie Benn (129th)
Max Pacioretty (22nd)
Wayne Simmonds (61st)
Logan Couture (9th)
P.K. Subban (43rd)
Ryan McDonagh (12th)
Kyle Turris (3rd)
James van Riemsdyk (2nd)
Karl Alzner (5th)
Jakub Voracek (7th)
Kevin Shattenkirk (14th)
Carl Hagelin (168th)
Patrick Maroon (161st)
Alex Killorn (77th)
Jake Muzzin (141st)
Alec Martinez (95th)
Scott Darling (153rd)
Mikael Backlund (24th)
David Perron (26th)
Nick Bonino (173rd)
Ian Cole (18th)
Brandon Sutter (11th)
Brendan Smith (27th)
Lars Eller (13th)
Sam Gagner (6th)
Paul Byron (179th)
Carl Gunnarsson (194th)
Thomas Hickey (4th)
Justin Braun (201st)

top-end speed, he didn't get invited to top-level tournaments, and it felt like he was playing in the middle of nowhere in Victoria. "You have to take a ferry or an airplane to get to where he played in junior," Holland said. "The Victoria Royals weren't in the Western Hockey League at the time, and it was a process to get over there. You lost a day and a half of travel because of the ferry."

Lucky for the Stars, Holland had an extra set of eyes on every home game in Victoria. His brother-in-law worked security for the team and was at every game. He would consistently give Holland updates on the winger that finished with 65 points in 33 BCHL games during his draft year.

With his brother-in-law's constant updates, Holland made another trip to Victoria and made sure the Stars had the winger on their draft board. "I kind of fell in love with him again," Holland said. "He had really taken good steps from the times I had seen him previously. I made sure Les Jackson and Tim Bernhardt [former director of amateur scouting] came in and liked what they saw."

Heading into the draft, the Stars had Benn ranked as a fourth-round pick, they had a pair of picks in the fourth round.

Instead of taking Benn in the fourth round, the Stars picked Sceviour and traded the other pick to the Columbus Blue Jackets for three additional fifth round picks, giving Dallas back-to-back selections.

With the 128th overall pick, the Stars picked Austin Smith, a Dallas native, and then selected Benn with the 129th selection. The pick may have flown under the radar that day, but the Stars quickly discovered they had a steal.

Instead of going to the University of Alaska–Fairbanks, where he had committed to play college hockey, Benn played for the Kelowna Rockets in the WHL the next season, had 65 points in 53 games, and helped his team win the WHL title.

The next season he was a member of Team Canada at the World Junior Championships and had six points in six games on his way to a gold medal.

16 Art Ross Winner

Jamie Benn entered the final game of the 2014–15 with a chance to make Dallas Stars history. The Stars never had an Art Ross Trophy winner before as the NHL's leading scorer, and entering Game 82 on April 11, 2015, Benn was still in a tight three-way race with Pittsburgh Penguins captain Sidney Crosby and New York Islanders captain John Tavares for the trophy.

With six games remaining in the regular season Benn had 72 points. Crosby had 79 and Tavares had 74. But over the next five games Benn had 11 points, Tavares had 10, and Crosby had five, setting up a Game 82 showdown with the Stars captain one point behind the others with 83 points.

That set the stage for a dramatic four-point night as Benn caught the others, getting a last-second assist to grab the Ross Trophy. Benn started strong and gave Dallas a 1–0 lead in the first period. He slipped a pass to Cody Eakin, who drew a pair of defenders and sent a backhand pass to Benn. Benn quickly one-timed Eakin's pass over Carter Hutton's glove with 12:25 remaining.

Benn scored his second goal of the game with 6:27 remaining in the period on the power play. Benn won the faceoff and sent the puck back to John Klingberg, who took a slap pass that Benn deflected into the upper corner for a 2–1 lead.

After the hot start, the game turned into a more defensive battle. The Stars were still leading 2–1 late in third period and seemed like they would end the season with a win, but Benn was likely going to come up short in his chase for the Ross Trophy.

But Nashville pulled the goalie, and with 2:05 remaining, Benn scored into the empty net after Dallas won a defensive zone faceoff. That goal pulled Benn into a tie with Tavares, who had two points that night, and was also at 86 points. If the game ended that way, Tavares would get the trophy because in case of a tie the player with more goals takes home the scoring title.

And with the score now 3–1, Nashville no longer had an empty net. It was a good story, but chances of Benn actually getting another point were slim.

With 10 seconds remaining, Nashville tried to clear the zone, but Benn knocked the puck down along the boards, and it landed on Trevor Daley's stick. Daley made a quick move and connected with Cody Eakin in front of the net, who scored with 8.5 seconds remaining. "I was still trying to get the point there, and if it

Franchise Record for Points in a Season

While Jamie Benn is the only Star to win the Art Ross Trophy, his trophy-winning season didn't even rank in the Top 10 for all-time points in franchise history.

1. Bobby Smith, 114 points (1981–82)
2. Dino Ciccarelli, 106 (1981–82)
3. Neal Broten, 105 (1985–86)
4. Dino Ciccarelli, 103 (1986–87)
5. Brian Bellows, 99 (1989–90)
6. Neal Broten, 98 (1981–82)
7. Tim Young, 95 (1976–77)
8. Bobby Smith, 93 (1980–81)
8. Al MacAdam, 93 (1979–80)
8. Mike Modano, 93 (1992–93)
8. Mike Modano, 93 (1993–94)

happened, it happened," Benn said after the game. "Trev made a great play to Eaks and found a way to get it in the net. Obviously, I've got to thank my teammates for what happened."

It was an even more impressive feat when you consider Benn's health—he would have double-hip surgery soon after that game— and the fact Tyler Seguin was a healthy scratch that night.

Seguin, who had 77 points that season, was late to practice the day before. Stars coach Lindy Ruff was a stickler for the rules. Earlier in the season he had scratched Erik Cole and Eakin for being late to practice, so even with Seguin's linemate looking for a bit of franchise history the center was watching from the press box. "That's the biggest thing that sucks," Seguin said at the time. "It's not even about me. I feel bad for Jamie just because I knew I could have helped him tonight. It's disappointing for myself and embarrassing for myself, but it's disappointing that I couldn't help my captain out, as well."

Turns out Benn didn't need Seguin that night, and the rest of the Stars looked at that season finale as a nice consolation after the team missed the postseason by seven points. "What a way to finish, to see a guy win a scoring title," Daley said. "It's a special thing to beat Tavares and Sidney Crosby. I think those are the two best players in the game."

For Benn it was a motivating factor. While he enjoyed hoisting the Art Ross Trophy, winning was always his primary goal. "It's a tough one. The No. 1 goal here is to make the playoffs and just give yourself a chance to win a Stanley Cup. We didn't do that this year, and it's disappointing," Benn said. "It's going to be a long summer, a lot of time to think. But at the same time, we've got to get back to work pretty soon here because it is so hard just to get into the NHL Playoffs. We got a lot of hard work to do."

Two months after his dramatic night, Benn was presented with the trophy at the NHL Awards Ceremony in Las Vegas. His acceptance speech? "Uhh...."

That's right. As part of a bit, the host Rob Riggle presented the award and asked Benn, "Jamie is there anything you'd like to say?"

Before Benn could answer cohesively, the music played him off, and the Stars captain waved to the crowd before walking away. It could have been perceived as a slight against Benn, but knowing the soft-spoken captain—particularly with the media—it was probably one his favorite interviews.

17 The Seguin Trade

On July 4, 2013, the Dallas Stars pulled off one of the biggest trades of the past decade, acquiring Tyler Seguin from the Boston Bruins in a seven-player deal. It was a statement-making move for new Stars general manager Jim Nill, who was hired away from the Detroit Red Wings in April of that year. After years of relatively slow summers in Dallas, Nill was bringing in one of the NHL's future stars and he was doing it with a one-sided deal that left much of the hockey world laughing at Boston.

So why did the Bruins trade Seguin?

He was only 21, recently signed to a six-year contract extension, and had 121 points in 203 games with Boston. By all accounts he was a star player about to take the next step in his career, and his team was just two weeks removed from playing for the Stanley Cup. But he didn't fit the Bruins culture, and his social life ending up on social media also irked the Bruins front office.

Thanks to an eye-opening episode of the Bruins television series *Behind the B,* we have the transcripts from the Bruins' conversations.

Peter Chiarelli, Bruins general manager: "We have to move a player, and the player I've been shopping is Seguin."

Keith Gretzky, Bruins scout: "I see work, hard, from Seguin, but a half a second late, and he won't pay the price. I thought he worked hard, and I give him credit. I agree with Denis that he's learning. I thought he learned, like, in the playoffs."

Scott Bradley, Bruins director of player personnel: "He's not a physical player. He relies on all on his skill."

Chiarelli: "Does that sound familiar?"

Bradley: "Yeah it does."

Bradley: "He's a star player. There's no doubt. But does he fit with our culture?"

One day later, the conversations about Seguin continued in Boston.

Bradley: "I just think there [are] too many red flags with him. He has a lot of talent, he should be scoring. I'm disappointed. Like, he brings up Kane…if he gives us half of Kane, we win the Stanley Cup. I don't like the way his game is going. He hasn't proven that he's tough enough or he plays our style of game. I don't know if a leopard ever changes its spots, but he's going to have to. Or else we're going to be sitting here next year doing the same thing."

Cam Neely, Bruins president: "Well, there [are] a couple issues from my perspective. The on ice and off the ice. And on the ice, [he] certainly has all kinds of skill. But I don't care what age you are, at three years in the league you should have some improvement in the areas that his coaches have talked to him about. And it's a little slower developing that it should be, and that's because it's the areas that it's difficult to get into in this game. For me, if we get the right deal for him, then it's something we need to do."

Chiarelli: "Questions? All right, I'll just man the phones here and see where we go."

Eventually Chiarelli ended up on the phone with Nill, and they came to an agreement on a seven-player trade. The Stars received Seguin, forward Rich Peverley, and defenseman Ryan Button. In return, the Bruins picked up forward Loui Eriksson and three prospects in Joe Morrow, Reilly Smith, and Matt Fraser.

Within four seasons Boston had nothing left from the deal. Fraser was lost on waivers, Eriksson left in free agency in 2016, Smith was traded away, and Morrow never got a qualifying offer as restricted free agent after three seasons in Boston.

And Seguin? He's now entering his sixth season in Dallas, still on the original contract he signed with Boston, and is averaging close to a point per game for the Stars.

18 Marty Turco

The Dallas Stars have a history of coming up with top players in the fifth round of the NHL draft. Marty Turco may have been the one to start that trend when Dallas selected him 124th overall in 1994.

He didn't make his NHL debut until 2000, six years after he was drafted, but once he took over in the Dallas crease, Turco re-wrote the franchise record books for goaltending. In nine seasons Turco won 262 games in 509 appearances. He set franchise records for wins, save percentage, and goals against average in a season. During the 2002–03 season, his first full season as the starter, Turco posted a then NHL record 1.73 goals against average and probably should have won the Vezina Trophy.

Throughout his career Turco was known for his ability to stop the puck and play it. His "Turco Grip" (which has its own chapter in this book) redefined how goalies handled the puck, and with his personality, the goalie quickly became a fan favorite in Texas.

Turco discussed his time in Dallas and some of his favorite teammates an interview for this book:

Q: You spent nine seasons in Dallas, but before you ever played a game you were well-versed in the franchise. What was that like?
A: Almost everybody forgets I was drafted in 1994, and my first training camp was 1998, and I didn't play a game until 2000. I've been around for a lot of shit. I've seen a lot of things going down.

I think the first thing I noticed, especially coming from Michigan and a highly-revered coach (Red Berenson), and coming here was just how older the team was. I couldn't quite call them mature because they are still hockey guys having fun, but just older and the leadership and the hockey sense in the locker room. The conversations were great.

And I don't think he gets enough credit, that's Bob Gainey. He was the GM and coach, obviously played and won lots of Stanley Cups and awards. The team just took on his persona. Team played with a lot of confidence, wanted to win, knew how to win, and he made great decisions to bring in Hitch, knew when to fire himself as coach, even knew when to fire Hitch.

Those guys with Les Jackson and Craig Button, they really had the pulse of the team. And then J.J. (McQueen), our strength coach, he's more than a strength coach; he had a military background and loves hockey and all the guys. That stuff was so important to give this franchise an opportunity, and it was all about winning.

And Mr. Hicks was a wonderful owner. His exit strategy wasn't that great, but when he was here he gave us every opportunity to win. To me the important part was he was around; he made himself accessible, invited us over to his house. He was a true Texas gentleman, and that was something we took with us as we tried to win. Those are the things that stood out to me on a serious note.

Q: What about on an unserious note?
A: Coming to play and sitting in the locker room with guys you watched. And then they are just regular hockey dudes, too. To hear Hully (Brett Hull) think he was a smart guy, always running his mouth, always hearing other guys telling him to shut up…that was just priceless stuff.

Overall in that locker room, that was great. The Mike Keanes and the Guy Carbonneaus, Mike Chambers playing on one knee at the end of his career, their value in that locker room was so evident when you look at that win and loss column. Brian Skrudland, too. He didn't play every game of the Stanley Cup Finals and he was still a key cog.

It was just great for me to start my career out…Brenden Morrow and I, we came in around the same time, and got to watch and be a part of it. That was pretty darn cool.

Q: What was it like being a "Black Ace" on the team that won the Stanley Cup in 1999?
A: It was great, it was a lot of fun. I just left college, we were young having a blast going to cities and watching important hockey, great hockey at that. It was such a great learning experience, and there are two ways for me to look at it.

I wasn't fortunate enough to play young. I didn't play a game until I was 25 years old. But before I played a game, I had three training camps, two four-round cup runs under my belt, was around for every second of it. So there was a lot of downtime where I got to hang out with veterans who weren't even playing or hurt. Also hanging around with the staff, the brass, the media, the other players' families, just everybody, I got to know them all really well.

By the time I finally played my first game, a few guys on the team were like, "Dude, why you putting so much money on the board?" And I told them, "It's my first game tonight, it's a big one for me." And they didn't believe me, they thought I had played. I remember telling Richard Matvichuk, "No, I have zero games played, I'm pretty sure I would know. Dude, I think I would know if it was my first game."

Q: Your last game with the Stars was also the last game for Jere Lehtinen. What do you remember about playing with him?
A: Every second of him playing, hockey sweat was dripping down his face. In practice we could be in Vancouver or Edmonton in a freezing cold practice facility, and sweat was dripping down his face. He works his tail off. Nobody could match his work ethic; it was almost impossible. Then locker room and weight room, he was just a dedicated guy. I remember one point I told him, "Dude, you've got to maybe work out a little less," but it didn't matter; he showed up every game and he could go forever.

He gets some credit for it now, but I don't think he did as much when he played, but he fixed everything. Somebody was struggling, you'd put Jere on his line, and they'd have to try and match his work ethic, or at least try to. And he'd get the puck nonstop and be (forcing) a turnover. Just a turnover and fore-checking machine. And just how he shot the puck…everything was coming in hard, not malicious or at my head or anything, but first shot of practice was just as hard as a game. He never stopped working.

Q: What about Brenden Morrow? You both joined the NHL team around the same time.
A: That's my best friend. See him almost every day. Dear friend and a hell of a hockey player. Another guy who worked his tail off, he was a quiet leader for us and scored some big goals, had some big hits. Kind of did it all. He held everyone accountable.

That guy is the toughest I've ever been around, and I've been around some tough cookies. His best attribute—being tough mentally and physically—could also have been his worst because he didn't know when to take a game or two off or let that injury run its course properly. He'd just plow through it. He's such warrior like that. It might have slowed him up a bit by the end of his career, but he battled, man. I loved seeing him get mad.

Q: What about Sergei Zubov?
A: I'll publicly say he is probably the best player I ever played with. And I played with some good ones. No. 9 was amazing, but his competitiveness, his skillset, his shooting and passing, I've just never seen anything like it. And he could stay out there for two minutes barely even breathing hard. He's just like an anomaly for hockey, probably could have scored more if he shot more, but he just enjoyed having the puck on his stick. He loved hockey and he's a great dude. Wasn't much of a guys' guy on the road, but at home and in the locker room he was there laughing. He was so underrated, seriously, he was a treat to play with.

He was just a freak. He never really worked out. From the time I met him, first time, 1998 training camp, I don't think his body composition changed, not even a hair turning grey. He wasn't ever hurt until the end, and I think when someone said, "Hey you're getting old, maybe you should start working out," that might have been his demise because he was never hurt before that.

Q: Who was the hardest player to stop in practice?
A: Probably would have been Zubie. He had such a good shot. Jere always shot like it was overtime of a big game, as hard as he could, and when I practiced with Hully, he always had a hell of a shot.

19 Game 6 of the 1999 Stanley Cup Finals

You already know how this chapter ends. Brett Hull collects a rebound in triple overtime, fires a wrist shot home, and the Dallas Stars hoist the Stanley Cup. Of course, it's still fun to relive that moment. And much less stressful when you already know the end result.

First Period
The Stars were the better team off the opening faceoff. Looking to end the series and win a championship, Dallas provided consistent pressure in the first half of the opening period against Buffalo goalie Dominik Hasek.

Dallas broke through and scored the opening goal at 8:09 of the period. Mike Modano chipped a pass to Jere Lehtinen, who carried the puck and somehow snuck a shot between Hasek's right pad and the post for a 1–0 lead.

Second Period
Buffalo responded in the second period, and Ed Belfour had his busiest period of the entire series. The Stars goalie faced 15 shots during the middle frame, many from high-danger areas.

Eventually Buffalo broke through with 1:39 remaining in the period. Stu Barnes, who would later play and coach in Dallas, picked a corner on a rush and beat Belfour with a perfect shot off the crossbar, tying the game 1–1 before the third period.

Third Period
Belfour and Hasek were perfect in a physical final period of regulation. Hasek stopped 10 shots, Belfour made six saves, and the officials swallowed their whistles.

First Overtime
The goalies were perfect, again.

This time each goalie had to make more acrobatic saves. Belfour seemingly misjudged a high shot but recovered to kick away the rebound with his left foot. On the other end, Hasek kicked out a juicy rebound, but he was quick enough to get over and thwart Sergei Zubov's slap shot.

Second Overtime
Buffalo nearly forced a Game 7 in the second overtime, but a point shot through a screen clanked off the crossbar.

That was the only shot that got past Belfour, who made 12 saves in the second overtime, going shot-for-shot with Hasek, who stopped 13. "I kept telling myself, hey the cup (is) in the building," Belfour said. "Just stay strong, keep making the saves. Those guys are gonna score. I know they're gonna score. I kept telling myself they're gonna score. Hang in there."

Third Overtime
Belfour hung in there and made 53 saves, only four in the third overtime period, and the Stars were able to finally celebrate when Hull scored at 14:51 of the sixth period. It was the longest cup-winning game in NHL history. "Honestly, it's been a long time

for me," Hull said after the game. "It's been a dream. And I think every kid—and I still consider myself a kid right now—you dream of getting that goal in overtime. And it's the greatest feeling ever. Very proud to be an NHL player and a Dallas Star right now."

Brett Hull scores a controversial and game-winning goal in the third overtime of Game 6 to give Dallas the Stanley Cup.

20 Game 7 of the 1999 Western Conference Finals

It was the most important home win in franchise history. While the Dallas Stars had their share of memorable moments, some of the biggest—including the Stanley Cup clinching victory—came on the road.

That's why Game 7 of the 1999 Western Conference Finals against the Colorado Avalanche holds a bit more meaning for Stars fans. It was a must-win, a do-or-die situation that the Stars needed to capitalize on if they were going to win the Stanley Cup and even have a chance against the Buffalo Sabres.

Heading into Game 7, the Stars were feeling good. They had lost Game 5 at home 7–5 and had been pushed to the brink of elimination. Game 6 was a chance for Colorado to close out the series in Denver, and the Avalanche were in good shape when Claude Lemieux gave his team a 1–0 lead late in the first period.

Dallas tied the game at 1–1 in the second period on a goal by Jere Lehtinen and went into the third period with a golden opportunity to even the series. And they capitalized with a dominant showing in that final 20 minutes. Jamie Langenbrunner scored twice and Richard Matvichuk scored his first goal of the postseason as Dallas won 4–1 and forced a Game 7. "That was a win where we got back to who we were," Stars coach Ken Hitchcock said. "We had lost ourselves a bit in Game 5 and we needed that Game 6 to get back to what we knew we could be."

The Stars looked like themselves in Game 7 with another 4–1 victory—this one even more dominant as they limited Colorado to just 19 shots.

First Period

After allowing an early goal in Game 6, the Stars were the better team from the start in Game 7. They pressured early, and at 8:25 of the period, Langenbrunner gave Dallas a 1–0 lead, finishing off a pass from Joe Nieuwendyk.

Second Period

Mike Keane scored five goals during the 1999 Playoffs; two of them came in a span of four minutes in the second period of Game 7. Pat

While Game 7 of the 1999 Western Conference Finals was billed to be tough battle between two powerhouse franchises, the Stars held strong and easily put away the Colorado Avalanche 4–1 to move on to the Finals.

Verbeek helped Keane give Dallas a 2–0 lead at 11:13 of the period, while Matvichuk delivered an assist on the goal that made it 3–0.

Third Period

Jere Lehtinen added an insurance goal to give Dallas a 4–0 lead. Joe Sakic did end the Stars shutout bid with a third-period goal, but it wasn't enough as Ed Belfour finished the game with 18 saves, and Dallas advanced to the Stanley Cup for the first time since moving to Texas.

21 Game 5 of the 1999 Stanley Cup Finals

As far as Stanley Cup Finals games go, Game 5 in 1999 was the biggest on home ice for the Dallas Stars. The series was tied at 2–2 after the Buffalo Sabres won 2–1 in Game 4 back at Marine Midland Arena. It was a defensive-minded, physical series that had been determined by the goaltenders.

In Game 4, Dallas outshot Buffalo 31–18, but Dominik Hasek outplayed Ed Belfour and had turned the best-of-seven series into a best-of-three for the Stanley Cup. Belfour made up for that in the first period of Game 5.

First Period

Buffalo was the better team at the start of Game 5 and outshot the Stars 9–8 in the period. Early in the period, Miroslav Satan had a chance that almost trickled through, but Belfour secured it with his glove and held the rebound.

With Belfour weathering the storm, Dallas had a couple chances later in the period—including a point blast by Sergei

Zubov—but neither goalie blinked, and the game was still scoreless heading into the second.

Second Period

Early in the second period, Jamie Langenbrunner drew a penalty, giving Dallas its first power play of the game. Less than a minute later the Stars capitalized on that opportunity.

Mike Modano carried the puck into the offensive zone along the right wing, stopped along the half wall, and fired a cross-ice pass to Darryl Sydor, who roofed a wrist shot past Hasek on the glove side.

The goal gave Dallas a bit of breathing room, and the Stars started to lock down defensively. Belfour only had to make five saves in the second period as Dallas lead 1–0 heading into the third period.

Third Period

Buffalo played like a desperate team in the third period, and spent much of the final frame in the offensive zone. Eventually, Dallas gained a key insurance goal after Modano forced a turnover in the defensive zone.

Modano stole the puck from Alexei Zhitnik along the boards and kicked the puck out to the neutral zone with his right skate. Richard Matvichuk, better known for his defense, carried the puck into the offensive zone on a rush with Pat Verbeek and then made a pass across. Verbeek faked a forehand shot and went to his backhand to give Dallas a 2–0 lead with 4:39 remaining in the game. Belfour made nine saves in the period to preserve the shutout, and Dallas moved within one game of winning the Stanley Cup.

22 Why "No Goal" Counted

Brett Hull's Stanley Cup-clinching goal against the Buffalo Sabres is rightfully considered one the most controversial moments in NHL history. When Hull scored on the Stars' 50th shot of the game in the third overtime, his left foot was in the crease. There is no doubting that, and the moment has been frozen in time in photos and video.

In that frozen moment, particularly an overhead shot, there is a moment where Hull's foot is in the crease and the puck isn't. Quickly grabbing the rulebook from the time, Buffalo fans seemed to have a case based on NHL rule 78-B:

> *Unless the puck is in the goal crease area, a player of the attacking side may not stand in the goal crease. If the puck should enter the net while such conditions prevail, the goal shall not be allowed. If an attacking player has physically interfered with the goalkeeper prior to or during the scoring of a goal, the goal will be disallowed and a penalty for goaltender interference will be assessed.*

While Hull's foot was in the crease when he scored on the rebound, the NHL had circulated a memo earlier that season clarifying a skate could be in the crease if a player was in control of the puck.

According to NHL officials—and this matches up as you watch the video—Hull initially put the puck in the crease on a deflected shot that was stopped by Dominik Hasek. Hull corralled the rebound, kicked the puck to himself, and shot the puck into the net.

While there were two shots on the play, it was deemed that Hull never lost possession and therefore was free to make a play with his foot in the crease.

So what's the issue? Why are Buffalo fans still upset today? You can blame the NHL for failing to publicly circulate that memo or make it well-known to their fans during the season. With it coming to light in the biggest game, it reeked of conspiracy for many fans across the league. "We all knew that they had changed the rule," Hull said around the time of his retirement. "But obviously the NHL decided they weren't going to tell anybody but the teams… They changed the rule to say if you have control in the crease, you can score the goal, and that's exactly what it was. "But nobody knows that. You can tell people that a million times, and they just will not listen."

Interestingly enough, that would be the final goal scrutinized under those rules. Before the 1999–2000 season, the NHL changed the wording of the rule to state that the player must be interfering with the goaltender's ability to play the puck.

23 Joe Nieuwendyk

Joe Nieuwendyk always showed up for the big games. In a career that spanned two decades, Nieuwendyk won the Stanley Cup three times, played in 158 career playoff games, and had 116 points (50 goals, 66 assists) in the postseason.

It was exactly what the Stars were hoping for when they acquired Nieuwendyk in a trade with the Calgary Flames on December 19, 1995. He was cornerstone of the Stars deep playoff runs in both 1999 and 2000.

In fact, Nieuwendyk's value in the postseason was unfortunately put on display in 1998 when he was injured and limited to one playoff game. The Stars reached the Western Conference Finals without Nieuwendyk but struggled to put the puck in the net in a six-game series loss to the Detroit Red Wings.

The next season Nieuwendyk made up for lost time as he won the Conn Smythe Trophy as the Playoffs MVP when the Stars won the Stanley Cup. He had 21 points and 11 goals in 23 playoff games; six of his goals were game-winning goals.

Nieuwendyk, then 33, helped the Stars reach the Stanley Cup Finals again in 2000, scoring seven goals and 10 points as Dallas came up just short against the New Jersey Devils in six games.

In 2002, the Stars traded Nieuwendyk to the Devils in exchange for Jason Arnott, Randy McKay, and a first-round draft pick. Nieuwendyk won another Stanley Cup with New Jersey in 2003—adding to the ones he won with Dallas and Calgary—and eventually retired in 2007 as a 40-year-old.

In his seven seasons with Dallas, he played 442 regular season games, had 178 goals and 162 assists for 340 points. In 2011 he was inducted into the Hockey Hall of Fame. Nieuwendyk later returned to the Stars in a management role and was named the team's general manager on May 31, 2009. Nieuwendyk had a rocky and difficult time as the GM for the Stars.

The team had come across difficult times financially and Nieuwendyk was the one who made the decision during the 2009–10 season that the Stars wouldn't be bringing back Mike Modano for a 21st season, an unpopular move at the time that hurt the relationship between the former teammates.

24 Brenden Morrow

Brenden Morrow signed his final NHL contract on March 17, 2016—a ceremonious one-day deal—and retired as a Dallas Star later that day. It was a fitting end for a player who had endeared himself to Stars fans during a 13-year career. Morrow was the everyman and the blue collar leader of the Stars. He also had a knack for scoring big goals and delivering big hits. "To the Stars fans, I know I wasn't the most skilled player," Morrow said at his retirement ceremony. "I relied a lot on grit. Thanks for appreciating that. You made me feel special in a way I could never repay."

Morrow was drafted by the Stars in the first round of the 1997 NHL Draft and turned pro during the 1999–2000 season, playing 21 games in the playoffs as the Stars tried to repeat as Stanley Cup champions. In 13 seasons with the team, Morrow played 835 games, recorded 528 points (243 goals, 285 assists), and was also named the fifth captain in Dallas Stars history in somewhat controversial fashion in 2006.

Mike Modano had been the captain since 2003 and was still very much the face of the franchise at the time. But Stars coach Dave Tippett and general manager Doug Armstrong decided that Morrow, who had given up a chance at free agency and recently signed a six-year contract, was entering the prime of his career and was ready for the official leadership position. The decision may have slightly splintered Modano's relationship with management, but it never hurt his relationship with Morrow. "I think he handled it, I think we both did, as best as we could," Modano said. "I think he felt in a way bad because of how it all went down."

After being a playoff fixture most of the 2000s, the final years of Morrow's captaincy came at the height of the team struggling with bankruptcy, and the product suffered on the ice. He ended up finishing his career by playing one season each with the Pittsburgh Penguins, St. Louis Blues, and Tampa Bay Lighting.

Morrow eventually retired at 37 without winning the Stanley Cup and came up nine games short of 1,000—a milestone he probably would have reached without numerous injuries in his career. "I know I didn't leave anything out there," Morrow said before retiring. "Every shift, every game, I gave everything I had. And I don't think you can regret anything if you play like that."

25 Stars' First Game in Texas

Without early success on the ice, hockey would have failed in Texas. "If we were just an expansion team and didn't have the base we did of a good team, I don't think the Dallas Stars would still be here today," Stars president Jim Lites said. "We needed a good product. Without that, without a winning team, the market would have never accepted the team like they did."

Having a winning debut went a long way in helping the Stars establish themselves as winners in a city that was looking for a second successful team to root for after the Dallas Cowboys.

And the Stars provided that in their first game at Reunion Arena on October 5, 1993, against the Detroit Red Wings. At 3:51 into the game, Neal Broten scored on a rebound to give Dallas a 1–0 lead. Less than 30 seconds later, Mike Modano scored his first goal as a Dallas Star on a backhand that beat Red Wings goalie Tim Cheveldae on the glove side.

Steve Yzerman cut the lead to 2–1 on a short-handed goal later in the first period, but Broten scored his second goal early in the second period to push the lead to 3–1. Dave Gagner and Jarkko Varvio also scored for Dallas in the middle stanza, taking a 5–3 lead into the third period.

In the third period, Grant Ledyard scored an insurance goal on the power play, and Andy Moog made 31 saves on 35 shots to preserve the first victory in the Stars new home in front of a sellout crowd.

Overall opening night in Dallas was a huge celebration, even before the puck dropped. Dignitaries from the city and the NHL who helped bring the team to Texas were both honored, while Dallas mayor Steve Bartlett welcomed the NHL with pregame remarks. "Welcome to Dallas, Texas, and the excitement of National Hockey League in Reunion Arena, brought to us by the Dallas Stars," Bartlett said. "Beginning tonight with the Dallas Stars in Reunion Arena, Dallas is home of the four major sports leagues in Dallas and will be for a long time to come. Reunion Arena will be rocking and rolling as we go to the Stanley Cup."

The Stars didn't reach the Stanley Cup in year one, but they were a playoff team. Dallas went 42–29–13 and finished third in the Central Division with 97 points. In the first round of the play-offs, Dallas swept the St. Louis Blues as Modano had five goals and three assists in the series.

In the second round, the Stars lost to the Vancouver Canucks in five games. Canucks right wing Pavel Bure was the star of the series with six goals and two assists in five games, and Vancouver eventually lost to the New York Rangers in the Stanley Cup Finals.

26 Hullenium

Supposedly the world was going to come to an end at midnight on December 31, 1999. As the clock struck midnight in the new millennium, computers were going to fail. Many systems were programed to record dates only using the last two digits of each year, so the year 2000 would potentially register as the year 1900, thus throwing off computer systems around the world, bringing world commerce to a sudden halt, and setting off an apocalyptic chain of events from which we would never recover.

That never happened.

January 1, 2000, arrived with a couple glitches (there actually were a couple power failures), but the Y2K bug never turned into the cataclysmic finale that many doomsday purveyors had pushed—and profited from—for much of 1999.

If the world had ended, the Dallas Stars would have gone out with a bang, and Brett Hull would have been the final 600-goal scorer in NHL history. Hull entered the New Year's Eve matchup with the Mighty Ducks of Anaheim with 599 career goals. Reaching 600 would have been memorable enough, but how Hull delivered in the third period made it one of the most iconic regular season games in franchise history.

It was a back-and-forth game dominated by great teams. In the second period, the Stars had scored twice on a power play, while the Mighty Ducks had tied the game on a short-handed goal from Paul Kariya. Anaheim then took a 4–3 lead when Ted Donato scored 1:40 into the third period, but Jason Marshall was called for cross-checking less than five minutes later.

That's when Hull struck for the second most iconic goal of his tenure with the Stars. Mike Modano won a puck battle along the wall and shoveled a backhand pass to Kirk Muller, who made a quick pass to Hull between the circles, and Hull fired home an iconic one-timer past Mighty Ducks goalie Guy Herbert.

With that goal Hull became the 12th player in NHL history to score 600 goals. He joined his father Bobby Hull—who had 610 career NHL goals—on the list, and news of his accomplishment flashed along the scroll in Times Square.

But Hull wasn't done.

After tying the game at 6:36 in the third period, he scored the game winner—and final NHL goal of the millennium—at 8:49. After a scramble in the Stars defensive end, Modano carried the puck into the offensive zone and stepped around a pair of defenders to set up a backhand pass to Hull. Hull caught the pass and lasered a snapshot past Herbert for 601.

A couple hours later, midnight struck, and the world didn't come to an end. Defeating the Mighty Ducks, and Y2K to an extent, was part of a New Year's Eve tradition for the Stars, who have a history of closing out the calendar year in style. The Stars have an 18–7–2 record when playing on the final day of the year and between 1991 and 2003 the Stars never suffered a loss as they were ringing in the New Year.

27 Modano, Lehtinen, and Turco Say Good-Bye

April 8, 2010 signaled the end of an era for the Dallas Stars. Three of the top 10 players in franchise history played their final home game in a 3–2 shootout win against the Anaheim Ducks. Mike Modano, the face of the franchise for two decades, was the biggest

name, but it would also be the final home game for his longtime
linemate Jere Lehtinen and franchise-defining goalie Marty Turco.

It was at the end of a disappointing season for the Stars where
they went 37–31–14 and missed the playoffs for the second straight
season. It was all but a certainty that Modano—who was playing
out the final year of his five-year contract—wouldn't be re-signed,
and many thought he would retire.

The Stars also didn't have plans to bring back Turco, their
starting goalie since 2002, or Lehtinen, who were both pending free
agents in the offseason.

Anaheim did everything it could to spoil the moment and led
2–1 late in the third period on a power play goal by Bobby Ryan.

With 1:47 remaining Modano tied the game when he tipped
Trevor Daley's point shot past Jonas Hiller. There was a brief
moment where it looked like Modano may have played it with a
high stick, but it was ruled a good goal that forced overtime.

Overtime hadn't been kind to Dallas that season. At that point,
in the 21 games that went to overtime or a shootout, the Stars had
lost 14. But this was a magical night, and Modano, Lehtinen, and
Turco would make sure their final home game was a success.

Brad Richards failed on his first attempt for the Stars, but Turco
kept it even by stopping Ducks rookie Dan Sexton with his right
pad. Modano went second and delivered in the big moment—like
he had many times before—with a wrist shot off the bar that left
Hiller looking in the wrong direction.

Turco then stopped Corey Perry, waiting out the forward and
poking the puck away, before Lehtinen sealed the victory with a
slick release on a wrister over Hiller's blocker. "I didn't have any
idea what to expect or how it was going to play out," Modano said.
"It was a nice way to possibly end it."

After the game there was a standing ovation for the Stars three
longtime stalwarts. A picture that Turco, Modano, and Lehtinen
took together is now part of the locker room facade at the team

practice facility in Frisco, Texas. "I think as the night went on it built and as the day progressed, it was getting tougher just to realize that could have been it," Modano said after the game. "The fans were fantastic. It's been a great relationship I've had with them. I can't say enough about them. I didn't expect the reception and the ovations throughout the night like that."

But that wasn't the Stars final game of the season, and Modano had one more emotional good-bye when Dallas traveled to Minnesota for a game against the Wild on April 10, 2010. That game also went to a shootout. Modano missed his chance this time, but Jamie Benn, the Stars' future captain, scored the game-winner in the fourth round to ensure Lehtinen, Turco, and Modano would go out on a winning note.

Just like the game in Dallas, Modano was named the first star of this game. When that honor was announced, Modano came out in a North Stars jersey and received a standing ovation from the crowd. "This is just as special," Modano said after the game. "Starting your career here...the fans, and the people that meant to a lot to my start and my life, I've been lucky to have the best set of fans I could possibly have."

After that game the Stars three icons went their separate ways. Modano played one season with the Detroit Red Wings before retiring, Turco played 34 combined games over the next two seasons with the Chicago Blackhawks and Boston Bruins, and Lehtinen retired as a player and entered a management role with Finland's national team.

28 2000 Stanley Cup Finals

In the 1970s and 1980s, repeat champions were fairly common in the NHL. The Philadelphia Flyers, Montreal Canadiens, New York Islanders, and Edmonton Oilers each had stretches where they won at least back-to-back championships.

Since the Oilers dynasty came to an end, repeat champions have become less common, and since 1990 only three franchises have won back-to-back titles.

The Dallas Stars almost became the third in 2000 when they reached the Stanley Cup Finals after winning their first championship in 1999. The Stars entered the 1999–2000 season as one of the favorites to once again contend for the cup.

They won the Pacific Division with a 43–23–10–6 record, and had the second seed heading into the Western Conference Playoffs behind the Presidents' Trophy-winning St. Louis Blues.

Dallas opened the postseason by making quick work of the seventh-seeded Edmonton Oilers in five games with Brett Hull scoring the game-winning goal in a 3–2 victory in Game 5.

While the Stars took care of business in the first round, the top-seeded Blues were upset by the No. 8 seed the San Jose Sharks, guaranteeing Dallas home-ice advantage for at least the next two rounds.

While the Sharks were too much for the Blues in seven games, the Stars cruised to a relatively easy victory once again in five games. Dallas won the first two games by matching 4–0 scores. San Jose won Game 3 by the score of 2–1, but Dallas won Game 4 at 5–4 and closed out the series with a 4–1 win in Game 5.

The third round wasn't nearly as easy against the Colorado Avalanche. Dallas and Colorado had past history. One year earlier

the Stars and Avalanche met in a classic seven-game series with
Dallas winning Game 7 and advancing to the Stanley Cup Finals
where it would eventually defeat the Buffalo Sabres in six games.

So the 2000 Western Conference Finals were a chance at
payback for the Avalanche. Colorado stole Game 1 in Dallas 2–0
with Patrick Roy posting a 24-save shutout. The Stars rebounded
with a 3–2 win in Game 2 but were once again shutout 2–0 in

*The 2000 Stanley Cup Finals between the Stars and the New Jersey Devils
lived up to its billing, but in the end, the Stars came up short in their bid to
repeat as champions.*

Game 3 by Roy. The Stars won 4–1 in Game 4 in Denver, then picked up a key 3–2 victory in Game 5 at home in overtime with Joe Nieuwendyk scoring the game-winning goal at 12:10 into sudden death.

The Avalanche forced Game 7 with a 2–1 victory at home in Game 6, setting up a one-game showdown for a trip to the Finals. In Game 7 the Stars were the better team from the start. Sergei Zubov gave Dallas a 1–0 lead 6:36 into the game, while Modano made it 2–0 with seconds remaining in the first period.

Rookie Roman Lyashenko gave Dallas a 3–0 lead early in the second period, and from there, Ed Belfour did the rest as he made 31 saves and preserved a 3–2 victory.

That set up a final matchup with the New Jersey Devils. While the Stars were the higher-seeded team, New Jersey had more points in the regular season and was granted home-ice advantage for the series.

New Jersey opened the series with a 7–3 win at home; it was the only lopsided game of the entire series.

Dallas won Game 2 by a 2–1 score, evening up the series and stealing a split before the series returned to Texas. When the series returned to Reunion Arena, the visiting Devils and their neutral zone trap prevailed.

New Jersey won 2–1 in Game 3 and won Game 4 by 3–1, taking a 3–1 series lead and setting up a chance to win the Stanley Cup in Game 5 back in New Jersey.

Game 5 ended up being a classic hard-fought game and a goalie duel between Belfour and Devils goalie Martin Brodeur. The latter made the first mistake, but it didn't happen until the third overtime when Modano scored on the Stars 41st shot of the game. Belfour made 48 saves, making sure there would be a Game 6 back at Reunion Arena.

Game 6 also needed overtime, and Belfour was brilliant once again. But this time the Devils got the final goal in a 2–1 victory as

Jason Arnott scored in double overtime on New Jersey's 45th shot of the game.

29 Roger Staubach

Roger Staubach is among the most revered Dallas sports icons. As a quarterback for the Dallas Cowboys, he won two Super Bowls and was a six-time Pro Bowler. Staubach, who also won the Heisman Trophy while at Navy, was inducted into the Pro Football Hall of Fame in 1985.

"Roger the Dodger" also played a key role in bringing the Stars to Texas. Back in 1990 future Stars owner Norm Green was a minority owner with the Calgary Flames. Green wanted a larger piece of a team and had flirted with the idea of buying an expansion franchise.

Green told Hartford Whalers owner Richard Gordon about his intentions and how Dallas could be a desirable location for an NHL team. Gordon suggested Green meet Staubach, who had moved into real estate after his playing days came to an end. Gordon and Green flew to Dallas for a meeting with Staubach. The former quarterback gave Green a tour of the town, and a friendship was born on that trip.

Soon after Green purchased the Minnesota North Stars, effectively ending any ideas of the owner pursuing an expansion franchise. But throughout Green's ownership in Minnesota, he would have phone conversations with Staubach and when Green decided it was time to move the team to Dallas he called his friend.

Staubach sold Green on Reunion Arena, which had originally been built for hockey in 1980. With some improvements, Staubach said it would be the perfect interim venue. With that encouragement Green asked Staubach to help quarterback the deal, and the former was a key part of the discussions (both public and private) as logistics were worked out to move the Stars to Dallas.

30 Neal Broten

If the Minnesota North Stars never left, Neal Broten would probably be the most iconic player in franchise history. Broten embodied hockey in Minnesota. In fact, you could argue it's not the "State of Hockey;" it's the "State of Broten."

Broten is from Roseau, a small town in northern Minnesota closer to Winnipeg than any major American city. In Roseau he played for a historical high school hockey powerhouse and went to the Minnesota State Tournament three straight years, and his team took third place in 1978.

In his final high school game, a 5–3 third-place win against Mounds View, Broten set a new state tournament record with four assists in one period. At that tournament he was heavily recruited by Herb Brooks, who landed a college commitment from the teenager.

The next season Broten had 71 points in 40 games with the University of Minnesota as a freshman and was named the WCHA Rookie of the Year playing for Brooks. Broten helped the Gophers to the 1979 NCAA Championship and scored the game-winning goal in a 4–3 victory against North Dakota in the National Championship Game at the Detroit Olympia.

The game-winning goal has lived on in Minnesota highlight reels. Broten deked around a defender, avoided an elbow, and dove as he chipped the puck over North Dakota goalie Bob Iwabuchi.

After the game Broten was overjoyed in an on-camera interview. "It's been about time," Broten said, while raising a No. 1 with his pointer finger. "I've been a state high school tournament three times and I haven't won yet, and this is the first time national tournament, am I happy!"

Broten then took a year off from college hockey to play for the U.S. Olympic team and Brooks during the 1979–80 season. To prepare for the Olympics, Brooks put his team through a demanding schedule that featured 61 exhibition games against international and college teams.

Broten played 55 games leading up to the Olympics and the 19-year-old had 55 points for the Americans, locking up a spot on the final roster. In the Olympics Broten had three points in seven games and helped the Americans complete the "Miracle on Ice" and win the Olympic gold medal.

With a gold medal, Broten returned to college hockey for his sophomore season and had 71 points in 36 games. He became the first winner of the Hobey Baker Award, which has since been presented annually to college hockey's most outstanding player.

That would be the end of Broten's college career, as he joined the North Stars—who drafted him in the third round in 1979—for the final three games of the regular season. He was then a key part of the 1981 Stanley Cup Finals push with eight points in 19 games.

Broten nearly won the Calder Memorial Trophy as a rookie the next season and had 98 points in 73 games. But instead of becoming the third North Star to grab top rookie honors, he was edged out by Winnipeg Jets rookie Dale Hawerchuk, who had 103 points in 80 games as an 18-year-old.

The Minnesota native quickly became a fan favorite in Bloomington. He was named the team MVP in 1984 and 1986 and during the 1985–86 season he became the first American-born player to record 100 points in a season. Broten's 76 assists during that 1985–86 season are still a club record today.

Broten scored at least 50 points in nine of his first 10 seasons with the only sub-50 showing coming during an injury-shortened campaign in 1987–88. One decade after helping the North Stars reach the Finals as a rookie, he was a catalyst with 22 points in 23 playoff games in 1991 as Minnesota had another Cinderella run to hockey's final series. "A player gifted with both natural talent and superior intelligence for the sport," former Stars coach and general manager Bob Gainey said. "When Neal Broten could add the emotional commitment and focus to this mix he was special… his play for the North Stars in the 1991 Playoffs was an example of Neal at his very best."

The Minnesota native was still part of the team when the franchise re-located from his home state to Texas in 1993. And on October 5, 1993, Broten scored the first goal in Dallas Stars history when he converted on a rebound in the first period against the Detroit Red Wings.

Broten played one full season in Dallas and had 52 points in 79 games. He was named the captain during a lockout-shortened 1994–95 season but was traded to the New Jersey Devils on February 27, 1995, in exchange for Corey Millen.

The trade to New Jersey worked out well for Broten, and four months later, he lifted the Stanley Cup after the Devils swept the Red Wings. With his Stanley Cup victory Broten joined an elusive group to have won an Olympic Gold Medal, NCAA Championship, and Stanley Cup in their career. He and former Stars goalie Ed Belfour are the only members of that elusive club.

Broten returned to Dallas to finish his career during the 1996–97 season. After a slow start to the season with both New Jersey and the Los Angeles Kings, Broten was placed on waivers on January 28, 1997, and claimed by Dallas.

A return to his old franchise provided a nice bookend to Broten's career. In 20 games he had 15 points and played his final

NHL game in a playoff contest against the Edmonton Oilers on April 29, 1997.

Broten finished his Stars career as the franchise all-time leader in games played (992), assists (593), and points (867), records that would be later surpassed by Mike Modano. The following season the Stars retired Broten's number on February 7, 1998, having his No. 7 hang alongside Bill Goldsworthy's No. 8 and Bill Masterton's No. 19 in the rafters. Two years later Broten was deservedly inducted into the USA Hockey Hall of Fame.

31 Bill Masterton

Each year the Bill Masterton Memorial Trophy is presented by the Professional Hockey Writers Association to the player who best exemplifies the qualities of perseverance, sportsmanship, and dedication to ice hockey. It's an award that comes from a somber place after its namesake became the first—and to this day only—player to die as a direct result from injuries in a game, and his number hangs in the rafters in Dallas.

In the early 1960s, Masterton had given up on an NHL future. It was the Original Six era, and jobs were scarce. After an 82-point AHL season with the Cleveland Barons during the 1962–63 season, Masterton went back to the University of Denver to finish a master's degree and had taken a job in Minneapolis with the technology company Honeywell.

He still played hockey for a senior team in the Twin Cities area called the St. Paul Steers, and also played for the U.S. national team in 1966, before NHL expansion in 1967 rekindled Masterton's chances at reaching the NHL.

List of Masterton Award Winners

Season	Winner	Team
2016–2017	Craig Anderson	Ottawa Senators
2015–2016	Jaromir Jagr	Florida Panthers
2014–2015	Devan Dubnyk	Minnesota Wild
2013–2014	Dominic Moore	New York Rangers
2012–2013	Josh Harding	Minnesota Wild
2011–2012	Max Pacioretty	Montreal Canadiens
2010–2011	Ian Laperriere	Philadelphia Flyers
2009–2010	Jose Theodore	Washington Capitals
2008–2009	Steve Sullivan	Nashville Predators
2007–2008	Jason Blake	Toronto Maple Leafs
2006–2007	Phil Kessel	Boston Bruins
2005–2006	Teemu Selanne	Mighty Ducks Of Anaheim
2004–2005	No award given due to NHL season lockout	
2003–2004	Bryan Berard	Chicago Blackhawks
2002–2003	Steve Yzerman	Detroit Red Wings
2001–2002	Saku Koivu	Montreal Canadiens
2000–2001	Adam Graves	New York Rangers
1999–2000	Ken Daneyko	New Jersey Devils
1998–1999	John Cullen	Tampa Bay Lightning
1997–1998	Jamie Mclennan	St. Louis Blues
1996–1997	Tony Granato	San Jose Sharks
1995–1996	Gary Roberts	Calgary Flames
1994–1995	Pat Lafontaine	Buffalo Sabres
1993–1994	Cam Neely	Boston Bruins
1992–1993	Mario Lemieux	Pittsburgh Penguins

The Montreal Canadiens still owned his rights, but traded him to the Minnesota North Stars after expansion, and Masterton was offered a tryout. "I looked at him and said, 'What are you going to do?' Because he was just starting a young family," Bill's brother Bob Masterton told the *Toronto Star* in 2011. "It was kind of one of those things where I asked the question, but I knew what he was going to do. It was always in the back of his mind."

1991–1992	Mark Fitzpatrick	New York Islanders
1990–1991	Dave Taylor	Los Angeles Kings
1989–1990	Gord Kluzak	Boston Bruins
1988–1989	Tim Kerr	Philadelphia Flyers
1987–1988	Bob Bourne	Los Angeles Kings
1986–1987	Doug Jarvis	Hartford Whalers
1985–1986	Charlie Simmer	Boston Bruins
1984–1985	Anders Hedberg	New York Rangers
1983–1984	Brad Park	Detroit Red Wings
1982–1983	Lanny Mcdonald	Calgary Flames
1981–1982	Glenn Resch	Colorado Rockies
1980–1981	Blake Dunlop	St. Louis Blues
1979–1980	Al Macadam	Minnesota North Stars
1978–1979	Serge Savard	Montreal Canadiens
1977–1978	Butch Goring	Los Angeles Kings
1976–1977	Ed Westfall	New York Islanders
1975–1976	Rod Gilbert	New York Rangers
1974–1975	Don Luce	Buffalo Sabres
1973–1974	Henri Richard	Montreal Canadiens
1972–1973	Lowell Macdonald	Pittsburgh Penguins
1971–1972	Bobby Clarke	Philadelphia Flyers
1070–1971	Jean Ratelle	New York Rangers
1969–1970	Pit Martin	Chicago Blackhawks
1968–1969	Ted Hampson	Oakland Seals
1967–1968	Claude Provost	Montreal Canadiens

Masterton made the team and he scored the first goal in franchise history. Four months later he was dead.

The final hit came on January 13, 1968, in a game against the Oakland Seals. He was crossing the Oakland blue line when he was checked by Seals defensemen Ron Harris and Larry Cahan. Masterton fell back and hit his head on the ice. "It sounded like a baseball bat hitting a ball," North Stars left winger Andre Boudrias told ESPN.com in 2016. "His eyes were gray at the time...it was like a horror picture. I knew he was done."

Masterton was taken to the hospital and never woke up. He was taken off life support at 1:55 in the morning on January 15, 1968. He was 29. "It bothers you for the rest of your life," Harris said in 2003. "It wasn't dirty and it wasn't meant to happen that way. Still, it's very hard because I made the play. It's always in the back of my mind."

Masterton wasn't wearing a helmet when he was hit—a common occurrence in the 1960s but a rarity for the North Stars center. Masterton had worn a helmet throughout college at Denver and had even worn a helmet in training camp that season, but to keep an NHL job, he had to ditch the head protection. "We were not allowed to wear helmets," North Stars left winger J.P. Parise told the *Toronto Star*. "You would get traded if you did. It was a no-no in no uncertain terms. You were a yellow belly if you wore a helmet."

Minnesota management wasn't bluffing. Boudrias was the only North Stars player to wear a helmet during the 1967–68 season and he was traded to the Chicago Blackhawks before the 1968–69 campaign. Even with Masterton's death wearing a helmet didn't become a rule until 1979. Players who signed a professional contract before June 1, 1979 were grandfathered in, and Craig MacTavish was the last helmetless player when he played for the St. Louis Blues in 1997.

It certainly didn't help that he wasn't wearing one, but a helmet might not have saved Masterton's life. In its 2011 investigation, the *Toronto Star* reported that a prior undiagnosed concussion may have killed Masterton. "I've never said this to anyone before," Wren Blair, the North Stars' coach told the paper. "I've never thought that it had anything to do with that. I think he had had a [pre-existing] cerebral brain hemorrhage."

Blair says it's something he had noticed prior to that fateful game. "I'd said to our trainer, 'Do you ever look at Billy when the game's on?'" Blair said. 'His face is blood red, almost purple. [The trainer] said, 'Yeah, I notice that, too.' I said, 'I wonder if we could have him checked. There's something wrong.'"

Masterton never got checked out. He was playing in an era where even thinking about wearing a helmet would get you traded. "We know the second hit can be fatal," said Dr. Charles Tator, a Toronto-based neurosurgeon and concussion expert. "There is evidence of massive brain swelling…that is out of proportion to the blow that he got. My interpretation is that the seeds of this catastrophic injury were sown days before."

The North Stars officially retired Masterton's No. 19 on January 17, 1987. It was the first number retired in franchise history and along with the other North Stars retired numbers it has a permanent space in the rafters in Texas.

32 Bill Goldsworthy

Bill Goldsworthy never played for the Dallas Stars. His career had been over for more than 25 years when the franchise moved from Minnesota to Texas. But there's a constant reminder of his place in franchise history whenever fans look up to the rafters at American Airlines Center, where Goldsworthy's No. 8 hangs alongside Neal Broten's No. 7, Mike Modano's No. 9, Bill Masterton's No. 19, and Jere Lehtinen's No. 26.

Goldsworthy was the original face of the franchise. He was a bit of a hockey journeyman before the 1967 NHL Expansion Draft, having played just 33 games in parts of three seasons with the Boston Bruins.

But the expanded league gave Goldsworthy a chance to make an impact in Minnesota. In the North Stars' first season, he had 33 points in 68 games, and fans at the Met Center were introduced to the "Goldy Shuffle," a signature celebration that Goldsworthy would break into after each goal.

Goldsworthy turned into a fan favorite in Minnesota and he backed it up with his play. He played in five All-Star games and set a then club record with 48 goals during the 1973–74 season. Goldsworthy was the first player in NHL history to score 250 goals with a single expansion club and he was part of Team Canada during the famed 1972 Summit Series against the USSR. He was the North Stars captain from 1974–1976 before he finished his NHL career with the New York Rangers and in the WHA with the Edmonton Oilers.

While he had his number retired, Goldsworthy wasn't the final player to wear No. 8 in franchise history. After his departure from Minnesota,the number remained in circulation. Kent-Erik Andersson, Dirk Graham, Brian Lawton, Terry Ruskowski, Larry Murphy, and Jim Johnson all wore No. 8 before the team decided to retire the number in a ceremony on February 15, 1992.

In that ceremony Johnson presented Goldsworthy with the No. 8 jersey and he switched back to No. 6 before a banner was raised to the rafters. "I want to thank Jimmy Johnson for giving up his sweater," Goldsworthy said in a speech after his number was retired. "You know it makes me proud that the last fellow that wore this sweater was a native Minnesotan."

For Goldsworthy it was special having his number retired next to Bill Masterton, who tragically died in 1968 from on-ice injuries. "I would also like to say that it's honor for me to have my number retired with Bill Masterton," Goldsworthy said. "As you well know, he scored the first goal in the history of the North Stars, and I scored the first goal here at the Met. He was my center iceman. And besides being a fine hockey player, he was a fine person. And for me to be up there beside him, I'm very proud and very honored."

Two years after his number was retired, Goldsworthy was coaching the San Antonio Iguanas in the Central Hockey League. He was hospitalized after fighting pneumonia and had blood clots that had moved from his legs to his lungs. That's when Goldsworthy found out that he had AIDS. He was the first known hockey player with the disease and he contracted it after he failed to take precautions in multiple sexual encounters after his divorce.

It was a difficult battle for Goldsworthy, who was told he had five years to live. Early on he did his part to fight the disease and even did benefits to raise awareness with Magic Johnson, the Los Angeles Lakers star who announced he was HIV positive in 1991.

While Johnson made an NBA return after a brief HIV-induced retirement and is still alive today, Goldsworthy passed away on March 29, 1996 at the age of 51. "My dad had a different perspective than Magic did," Tammy Goldsworthy told the *Los Angeles Times* in 1996. "My dad has a real zest for life, and then it was really hard for him to realize he was dying. Magic has such a positive outlook on life."

Things took a turn for the worse early in 1996 for Goldsworthy when the weight of the disease further pushed a bad drinking habit. "He went to the doctor in January or February, and the doctor told him as far as the AIDS was concerned, he was in great shape. He had gotten through the winter without any infections or setbacks and the doctor said he could live for a year or more," Linda Loerch, Goldsworthy's longtime companion told the *Los Angeles Times*. "He was dead within six weeks. He drank himself to death. Bill looked very healthy until the last few months, and that was because he started drinking. Bill was in good shape. Alcohol just takes a toll on your body."

33 Iginla for Nieuwendyk

Trades rarely turn into a win-win situation. While both general managers in a deal often believe they are making their team better, hindsight often reveals that one side truly got the better side of an exchange. But a trade on December 19, 1995 between the Dallas Stars and Calgary Flames truly turned into a win-win situation for both teams.

Joe Nieuwendyk wasn't happy with his contract heading into the 1995–96 season. He and the Flames hadn't been able to hammer out a deal, and Nieuwendyk was awarded a one-year, $1.85 million contract in arbitration. Nieuwendyk wanted longer terms on the deal and wanted to renegotiate the contract into a longer term extension. The Flames made an offer of $6 million for three seasons, but it wasn't sufficient for Nieuwendyk, and he didn't join Calgary at the start of the season.

At the same time, the Stars were looking for another elite forward to help Mike Modano. The top contenders in the Western Conference at the time had elite twosomes. The Detroit Red Wings had Steve Yzerman and Sergei Fedorov. The Colorado Avalanche had Peter Forsberg and Joe Sakic.

As December rolled around, the Stars started to work on a deal for Nieuwendyk. At the same time, Jarome Iginla was one of the best prospects in hockey. The Stars had drafted him 11th overall in 1995 NHL Draft, and it was a bit of a steal after many had projected Iginla would be a top 10 pick.

Iginla was living up to the hype after getting drafted. He was having a dominant season for the Kamloops Blazers in the WHL and would finish the 1995–96 season with 136 points in 63 games. He also added a gold medal at the World Junior Championships.

After coming to the team in a trade for prospect Jarome Iginla, Joe Nieuwendyk provided big plays, winning the Conn Smythe Trophy as playoff MVP during the Stars' championship season.

The right winger was the Stars' best can't-miss prospect since the franchise drafted Modano with the first overall pick in 1988, and you could argue he's still second on that list today.

But trading for Nieuwendyk—if the Stars could hammer out a contract—was deemed more than worth it. Nieuwendyk was a Stanley Cup champion and a clutch performer. Before the salary cap era, players like that didn't often move teams freely.

So on December 19, 1995 the Stars officially traded Jarome Iginla and Corey Millen to Calgary in exchange for Nieuwendyk.

The deal came as a shock to the then teenaged Iginla. "After you are picked, your next goal is to play your first NHL game," Iginla told *The Hockey News*. "At the time I was imagining it would be with the Stars. The truth is, whatever team picked me was going to automatically become my new favorite team. I was at the World Junior Camp and I got a call from the coach," Iginla added. "He told me I had just been traded, and my first thought was I had been traded by Kamloops to another WHL team. I was relieved that it was an NHL trade."

That's not a knock on the Stars; Kamloops was a very good team that season and had legitimate aspirations for both a WHL Championship and appearance in the Memorial Cup.

After the trade Dallas quickly resolved the contract issue and signed Nieuwendyk to a five-year, $11.3 million contract extension, and the winger became part of a core that helped the Stars reach back-to-back Stanley Cup Finals and win a championship in 1999.

During that championship season Nieuwendyk had 11 goals and 10 assists in 23 games. Six of his goals were game-winning markers and he won the Conn Smythe Trophy as the playoff MVP. While his regular season numbers in Dallas took a hit because of injuries, without Nieuwendyk's playoff production, the Stars likely wouldn't have a black banner with "Stanley Cup Champions" hanging in the rafters.

Nieuwendyk provided an immediate remedy for the Stars, while Iginla was the long-term player the Flames were looking for.

Iginla made his NHL debut during the 1996 Playoffs with Calgary before starting his full NHL career the following fall and establishing himself as the new face of a franchise. Iginla played 16 seasons for Calgary and was named the captain before the 2003–04 season. During that time he set new franchise records in points and goals, passing Nieuwendyk to achieve the latter.

More than two decades later, both franchises can look back fondly on that trade. Sooner than later Iginla's name will be in the Hockey Hall of Fame and his number will be retired in Calgary and the Stars likely wouldn't have won a Stanley Cup without Nieuwendyk.

34 Tyler Seguin

Tyler Seguin was a controversial player before he even stepped foot in the NHL. Throughout the 2009–10 season, there was an ongoing debate in the hockey world: who was the top prospect in hockey and who should be the No. 1 pick in the 2010 NHL Draft? Tyler Seguin or Taylor Hall?

There was never a true consensus in the Tyler vs. Taylor debate, and eventually the Edmonton Oilers made the final decision when they took Hall with the No. 1 overall pick. Seguin was picked No. 2 overall by the Boston Bruins.

It was a draft that worked out better for Seguin than Hall. In his rookie season, a 19-year-old Seguin lifted the Stanley Cup when the Bruins beat the Vancouver Canucks in seven games. Two seasons later, now 21, he reached the Finals again as the Bruins lost to the Chicago Blackhawks in six games.

That Game 6 loss to Chicago was Seguin's final game for the Bruins. Two weeks later he was traded to the Stars in a blockbuster deal on July 4, 2013 (there is a whole chapter on that trade in this book). The Stars reaped immediate rewards in the Seguin trade. In his first season with Dallas, the center had a career-high 37 goals and 84 points and has since scored as least 70 points in each season with the Stars.

In his relatively short time with Dallas, Seguin already holds the record for most hat tricks by a Dallas Star with seven. The franchise record is still 14 held by Dino Ciccarelli while with the North Stars. Seguin could track that record down if he remains in Dallas long term after the 2018–19 season.

35 Jim Nill

Jim Nill was one of the biggest names on the market when the Dallas Stars were looking for a new general manager in 2013. The assistant general manager in Detroit, Nill had been one of the key builders of a Red Wings franchise that won Stanley Cups in 1997, 1998, 2002, and 2008. "It was 2013, and we were gonna make a change and let go of Joe Nieuwendyk," Stars president Jim Lites said. "I got with Les Jackson and said okay, let's make a list. Think overnight, anybody that could be out there, let's do it."

Lites made one phone call that night: a direct call to Nill. "I called Jim and asked one question. 'Would you come to Dallas if I asked? No pressure, just want to know,'" Lites said. "He said,

'Absolutely, I'm ready to come down,' and I told him 'say no more, I'll be back to you in a couple days.'"

A couple years earlier, Nill had turned down a job offer from the Montreal Canadiens. His wife, Becky, was battling breast cancer, and it wasn't the right time for the Nill family to leave Detroit. So the morning after Lites and Nill had a short conversation, Lites met with Jackson in his office to review the list. Nill wasn't on Jackson's list. "I asked Les why Jim wasn't on his list," Lites said. "And Les said, 'well, if you can get Jim Nill to leave Detroit, you don't need a list. He'd be the most qualified guy.'"

Lites called Stars owner Tom Gaglardi. The owner wanted to go through a long list, but Lites said he could get Nill and that this was the best option. He asked the owner to let him make a deal. With Gagliardi's approval, Lites called Nill. Nill had permission from Red Wings general manager Ken Holland; he had an out in his contract with Detroit as long as it was for a general manager position.

Lites called Nill with two games left in the 2012–13 regular season and told Nill he wanted to get things hammered away quickly because the Stars wanted to move right after the season came to an end.

While Nill and Lites worked on details, there was one minor snafu. Gaglardi had made a promise to Brian Burke that he would interview the former Vancouver Canucks, Anaheim Ducks, and Toronto Maple Leafs executive if he ever had an opening for GM. "We basically have it done and Tom tells me about this promise and that he's got to interview Brian Burke," Lites said. "I told him, 'Why would you do that? I've just given the job at your suggestion to Jim Nill. Don't even think about interviewing Brian Burke because Brian Burke has no discretion. He'll tell everybody he's got the job.'"

Lites convinced Gaglardi not to interview Burke. Instead he set up a meeting between Nill and Gaglardi in Vancouver. It was a two-day meeting, and the owner never called Burke. "I didn't want

Jim Nill to ever think that he was anything but our first priority," Lites said. "Because this was the most coveted guy in our business. And Tom, to his word, did that."

On April 29, 2013, Nill was formally hired as the 11th general manager in team history. Nill discussed his time with Dallas in an interview for this book:

Q: What was it like leaving Detroit for Dallas?
A: I was with Detroit for almost 23 years. It doesn't matter what you do, you live your whole life somewhere…my kids grew up there with the franchise, we won four cups, so some great memories, but it was kind of time to (go). In the end Dallas was a very good fit, and somewhere we were really intrigued about. When I talked to Jim Lites and Tom Gaglardi, it really intrigued me and here we are today.

Q: What was the transition like to the top chair?
A: It is different. It goes to now you have to make the final decision. In the past I was with Kenny Holland, or Scotty Bowman, or Jimmy Devellano or Mr. Ilitch and voiced my opinion, and we'd fight and argue about different things, but in the end Kenny Holland had to make that final call. And that's where I'm at now. It is different, now your preparation is the same. You just have to make that final decision that goes with the territory. I think the biggest part is—and you don't realize it until you get into that position and you know about it—but until you are there, you don't realize how much it's dealing with people every day.

You're managing people, and I managed people in Detroit, but Kenny had to make the final call, and it was a lot more everyday hockey. In the GM position, you're making decisions that have to do with the franchise. It's dealing with people, it's dealing with coaches, it's dealing with ownership. It gets to be less hockey; it's more dealing with people.

And that's one thing I learned when I interviewed for some other jobs and I realized I wasn't ready for it. I saw myself as real good and I worked hard on the hockey side, but I didn't understand, 'Okay, now you've got to manage people.' I'm not the guy going out and seeing all the players all the time, not seeing all the draft picks. I've got to go out and hire good people and I've got to manage those people, and that's the biggest change. You go from being a doer, and you're still a doer, but you've got to manage more doers now and let them grow and let other people make you better. My whole goal is to hire good people, help them in any way I can, listen to them—hopefully they make me better—and I know that if they are gonna grow and eventually get jobs somewhere else, that's going to make our organization better.

Q: How do you manage winning now and planning for the future?
A: It's changed a lot because of the (salary) cap. The cap has really changed it, and I think the parity has really changed it. I think one of the biggest hurdles right now is managing expectations. Managing the expectations of the media, fans, ownership. The game is so close right now, and that's the hardest part. I think if you look at the standings right now, whoever gets into the playoffs can win the Stanley Cup. It used to be that when the year started you could say, 'There are five teams that could win.' It's not that way anymore, I think there are 20 teams that have a legitimate chance to win the Stanley Cup, and now you've got to be built for the playoffs to go through it.

The biggest hurdle is managing that consistency, and that's where we've got to get to: where we are in the playoffs year after year. You might stumble here and there, and injuries are going to dictate that, but it's being that consistent team. That's where we've got to get to. I like the players we've accumulated, what we've done. Now it's figuring out where is that consistency? When we go into a game and we don't have it that night, how do you find a way to win? That's where we've got to get to.

Q: You've brought quite a few former Detroit employees into Dallas. Was it difficult to get them to join the Stars?
A: Detroit was kind of in the process of making changes, and in the end, when people have a chance to go somewhere, you're not going to hold them back. And that's kind of what was going on in Detroit. So really it was up to them and their comfort level. I feel like I had built up a pretty good relationship, I feel like I'm a people person and I think I'm getting better at managing people, and that's something those people (leaving the Red Wings) had to trust.

Q: One of your first big moves was trading for Tyler Seguin. What do you remember about that deal?
A: It was a salary cap situation. They were in a salary cap situation. It was a perfect storm for them: contracts were coming up, they had bonuses, guys that had just signed new deals—going from $3 million to $4 million to guys that were making $7 million. Somebody had to go. They had just gotten to the Finals and they had the core built. Are you going to rip away the core of a (Patrice) Bergeron or somebody like that, (Tuukka) Rask, or a young kid that's coming up. Somebody had to go, and they had to make that decision. But you're seeing more and more of it. I think now in today's game you're seeing more and more deals like that where the cap comes into play, and you have to be aware as another team of what deal might come up because of that.

Q: As you've said, the cap has had a big impact on the game. Can you expand on that?
A: This is going to be bad English, but it used to be a league of who has the most *best* players. But now it doesn't mean you're going

to win. You almost want to have more *better* players. If you can have just 14 really good players, is that better than having six elite players? That's what everyone is trying to find out.

That's what we're trying to manage. Our sport is different than most sports. Basketball, you see two guys or three guys win championships—they are on the floor all the time. Hockey isn't that way. We're a game of 20 players, and they all affect the game. Whereas other sports, three or four players can have more of an impact than our two or three. Especially with how good the game is now.

The game has gotten so good that the difference between the elite players and the good players has shrunk. Good example is you watch the Olympics where everyone has the best players, the games are 1–0, 0–0 because everyone is good. Everybody can skate and handle the puck nowadays, so you can eliminate the impact of other players on another level.

Q: Have you checked notes and discussed management with GMs from other sports?
A: We've talked quite a bit actually. We did that a lot in Detroit, especially when we were coming into the cap era. Football and basketball. And we were fortunate that Mr. I owned the (Detroit) Tigers, so we talked all the time with (former Tigers president) Dave Dombrowski. How he dealt with agents, how you develop players…and we still do that quite a bit, talking with other teams here.

Q: You didn't come to Dallas until 2013, but as someone in the hockey world, what was it like to watch the NHL move a team from the "State of Hockey" to Texas and succeed?
A: It's doing really well here. Right away when something arrives there is so much excitement, and can they sustain it? Winning the cup helps, I think the biggest challenge now is competing for people's interest. That's the biggest thing.

And that's why we have to win consistently. If you're a fan sitting out there, you can go to a football game, baseball game, basketball game, high school football game, college football game—there is a lot competition, and there is beautiful weather to watch things outdoors. That's where our consistency is important. If we can build that up, we can have a more consistent fanbase.

Q: How close are you to that consistency?
A: We've been close. We made (the playoffs), missed, made it, missed. I think (the 2015–16 season) was a real blip. It was a year that could happen to any team, and the injuries were devastating. I'm not a big excuse guy, but facts are facts. That was a tough year to swallow, it was actually my toughest year in hockey. You just couldn't control some things that happened.

But I would say we are getting pretty close to where we want to be overall. Now we've got to do it on the ice. I like where the organization is. I like where situations in Austin (with the AHL team), they've got a good organization down there. We've got some good young kids coming. We've had some good years of drafts, we've got some young guys that are playing for their countries at World Juniors. And it's some high-end guys: (Miro) Heiskanen I think is going to be a high end guy, (Jake) Oettinger is going to be a high-end goalie. We've got some good guys coming. Now the biggest word in sports is patience.

We've got to let it happen. We're not going to rush some things. I know how fans are. And it's really our society. They want it now, and then they can always find something that's happened somewhere else and say, 'Well it's working there.' Well there might be something might not be working there. So you have to be careful. But I think we're in a good spot. I like how everything is coming together, but we've got to go do it now.

36 Peverley Lives

The Dallas Stars thought they lost Rich Peverley on March 10, 2014. Six minutes and 23 seconds into a game against the Columbus Blue Jackets, the center had just completed a shift, had taken a seat on the bench, and then everything changed. "Rich had just come off a shift, and I don't think I'll ever forget what happened," Stars coach Lindy Ruff said. "And I called the next line and within a few seconds Rich was slumped over on [Alex] Chiasson and Jamie Benn."

"He just fell right into my lap and we kind of knew right away that something was wrong," Benn said.

Stars head trainer Dave Zeis was standing behind Peverley when he collapsed and immediately attended to the player. He was joined immediately by Dr. William Robertson, who was sitting three rows behind the bench.

There wasn't any time to waste. Zeis and Robertson grabbed Peverley and pulled him into the hallway between the benches and the locker rooms at American Airlines Center. They were quickly joined by Dr. Robert Dimeff, Dr. Gil Salazar, and a nurse that happened to be sitting close to Robertson.

It took just 13 seconds for the makeshift medical team to start working on Peverley after he collapsed. CPR wasn't enough. The medical team applied a shock that, combined with quick thinking from Zeis and the doctors, saved Peverley's life. "Rich came through right away," Zeis said. "A little bit out of it, but knew somewhat where he was that he asked to go out there the next shift."

Ruff was with Peverley throughout the chaos, from the time he and multiple players were screaming for doctors to the moments he stood a couple feet away from a makeshift triage unit in the hallway behind the bench.

Peverley's wife, Nathalie, later wrote a thank you note to Ruff that he kept pinned on his office wall throughout his coaching tenure in Texas. Nathalie was there when her husband regained consciousness. She had scrambled down to the hallway after Peverley collapsed. "And then seeing my wife's face," Peverley said. "She was white."

For Peverley, looking back on the incident is like retelling someone else's story. He remembers putting his head on his glove, and that's it. He's watched the video of the incident, but it's not focused on the bench, and it was a moment of pure confusion for both fans and broadcasters. "For me it's like—I hate to say this—but it's like it never really happened," Peverley said. "I had to deal with the emotions and everything, the aftermath. But, you know, I didn't deal with the fact that I could have died in front of people."

For those in attendance, it was pure confusion. Those watching on television were also in the dark after watching the Stars bench slam their sticks violently on the ice trying to get people's attention, anyone that could help, in a moment of panic.

Shawn Horcoff had the puck when Peverley collapsed. "I kind of looked back and wasn't really sure at first what happened," Horcoff said. "[I] thought maybe there was an offside or something, or too many men or something."

The American Airlines Center went silent. The broadcasters, Daryl Reaugh and Ralph Strangis, had figured out Peverley was the one missing from the bench, but like everyone else they were in the dark on what was happening in the hallway.

Once Peverley regained consciousness and was taken to the hospital Ruff had a conversation with his captain. It was still early in the game, and the Stars were still fighting for a playoff spot. "I don't think you'll ever forget the look on some of those guys' faces," Ruff said. "When we discussed whether we were going to restart this game…Jamie said there is no way I can play this game anymore."

Officials from the league and both teams agreed. Stars general manager Jim Nill was in Florida for the annual GM meetings at the time of the incident and had a meeting with NHL commissioner Gary Bettman and other officials: they were going to end the game.

That's when fans in the building got confirmation Peverley was the afflicted player and that he was still alive. Peverley had collapsed at 7:50 in the evening local time. At 8:23—33 minutes later—an announcement was made that game was being postponed.

It was a tough night for all of the Stars, who immediately had to fly to St. Louis with back-to-back games on the schedule. Chiasson, who Peverley had partially collapsed onto, was taken to the hospital dealing with shock. Once they were in St. Louis, Alex Goligoski and Erik Cole didn't get much sleep and talked through the incident together late into the evening.

The game against the Blues was an emotionally charged and difficult game for the Stars, but they won for Peverley. St. Louis took an early 1–0 lead before Colton Sceviour scored on a rebound to tie the game at 1–1. Antoine Roussel later gave Dallas a 2–1 lead on a breakaway, but St. Louis tied the game at 2–2 on a scramble in the third period.

In overtime, Benn scored on a pass from Trevor Daley, completing an emotional 24-hour stretch with a victory. "Those are moments that you can't coach, you can't teach," Ruff said.

Back in Dallas, Peverley was still trying to comprehend what happened. A week later he had surgery to correct an abnormal heart rhythm. For a while, Peverley hoped to return to the ice. He worked out and got second and third opinions from doctors on his heart. He also spoke to former Detroit Red Wing Jiri Fischer, who suffered a similar incident on November 21, 2005, that ended his career.

In the end Peverley made the difficult decision to retire. "I could have kept looking around to find a way to play, but it wasn't worth it," Peverley said. "I had a family, and my new job made it a lot easier. I'm very thankful for the Stars helping me make that transition."

With the Stars' help, Peverley found a second career in hockey. Peverley is now the player development coordinator for the Stars, a role he worked to create with Stars general manager Jim Nill during the 2014–15 season as he spent time in Dallas working closely with several of the Stars top executives. "It would have been easy to say, 'Okay, Rich, you've got a year left on your contract, have a good life,'" Nill said. "But it was important for us to not just throw him to the side of the street. Even if it wasn't in hockey, we wanted to help him. But he showed a passion for staying in the game."

Peverley has also shown a passion for helping save lives. After his heart stopped, he and Nathalie started an organization called Pevs Protects, which works to raise money and awareness for heart health. "I'm lucky that I'm put in a position to help people and connect. It was unfortunate how it happened, but I've been able to meet a great amount of people who have had some mishaps in their lives and issues like I did," Peverley said. "I feel fortunate that I've been able to connect with people like that, and that we both are here to talk about it when those discussions happen."

37 The "Turco Grip"

Goaltending has greatly evolved over the course of hockey history. In the late 1800s, the goalie was another skater whose main responsibility was checking opposing forwards in front of the goal markers. He wasn't allowed to kneel, lay on the ice, or catch the puck—stand-up goalie wasn't a style; it was a rule.

Clint Benedict was the first goalie to challenge that rule and often dropped to the ice to make saves, rolling and flailing to keep the puck out of the net. In 1918, the second year of the organized NHL, rules were changed to account for Benedict's style and those copycats that would follow.

While goalies were allowed to drop the ice, most didn't do it. This was an age before masks, and few had the courage to drop to their knees and make saves in that manner like Glenn Hall did with the Detroit Red Wings and Chicago Blackhawks in the 1950s.

Hall was ahead of his time. While Roger Crozier and Tony Esposito used a similar technique in the NHL in the 1970s and Vladislav Tretiak baffled Canadians during the 1972 USSR-Canada Summit Series as a butterfly goalie, it didn't truly become the modern medium of goaltending until Patrick Roy popularized the style in the mid-1980s.

Around the same time Roy was redefining standard positioning with the Montreal Canadiens, Philadelphia Flyers goalie Ron Hextall was changing another key part of a goalie's arsenal. Hextall was a trailblazing puck handler. For the first time in modern NHL history a goalie was both good enough and confident enough to make passes and even take shots at the opposing net.

Hextall inspired an entire generation of puck-handling goalies, including Marty Turco. The longtime Star had 22 assists in his career and quickly established himself as one of the NHL's best puck handling goalies when he made his debut in 2000.

Turco wasn't just one of the best, he was also an innovator and redefined how goalies played the puck. Before Turco entered the NHL, goalies didn't have an ideal grip on their stick. The glove hand would be used as more of a pushing mechanism, and goalies were one dimensional and predictable in where they would pass the puck.

But Turco flipped his glove hand over to the other side of the stick. It gave him better control and more options, instead of being limited to straight passes. Turco could change the angles and could actually make a seamless backhand pass. With better leverage on the stick he could make hard, accurate saucer passes. "I couldn't shoot it as high that way on my forehand, but it was flatter, it was more accurate; my ability to change angles went from about 15 percent dispersion to about 60, 65 percent," Turco said. "Better yet, I had a backhand. I had a legit one. One where I could get it up on the glass even and make little more pinpoint passes as opposed to just shoveling it over there. The whole point of playing it is to get your defenseman the puck quicker, so they can take less of a beating from forecheckers. Once you have a backhand, it changes your dynamics, and the forechecker has to make a decision."

Other goalies started to notice Turco's success and copied the Stars goalie, starting with former Dallas prospects like Mike Smith and Dan Ellis. Eventually the "Turco Grip" became standard teaching in goalie schools, and you'd be hard pressed to find an NHL goalie that doesn't mimic Turco's technique in today's game. "I've been out of the game so long that I start reminding the young goalies, like 'Hey, you know who started that?'" Turco said. "You're welcome."

The "Turco Grip" was born in a practice when Turco was playing for the IHL's Michigan K-Wings during the 1998–99 season. During a drill Turco was having trouble stopping the puck behind the net on his backhand with a more traditional grip. "You just don't have much leverage on your toe on your backhand. And then I kept losing the puck and had to chase it and finally I just got pissed off and turned my hand over and jammed it into the boards," Turco said. "And of course I flipped my hand back over to play it the traditional way. Then we introduced a forechecker to the drill and the forechecker was on me quick one time, and I flipped my glove over to stop it and I slid it over to my partner—or my defenseman—behind the goal on a perfect little pass," Turco added. "I was like, 'That felt pretty good,' and I just went from there and started playing it."

When he got to the NHL the circumstances were in place for Turco's puck-handling style to thrive and truly popularize his grip. The Stars wanted their goalies to move the puck and help eliminate forecheckers with quick passes. "By the time I got here the door was cracked open for me and I kicked that thing through," Turco said. "[Ken Hitchcock] didn't have a handle on me and Dave Tippett had all the confidence in the world in me and saw that every mistake that I made was bettered by 20 to 30 good plays; we thought that outweighed it."

Turco said he never planned to be an innovator, but passing the technique on to younger goalies became a natural conversation when other goalies in Stars training camp would ask Turco why he was so good at puck handling. "By the time I was the starter and young guys would talk to me, I'd say, 'Come on, try this, it'll make you better,'" Turco said. "We were all on the same team and trying to win hockey games, so I thought it was my duty to pass on information to the next generation, next line of players."

38 Strader Strong

Dave Strader only spent one full season as the voice of the Dallas Stars, but in that short time he endeared himself to Stars fans with both his talent to call a game and his passion for the sport.

At the end of the 2016 Playoffs, Strader was diagnosed with cholangiocarcinoma, a rare and aggressive form of bile duct cancer. From that moment the Stars adopted "Strader Strong" as

Strader's Fight
This was one of the last chapters I wrote for the book. I actually avoided writing it until the final week before my first draft deadline because I wasn't sure how to best write this chapter. I'm happy with the finished product, but I also wanted to share another story, which was originally published in Wrong Side of the Red Line on the day he passed away:

"The Voice" may be gone, but Dave Strader beat cancer
As weird as it sounds, thanks to Twitter I knew Dave Strader was still with us.

I last spoke to Dave in April, around the time it was announced the Hockey Hall of Fame would honor him with the 2017 Foster Hewitt Memorial Award.

But over the last five months Dave was active on Twitter. Simply seeing him retweet line rushes from a September practice or a factoid that Martin Hanzal was practicing, it was a constant reminder that one of hockey's greatest broadcasters was still with us.

And not just with us, but still honing a craft that he'd mastered in close to four decades of hockey play-by-play.

Simple little retweets. You probably didn't think anything about them at the time, but it was a small reminder that while he was fighting for his life Dave Strader was still taking notes on line combinations and was prepared to call a game at a moment's notice.

So checking my email on Sunday morning and seeing "Dallas Stars Mourn The Passing Of Dave Strader" in the subject line felt like a punch to the gut. That feeling is still there hours later, and I'm sure it'll be even worse when the Stars inevitably honor Strader in some

a mantra. Players and fans kept Strader in their thoughts, while he was flooded with support from both traditional mail and social media.

On February 18, 2017, Strader returned to the broadcast booth to start a five-game stint, his first game since the diagnosis. The Stars won 4–3 in overtime that night with Jamie Benn scoring the game-winning goal. After the win the Stars raised their sticks in a fashion before their opening night game against the Vegas Golden Knights on Friday.

And I only knew Dave in a limited capacity. I can't imagine how his family and close friends are feeling today.

The five games he worked last season were the highlight of the Stars season. Normally I don't listen to the broadcast while covering a game, if anything I might have it playing in the background and pop in a headphone after a highlight or questionable play.

But when Dave Strader was back in the booth for five games I listened to every second of the broadcast. He wasn't sick on the broadcast, he was still "The Voice" and it was a joy to listen to.

Cancer sucks.

It's a frustrating, destructive disease. It's impacted everyone.

We often say someone beats cancer if they live, and that's true. But it's not a blanket statement.

My mom has had cancer twice, I called her this morning. She beat cancer.

I can't call my one grandfather, who I called "grand daddy," anymore, he had cancer. But he still beat it. He may not have lived, but he beat cancer with his sense of humor. He had to wear an eye patch at times, and he let his grandson pretend he was a pirate while playing pirate LEGOs up until the end of his life.

And Dave Strader beat cancer.

Dave beat cancer when he returned to the booth. He beat cancer when the Stars saluted him after his first game back. He beat it when he called a playoff game on national TV while a disease tried to destroy his body.

Cancer sucks, but it doesn't have to win. Dave knew that.

salute to the broadcaster, who eventually passed away on October 1, 2017. "I think it's nice that we had a moment to acknowledge him," Dallas forward Jason Spezza said. "I think he knew everyone was thinking about him, but to have a forum where we could acknowledge him, I think it'll be a memory that will stick with the organization for a long time. He was dedicated to the game of hockey and a great man."

A large print photo of that salute hangs in the hallway of the Stars practice facility in Frisco, Texas. The Stars also wore stickers with his initials and a microphone on their helmets during the 2017–18 season.

Born in Glens Falls, New York, Strader graduated from the University of Massachusetts with a bachelor's degree in communication studies while working at the college radio station. He began his broadcasting career as the radio voice of the Adirondack Flames, the Detroit Red Wings' American Hockey League affiliate, and their director of public relations from 1979 to 1985. Twice honored by the New York Broadcasters Association for excellence in play-by-play broadcasting, Strader earned the Ken McKenzie Award as the AHL's top PR professional in 1984 and was inducted into the Adirondack Hockey Hall of Fame in 2012. "I don't think Dave ever [for] one second took any of that for granted," Strader's broadcast partner Daryl Reaugh said. "Whether he was calling games in the minors, he loves calling games and he loves being around hockey. He loved it."

Strader spent 11 years as the television voice of the Red Wings (1985–1996) while also calling national games for FOX and ESPN. He also called games for the Florida Panthers and Arizona Coyotes before joining NBC full time in 2011.

Trevor Strader, Dave's youngest son, said the entire hockey community made a difference to his father, who was honored by the Hockey Hall of Fame as the 2017 winner of the Foster Hewitt Memorial Award for his outstanding contributions as a hockey broadcaster. "From fans, from people's he worked with, to the [Red Wings] to the Panthers to the Coyotes, to NBC, every organization he worked with was so supportive of him," Strader said. "Little touches of continued support kept him fighting as long as he did with all the setbacks he had throughout his treatment."

And the best moments for Dave came in the broadcast booth. When he was back behind the microphone calling a game, he was fighting cancer. "He said that was the best treatment he could have ever asked for," Trevor said. "He said after that game in Dallas that it felt like the last nine months hadn't happened. He felt so alive and at home; it really kept him going throughout the whole spring and the summer."

He also planned to call as many games as possible during the 2017–18 season. Trevor said his dad was keeping track of Stars training camp from afar, and nothing was going to keep him from returning to the booth. "We found on his iPad he had the whole NHL season scheduled and he had games marked off that would be potential games that would fit around his medical appointments that he was going to try and call," he said. "There was never going be a moment where he was not going to call games. I think that's a testament; his mind-set was never giving up. His mind-set was always what can I do next, what can I call? That was just how he was."

39 Craig Ludwig

Craig Ludwig was a cult hero for Dallas Stars fans. The defenseman was part of the original team that moved from Minnesota to Dallas, played eight seasons in Texas, and retired after winning the Stanley Cup in 1999.

Ludwig helped personify the Stars' early vibe. It was rock-n-roll, hard-hitting hockey, and Ludwig's large shin pads—the only pair he wore for his entire career—became part of franchise lore.

Ludwig continued to hold a role in the organization after his playing days, working as an advisor to the front office, a liaison for the coaches, and eventually stepping into a role as color analyst full-time during the 2017–18 season. Ludwig discussed his time in Dallas in an interview for this book:

Q: What do you remember about making the transition to Dallas from Minnesota?
A: I think what stood out for me, and probably for all the guys, was, "What the fuck are we getting into, coming to Texas?" I remember sitting—and it was one of the preseason games, and there were about four of us sitting—and we weren't playing that night, and there were guys sitting behind us talking about how the scorekeepers didn't know how to keep score.

And I was kind of listening, and the one guy says to the other, "They only [have] one point up on the board." That's how bad it was. They thought it was supposed to be three points like a field goal. It was like, what are we getting ourselves into here?

Q: There was a football mentality. Fans liked fighting and hits right away, right?
A: Mike Modano wasn't the most popular guy here. Guys that were a little more physical and the ones that had a few fights, they were the favorites and people wanted those jerseys. But what they loved about it, was it was as close to football as they could get. It was physical, and guys were playing on these little blades that they couldn't comprehend, so it was something to where—and I don't want to say comical—but it was a point where you would wonder if the fans even knew what the hell happened that night.

They started doing these 101s during intermissions. They were actually going out on the ice and explaining what icing was and offsides. Which was a great idea, but for us, it was like, "You've gotta be kidding me." Like what are we doing here?

Q: But did it turn out well?

A: For sure, we ended up loving it down here, and a lot of guys never left and still live here today. You could go out to eat, you could do something with the family, and not be bothered. That did get a bit annoying after a while—to be on the pecking order behind the Rangers and Cowboys—but you took advantage of it.

And as we got pretty good, made the playoffs, it started to become the thing to do. People were interested and started to understand the game. It became a nice place to play. Reunion was tough for the opponents, and hockey just grew. In the end I loved it, and I don't know a guy that didn't.

Q: You're on the media side of things now on the broadcast. What do you remember about the media coverage of hockey in the early days in Dallas?

A: One of the downsides was we had one reporter. For guys like myself, who had come from Montreal, it was too easy. When you'd have a bad game, it was always natural to pick up the paper, and it was always, "Oh geez, what are they going to write about me today?" And there was none of that. It wasn't one of those places where you'd have a bad game and then catch a little bit of hell media-wise. Sometimes it's a benefit when you suck to get called out; that's something that may have helped more.

Q: But the team was a winner early. How important was that to ensuring long-term success?

A: I mean they expect a championship in every city right? But here you had the Cowboys, and that was your standard. What was great for us was actually all those guys were coming to our games.

We were over at Troy (Aikman)'s house once a week playing poker. Daryl Johnston was there, and right down the street from the practice rink was the Cowboys Cafe, so we were there every day, and they were there every day. So it was a nice opportunity to get know those guys and know those guys that were the king of the castle over here. So from that standpoint it was nice to rub elbows and say, "Oh, I was out with so-and-so last night." And people started to know us, and they would come to our games.

Q: So they got the sport then?
A: No, they didn't get it. Religion here is those guys (the Cowboys) right down the road. But it was actually kind of fun sitting there and trying to explain to them what offsides was and what icing was. Because they were just fascinated that you could just run somebody over, you could get in a fight, and that was all legal. That kind of stuff that they didn't understand, but they liked it.

But I think guys actually enjoyed that. You had people glued to every word you said and weren't so concerned as much about who you were but wanted to learn the game. I never found it to be a pain in the ass to answer these question; it was nice to see people interested. Sure there were more free dinners in Montreal than there were in Dallas, but an expectation grew, and people wanted to learn more.

Q: Bob Gainey really defined the franchise, as both a coach and general manager. You also played with him in Montreal. What do you remember about his time in Dallas?
A: Early on I remember Bob complaining about having all these .500 guys that had come from Minnesota; guys who would win one and lose one and be okay with that. And he started bringing in these guys from Montreal, where they won and were used to winning.

And you could feel it changing. Then we had a pretty good couple years, and Bob really understood how things worked. It's not easy to fire yourself, but he made the right decisions, and that meant winning. That's what Bob did. He put winning over his own ego. He didn't say much, but when he did, it put us in the right direction.

Bob was my Scotty Bowman because I spent a lot of years with him in Montreal. When I was a rookie in Montreal, he would come back to me on the plane and sit down with a paper and pencil and ask me what I thought about the penalty kill that night. And he was that kind of a guy where you'd give him an answer, then he'd look at it, and then he'd look at you, and then it would get more uncomfortable by the moment. Then he'd go, "no." And then tell you how you were wrong because Bob was always teaching. He was put here to be a hockey guy. You know what I mean? He was 24/7 in hockey. When he was a captain in Montreal, he didn't lose his mind every day, where some guys and coaches can go and snap.

He expected you to win. An example of Bob: we were in the season one time and we'd stretch and come to the middle of the ice and you'd expect your coach to speak. And he'd say...if we had a game the next night, he'd look at one guy, and—say we're playing Philly—he'd ask one guy, "What was the score of Philly's last game?" And you're thinking, what the fuck's that gotta do with anything?

And then he'd ask another guy, "Well, who got the game-winning goal?" And if you got that answer right or wrong, then he'd ask someone else the same question. So he did that three or four days in a row, and we're thinking this fucking guy is going to do this every day. So when we came in there were all these *USA Today* papers, and we were all staring at the box scores and looking at the schedule because he might ask you, "Who did they play the last two games?" And what he was doing was getting you dialed in and ready for your next opponent.

In everything he did, it was about doing it right. As a player when you're doing your down and backs, he'd touch the glass, do a perfect two-foot stop. He didn't give a shit if he was four lines behind everybody else. He was going to do it right. That's how he was and that's how he was as a coach and a general manager. The benefits will come if you do it the right way.

Q: What about Ken Hitchcock? Was he the Hitch that everyone thinks about right away?
A: He turned into Hitch that we know about now. The first time he came in, I think it was when he was coaching Kalamazoo or something like that, and he was quiet and said, "Oh it's okay, it's alright," things like that when he was with the team in training camp. Than a year later, when he was the coach, he came in and he was Hitch, and was like, "Is this the same fucking guy?"

He's the kind of guy that you've got to keep guys in check and you've got to talk to him and he's hard. I'd say to guys, "We just won six out of the last seven games. What do you want?" He came in like a lamb and turned into a lion real quick, and it paid off.

I think he understood that he had the players that could handle that style of coaching, the ones that needed this little tap on the ass. There weren't many of them. He kept everyone in line, and those guys that couldn't handle it were dragged in by the rest of the group.

What's different about Hitch—especially compared to a lot of coaches I had—is he was just as hard as those top guys. And it was really refreshing to see him hard on the top guys, the guys that scored goals and made money. It was a moment like, yes, know you know what the fuck it's like for the rest of us. I think that made the team closer together; everyone was treated the same. I mean, he yelled at everyone, except Jere Lehtinen. How could you ever yell at Jere Lehtinen? It's refreshing, he yells at everyone. But that's why Hitch has that shelf life.

Q: What did that 1999 season feel like?

A: You could feel it. You could feel it from the couple years prior when we were close. We kept getting close, we had a great team. We had a team the way Hitch coached, it made us stronger. What he's all about: you have your captains, but our role as captains, and everyone thinks those three or five guys with letters, however you do it, that their job is to be the leadership. That's not what their job is. Their job is to make that group bigger and bigger and keep pulling guys into a leadership role. The more you do that, the stronger you're gonna be.

We knew that we had a huge group like that, and both Hitch and Bob [Gainey] helped push that. Bob kept pulling guys in from Montreal, guys who knew how to win. A lot of us had won in 86 or 93 with Montreal, so we had a lot of guys that knew it wasn't a light switch; this is not something you can just turn on. We had to do it from game-to-game, day-to-day, and Hitch kept keeping the foot on the gas. The practices would get harder and harder, but we'd keep winning and winning. And in the moment you'd think, "Why the fuck do these keep getting harder? We're winning?" But when you realized that we weren't going to change our game and roll into Game 1 of the playoffs playing the same game, we were ready for the playoffs. You got ready for the playoffs with Game 1 of the regular season. We played the same way in Game 1, Game 40, Game 50. When you play like that, you have a feeling this could be a long season.

40 Pantera

If you've ever been to Dallas Stars game, you've likely heard "Puck Off" by Pantera. The song—a Dallas Stars anthem by the Arlington-based heavy metal group—has a history as both a goal song and warmup mix for the team, and was birthed into reality before the night before the 1999 Stanley Cup Playoffs.

Craig Ludwig was golfing with Vinnie Paul the day before the first-round series with the Edmonton Oilers when he asked the rocker to put something together. They finished the round of golf, Paul and his brother, Dimebag Darrell, went back to the studio that night and wrote and recorded the song. They delivered the song to Ludwig on a CD the next morning, and it was part of the pregame mix that night.

The song became a playoff fixture. It played before each game, and the Stars listened to it before each home game. And the best story about that song comes from Game 6 of the second round against the St. Louis Blues. The day before Game 6, Ludwig called Paul and asked him to get him a copy of the CD for the road. The Stars had been 5–0 at home when the song had played and they needed some extra juice as they were trying to close out the series.

The disc didn't make it before the game; a storm caused a delay in delivery. It also didn't arrive before the first intermission or second intermission. But it did arrive right as regulation came to a close with the Stars and Blues tied at 1–1. Ludwig took the CD, put it on the stereo in the locker room, and the familiar "Dallas! Stars! Dallas! Stars!" was blasted right before overtime started. Two minutes and 21 seconds into overtime, Mike Modano scored to end the series.

Fittingly, the members of Pantera were a big part of the Stanley Cup celebration a month later. Depending on who you ask, a party at Paul's house lasted somewhere between three and five days, only taking a break for the championship parade where some of the players showed up an hour late after trying to sober up.

And that likely explains the large dent that was found in the base of the Stanley Cup, which has since been buffed out, after the Stars celebration. There were other explanations and theories, including the cup being dropped in the locker room in Buffalo or being mishandled at the DFW Airport, but the more likely explanation starts and ends with the Pantera party.

During the partying the Stanley Cup ended up in the pool, when Guy Carbonneau threw the chalice from a second-story window and it hit the lip of the pool before taking a splash in the water. Carbonneau denies this fact, but it fits with his past celebrations after he had tossed the Stanley Cup into Patrick Roy's pool when the Montreal Canadiens won in 1993.

41 Shane Churla

With 1,883 penalty minutes, Shane Churla still holds the franchise record for time spent in the box. And when the Dallas Stars moved from Minnesota to Texas, the 6'1", 200-pound right winger was the original enforcer.

During the first season in Dallas he set a franchise record with 26 fights in one season, but he also had a career year offensively with six goals. He was an instant fan favorite at Reunion Arena. Churla—who now works for the Montreal Canadiens—discussed his time in Dallas in a Q&A for this book:

Q: What do you remember about the move from Minnesota to Dallas?

A: I think it was unique because normally when you move it's a trade and you're normally by yourself. And you may go to a team and know one or two guys, while we moved as a group. So all we had was each other because nobody really knew anybody here. In turn I think it helped our team come together. I thought we were a pretty tight group at that point, so that was the intriguing part about it.

Q: What were the early hockey fans like in Dallas?

A: I think there was an education period just as far as some of the people learning the game, but I think they really liked the speed and physicality of it. In turn I think that brought more people to the table.

Q: You were a fan favorite right away. What was that like?

A: I always liken it to that it's a football city, so they like the physicality part of it. As I've said before, no place has treated me as well for the role I was in. They really appreciated it. They seemed to like it, and in turn I fed off it.

Q: How important was early success on the ice for the franchise to succeed in Dallas?

A: I think it was crucial. That and the fact that they grew it internally with building the rinks and grew their fanbase that way; I think that was a very key part. But the fact that we came in and played hard, I think it helped sell the game in Texas, for sure.

Q: You had quite a role in one of the Stars' true rivalries with the Chicago Blackhawks in the late 1980s in Minnesota, and that followed the team to Dallas in the early 1990s. What was that like?
A: The Chuck Norris Division. It was a tough grind, every team was loaded up that way. You knew going in, there (were) going to be no easy games. It's funny now that I'm on the scouting side I see a 3–0 or 4–0 game, and nothing happens. Well back in the day, that turned into a four or five-hour game with dustups and everything else.

Q: What do you think of fighting's diminishing role in hockey?
A: I think it was time, probably. They had to put some things in place with the concussions and everything else to protect the players and protect the game. I don't think they totally need to take it all out of the game; I think players need an avenue to release some pressure. If not (fighting) it's going to be stick work, and you don't want that. It's definitely morphing to speed and skill, and that's a direction in today's game.

Q: Is that something you noticed during your career? Or only after?
A: Not in my time. I think they talked about it, they talked about shortening the benches and stuff like that. You know, as far as my period of time in the National Hockey League, it was never talked about getting rid of or limiting fights.

Q: How do you think you would fare in today's NHL?
A: With the slashing and hooking calls, I would probably be in the box twice as much, but I could skate and I could get there. But you can weigh it both ways. Nobody would be able to hold me up. That would be an advantage. I could get in there and pressure. It's gone to speed and skill, and guys that played my role also have to play a special team now. You can't just be a guy at the end of the bench.

And I don't think I was. I did get those opportunities and I think I went out there and contributed more than just a fight.

42 Guy Carbonneau

Guy Carbonneau was past his prime when he arrived in Dallas. He was already 35 years old when he was traded from the St. Louis Blues to the Dallas Stars on October 2, 1995. He had gotten a bit slower with age, he wasn't going to win any more Selke Trophies, and he wasn't going to score close to 50 points a season like he did in his late 20s with the Montreal Canadiens.

But Carbonneau was a winner who helped reshape and ultimately define the team that won the Stanley Cup in 1999. In order for Ken Hitchcock and Bob Gainey's system to work, they needed players that bought in and lived smart, defensive, winning hockey.

That was Carbonneau. "He wasn't the fastest guy or the guy that would score a goal when you needed with us, but he helped define that group," Hitchcock said. "You need your leaders to sell your message, and Guy was a winner. He sold winning and everyone can follow that."

In five seasons with Dallas, Carbonneau appeared in 364 games, had 34 goals, and 66 assists. He won his third Stanley Cup with the Stars in 1999, adding to cup wins in 1986 and 1993 with Montreal before retiring after the 1999–2000 season with 1,318 career games—good for 56th in NHL history at the time of this book. On top of that, in his final season as a 39-year-old, Carbonneau still received a pair of first-place votes for the Selke as the NHL's top defensive forward. Carbonneau discussed his time in Dallas in an interview for this book:

Q: What does this franchise mean to you?

A: For me it's always special…my two daughters still live in Dallas. Every time I always go back, it's an occasion to see them and see the grandkids. Not too often when I go back I have the chance to go to a hockey game. Most of the times I'm here in the summer, or it's a quick in and out. So having a chance the week before for Jere's jersey retirement and going back for the little ceremony, it's always fun. It's always fun to be recognized. You do this because you love it. As much as we don't want to be recognized when we play, it's

Though past his prime when he arrived in Dallas, Guy Carbonneau provided some much-needed smart, defensive stability to balance the team's big playmakers.

different (after you retire). It's always fun to come and see the guys again. If you talk to everyone once they retire, the thing they miss the most is seeing the guys every day.

Q: What was it like coming to Dallas in 1995?
A: It was kind of awkward at the start. I was probably one of the lucky ones starting my career here in Montreal. Playing with guys like Guy Lafleur, and Larry Robinson, and Bob Gainey, guys that were really successful for long periods of time. And you can name a lot of people that won one cup or two cups, but having a chance to start your career with guys that won six or seven, and being around guys like Henri Richard, who won 11, it was a good way to start. The franchise was the talk of the town. Hockey is a passion here in Montreal, especially in Canada. So the first couple weeks in Dallas it was awkward and different.

It was football, baseball, and basketball and not as much as hockey. I knew Bob (Gainey) and I knew that they wanted to build a winner, and having guys like (Brian) Skrudland, and Mike Keane, and (Craig) Ludwig, those guys around made us feel like we were going in the right way. But it's one thing to say that you are going to build a winner, and it's another thing to say that you are going to do it. So the start was funny; not a lot of reporters, not a lot of people around, which was kind of fun at one point. I think we kind of gelled together and became one of the good teams in the NHL, so the process was really fun.

Q: How far into that process did you realize it was a group that could win a championship?
A: I think it took a couple seasons. My first year, or the first two years, Bob was trying to have a feeling for what we had and what he needed for the missing pieces. The third season, in 1998, we had a good run and had a hard loss. It was a hard loss, but I always

said that you build character by losing. It's hard to get to the end. It's a long process, there are a lot of ups and a lot of downs. I really believe that we lost in 1998 and that kind of made us stronger and more determined to achieve our goal. And the team came back with a vengeance the year after, and almost did it again in 2000.

Q: A couple people have said the team was a reflection of Bob Gainey. What does that mean to you?
A: He was one of the guys that built this thing. He made the decision to go get Eddie Belfour and then get Brett Hull, and then go get Joe Nieuwendyk when we knew we needed some help to help (Mike) Modano and guys like Derian Hatcher. I think he brought guys that had a lot of character, and that was Bob. Bob was pretty quiet and had an attitude of never quit, and I think that's the kind of guys that he brought in. And we meshed really, really well.

Q: You were here for Jere Lehtinen's jersey retirement ceremony. As a Selke winner yourself, what was it like watching him in his prime?
A: It's always fun. I learned by playing with Bob, who was already a Selke winner, and I learned a lot from him talking with him— talking the game, talking about what you needed to do to be a better player or a better person. And I think I saw Jere look that early in his career.

He was somebody that had a really, really good work ethic. Just never quit, worked really hard in practice, wanted to be a good player, and having the chance to play with Mike Modano and Brett Hull for a while doesn't hurt either. But he was always somebody that just knew what he needed to do to play well defensively. He was a no-question player, just showed up every morning, worked hard in practice, got ready for the game, and said…well he didn't really say it, but you knew he was just thinking, "Let's do it again tomorrow."

Q: What about that Stanley Cup-winning team? I've heard it was a really close group off the ice. Is that a fair assessment?

A: There is always that connection with most of the players. I'm not saying that every team kind of meshes like that and likes everybody. There are 23, 24, 25 guys that are different characters and have different goals; that's the beauty about a sports team. And I think we understood that. We had a veteran team. There were some rookies and young guys but not that many. We were all at the end of our career or mid career and we all had the same goal. Even when there was bullshit, we didn't take long to resolve.

We had one goal, and that was to win the Stanley Cup. We addressed the issues and put it aside and just kept going. You were talking early how we reflected Bob Gainey, and I think that's what Bob was. Bob was a "no bullshit" guy. If he had a problem, he would tell you and that was it.

When things are going well on the ice, things are usually going well off of the ice. Like I said, we had a veteran team. And a lot of us had bikes and motorcycles, so we used to come to practice on the bikes, and then after practice do rides. So there was a lot of togetherness; that was normal for those years in Dallas.

Q: Your family still lives in Dallas, you have grandkids playing youth hockey here. Is that something you would have ever imagined when you first heard about the NHL moving to Texas in 1993?

A: We had teams in L.A. for a while. We knew that hockey was popular in Canada and (eastern) North America, like Boston and New York, those places. They were trying to put teams out west where it was more football, basketball, and baseball. I think it took time, but I think what Dallas did better than any other franchise—and I think now the new franchises understand what they did—they started to build the rinks.

They wanted to not only to go to Dallas and be a good sports franchise, rack up the money, and that would be it. I think they had a bigger idea in their heads and they started to build rinks, and hockey became popular, and they hit the root. They had to come to get the people who play baseball or football or basketball to enjoy hockey, and I think now you see the result.

I notice this now. I have grandkids who play hockey. And every time I'm back in Dallas, I go to the rink and you see it. You see the kids getting involved, the parents getting involved. And that's the success. Yes, we won the cup in 1999 and almost did it in 2000, but I think they're more successful out of the rink and building hockey for everyone else.

43 Hockey Players Want to Come to Texas

Thanks to a trio of key factors the Dallas Stars have turned into a destination team for NHL players. Whether that's via trade or free agency, rarely do the Stars end up on a no-fly list for a player or agent. "I've been with this team since the beginning and I've never heard a player say 'We won't go there,' about Dallas," Stars president Jim Lites said. "We've had players waive their no-trade clause to come here. In fact, the only guy that ever turned us down and enforced his no-trade is Joe Thornton because he wasn't going anywhere. He had his deal, his kids were young, he loved his house; he wasn't going anywhere. "He got into a 'fuck you' with the GM there [in San Jose]. "Before we acquired Jason Spezza, the same offer had been made to San Jose for Joe Thornton, and it was accepted, but Joe wasn't going to make it happen."

So with the exception of Joe Thornton, why do players circle Dallas as a destination? "There are a couple reasons," Stars general manager Jim Nill said. "If you're an NHL player, you look at Dallas and you see them as a hard team to play against. They play fast, they've got some good players, and they are willing to make moves to win. That's appealing to players. You also have the tax situation, which works well in our favor, and it's a beautiful city where players are recognized, but not overwhelmed."

The lack of state income tax goes a long way, especially when the Stars are bidding for the services of a player considering a tax-heavy market like Canada or California. For example, during the 2017 offseason, Alexander Radulov picked Dallas over a similar offer from the Montreal Canadiens. While on paper it was the same deal with $31.25 million over five seasons, Montreal would have had to offer an extra $2 million in salary to make up for the taxes Radulov would have to pay in Quebec.

Dallas also has that ideal balance of an untraditional market mixed with a passionate fanbase. It's not a Canadian city where players are mobbed and struggle to live a normal life, but it is a place that appreciates a winner and demonstrates southern hospitality that players have come to enjoy. "Here people go out and shake their hand and say, 'Good luck tonight,' but they don't overwhelm them," Nill said.

Proof of that is how many players end up living in Dallas after they retire. "I retired here for a reason," Vernon Fiddler said. "This became home. The city and the people were always great to me and my family, and every year it gets better as a hockey town."

44 Dino Ciccarelli

If Dino Ciccarelli had played in Dallas, his No. 20 likely would be hanging from the rafters alongside Neal Broten's No. 7 at American Airlines Center. Ciccarelli had all the makings to be a fan favorite. He was an unexpected success story, played with an edge, and was pretty good at putting the puck in the net, particularly in the playoffs.

As a teenager Ciccarelli was a dominant force for the London Knights, but an injury during his draft year limited him to 19 points in 30 games. With less of a sample size to go off, Ciccarelli went undrafted.

He eventually signed with the North Stars as a free agent, picking Minnesota over an offer from the Buffalo Sabres since general manager Lou Nanne had a better offer for early playing time. In his final season with London, he had 103 points in 62 games and joined the CHL's Oklahoma City Stars at the end of the season. The next season Ciccarelli started the season in Oklahoma before being called up for good halfway through the season.

He finished his rookie season with 30 points in 32 NHL games and then starred as the North Stars made a miraculous run to the 1981 Stanley Cup Finals. Ciccarelli set an NHL rookie record with 21 points and 14 goals that postseason. His 14 goals are still a record today, and it kicked off a successful nine-season stint in Minnesota. "What a turnaround for me," Ciccarelli said after his career came to an end. "I just wanted to continue and play in the league. You don't think about scoring 600 goals or playing 19 years."

In his second season, Ciccarelli scored 55 goals—a franchise record he still shares with Brian Bellows—and scored at least 30 goals in seven of the next eight seasons. In 602 games with the franchise he had 651 points, including 332 goals and 319 assists, he still ranks third in franchise history for goals and fourth in points.

Ciccarelli was traded to the Washington Capitals late during 1988–89 season and ended his career with 1,200 points in 1,232 career games between five franchises. His 608 career goals are the most by any player that was draft eligible but went undrafted.

In 2010, Ciccarelli was inducted into the Hockey Hall of Fame. Ciccarelli had to wait eight years to get inducted. It was a combination of questions about his candidacy—he never won a cup and never won a major individual award—and he ran into legal troubles throughout his career.

When he was finally elected, Ciccarelli wanted to make sure it wasn't a hoax before celebrating. "I guess you start thinking that way," Ciccarelli said. "I was hoping it would come. In past years, people would call me and say they heard I was in. I tried not to get too excited this year and when I got the call I was very excited. It would have been nice to enjoy it with my [parents, both deceased], but I've got my kids and my family to share it with."

45 The Tent

Dallas Stars fans from the 1990s affectionately remember "The Tent." While Reunion Arena was a raucous and exciting venue for the Stars, it didn't have the modern conveniences fans can now enjoy at American Airlines Center. There were no suites, there was no club level, and the building was old.

And for the Stars, one makeshift remedy was "The Tent." It was essentially a postgame club set up outside of Reunion Arena. "It was big white tent, there was a DJ and a dance area, a bar along the one side, and it was the place to go after the game," Craig Ludwig said. "It was great. As players we'd go hang out there after the games. Fans would have a great time, it really was a fucking genius idea."

"It was the best singles bar in Dallas," Stars president Jim Lites said. "We didn't have the club area and things like that that we have at American Airlines Center, so you have to create something like that outside."

"It was open for a couple hours after the game, so it became a real kind of spot to hang out," Shane Churla said. "Some weekends it was packed, and people would be in there all night."

For the Stars players it turned into a way to both sell the sport and unwind after a game.

"It was a thing where the guys would get together for a couple beers, and for me it was nice to stand outside in the winter after spending years in Montreal," Guy Carbonneau said. "And it was great for fans. They could come up and get autographs and things like that, while they also had a good time."

"We were told to go up there and go socialize. I don't know if you'd get that from the management today," Mike Modano said. "But it was interesting. It was a different group of people every night. You joined in with the fans, and I think it helped some fans grasp the sport more right away."

It was also a bonding point for those teams that won the Stanley Cup in the late 1990s. While all players wouldn't go to the tent after every game, there was an unofficial team rule that wives and girlfriends didn't enter the tent. "We were behind the bar, and it was bonding as a team. It was important and we were a close group," Ludwig said. "There was a player one time that had his wife at the game that night, and we decided it was a tent night for the whole team. So after the game his wife waited outside the tent doors the entire time. Now that's a fucking teammate."

46 Hartsburg, Klingberg, and Hips

While Sergei Zubov is the gold standard for Stars offensive-minded defensemen, Craig Hartsburg set the bar early with his play in Minnesota from 1979 to 1989.

Hartsburg started his pro career during the 1978–79 as an underage free agent with the Birmingham Bulls in the WHA. That would be the final season for the financially struggling league, and since Hartsburg was still only 19, he was eligible for the 1979 NHL Draft where the North Stars picked him with the sixth overall pick in the first round.

Hartsburg quickly established himself as an offensive force from the blue line with the North Stars. In his first NHL season, he had 44 points in 79 games and he followed that up with 43 points during the 1980–81 season.

The left-handed defender had his best season—and one of the best in franchise history—during the 1981–82 campaign. Then 22, Hartsburg set franchise records for defensemen with 60 assists and 77 points, two marks that still stand. He finished fourth in the Norris Trophy voting for the NHL's top defenseman.

Hartsburg received seven first-place votes, five second-place votes, and four third-place votes. In total he received 17.14 percent of the total votes, finishing behind three future Hockey Hall of Famers—the Edmonton Oilers' Paul Coffey, Boston Bruins' Ray Bourque, and the Norris winner that season, Chicago Blackhawks defenseman Doug Wilson.

Unfortunately, that would be the peak of Hartsburg's career as hip injuries hindered him. While he had 62 points the next season, Hartsburg was limited to 58 games between 1984 and 1985. He battled back with 57 points during the 1985–86 season, and was once again a Norris Trophy candidate with 61 points as a 27-year-old during the 1986–87 season.

Hartsburg only played 27 games during the 1987–88 season and was limited to 30 during the 1988–89 season, prompting him to retire before his 30th birthday. He finished his playing career with 413 points in 570 games with the North Stars, an average of 0.72 points per game.

Hartsburg later recalled in an interview with *The Hockey News* that having to retire was one of his most painful memories. "I felt I still had a lot of hockey left, but, unfortunately, I couldn't perform," Hartsburg said.

While his playing career was over, Hartsburg used those late injuries to springboard into a career in coaching. He was an assistant with the North Stars the year after he retired and later served as the head coach for the Blackhawks, Anaheim Ducks, and Ottawa Senators. "The last two years I wasn't playing because I had lots of injuries and I started thinking about [coaching]," Hartsburg told the *Ottawa Sun* in 2008. "I got lucky because Pierre Page gave me an opportunity to come in as the third assistant. There wasn't a lot of responsibility, but I watched and was able to see what the life of a coach was about."

Even with his hips holding him back, Hartsburg still ranks second in franchise history among defenders with 98 goals, 315 assists, 413 points, 40 power play goals, and 1,492 shots. But you can't help but wonder what Hartsburg would have been able to do without bum hips.

Almost three decades later, advancements in modern medicine may have helped Stars fans from asking a similar question about John Klingberg, who had hip surgery in 2012 when he was still a Stars prospect playing back in Europe. He then had double hip surgery before the 2014–15 season but recovered in time to lead all NHL rookie defenseman in scoring with 40 points that season.

After that rookie campaign, the Stars smartly signed Klingberg to a seven-year contract extension. In the first season of that contract Klingberg finished sixth in the Norris Trophy voting as a 23-year-old. Now entering the prime of his career, the Swedish defender has potential to climb the Stars all-time record books and appears set to be a fixture on the blue line well into his 30s. It's amazing what modern medicine can do.

47 Cinco de Morrow

The game started on May 4, 2008. It didn't end until 1:24 in the morning on May 5, 2008 with the Dallas Stars celebrating their first trip to the Western Conference Finals since 2000.

Overtime had been common practice between the Stars and San Jose Sharks that series. Three of the first five games required a sudden-death session, including a Game 5 win by the Sharks that extended the series.

So heading into Game 6 there was almost an expectation that the teams would play more than 60 minutes. But no one expected the teams to play more than 60 minutes of overtime.

First Period
Only 72 seconds into the game, Stars forward Joel Lundqvist checked Douglas Murray in the corner and knocked out a piece of plexiglass. That was the first sign this was going to be a long night.

Second Period
After a scoreless first period, the Stars broke through at 4:49 of the second period. Sergei Zubov's shot was stopped by Sharks goalie

Brenden Morrow celebrates his game-winning goal against the San Jose Sharks in the fourth overtime of Game 6 to send the Stars to the Western Conference Finals.

Evgeni Nabokov, but the goalie then got tangled up with Niklas Hagman. Nabokov tried to recover and dove for a rebound but couldn't stop Antti Miettinen's shot that gave Dallas a 1–0 lead. Marty Turco made 11 saves in the period to help Dallas hold the lead entering the third period.

Third Period
San Jose finally ended Turco's shutout bid 1:39 into the third period. After making a series of sharp saves earlier in the sequence, the Stars goalie was caught off guard on a turnaround shot by Ryane Clowe that hit off the right post and into the net.

That goal swung the momentum for the Sharks, who controlled possession and outshot the Stars 12–7 in the period. San Jose likely would have went into overtime feeling confident, but Stars captain Brenden Morrow hammered Sharks right wing Milan Michalek with less than 10 seconds remaining in regulation. The hit knocked Michalek out of the game and sent a jolt to the Stars heading into the locker room.

First Overtime
Motivated by their captain's big hit, the Stars were the better team in the first overtime and nearly won the series 91 seconds into the first session. Brad Richards had a clean point-blank one-timer from below the faceoff circle, but Nabokov got across and made one of the greatest glove saves in NHL history.

The Stars argued the puck had crossed the line while it was in Nabokov's glove, and the red light had flashed, but overhead reviews confirmed the goalie had made a miraculous stop. That was one of 18 saves Nabokov made that period. Turco made 11, and the game rolled into the second overtime.

Second Overtime

This was the period where Turco ultimately saved the game for the Stars. Dallas seemingly emptied the tank in the first overtime and couldn't generate any offense in the fifth period. Nabokov was only required to make two saves, while Turco made 11.

Third Overtime

With energy draining, scoring chances became more infrequent in the third overtime as Nabokov (six) and Turco (eight) only had to combine for 14 saves. San Jose thought it scored a game-winner midway through when Clowe seemed to poke a shot past Turco, but it was under the goalie's glove. San Jose also had a power play early in the period, but the Stars penalty kill only allowed one shot while Nicklas Grossmann was in the box for hooking.

Fourth Overtime

At 8:14 of the period, Sharks defenseman Brian Campbell was called for tripping, giving the Stars their first power play since the second period.

Finally somebody capitalized.

Working the point, Mike Modano made a pass to Stephane Robidas and received a pass back. Moving to the right side of the ice, Modano made a pass to Mike Ribeiro, who had taken Modano's spot on the left point.

Robidas had moved down the half wall during this sequence, and Ribeiro made a cross ice pass to the defender. While this was happening, Morrow had taken up residence in front of the net. His stick was on the ice, and Robidas found him with a pass to the slot, where Morrow deflected the puck past Nabokov's right pad.

After 69 minutes and three seconds of overtime the game was over. Five hours and 14 minutes after the opening faceoff, the Stars were headed back to the Western Conference Finals. Turco only had to make one save in the fourth overtime, his 61st of the night, a franchise record that still stands today.

# District 5

A pee wee hockey team from District 5 in Minneapolis helped change the course of Dallas Stars history.

Seriously.

Before Norm Green decided to move the North Stars from Minnesota to Dallas, it was almost a certainty the team would be moving to Southern California. The team would have moved to Anaheim, been known as the L.A. Stars, and played at the brand new Anaheim Arena (now known as the Honda Center).

It was the perfect fit for Green and a deal was in place. But Disney got in the way. On October 2, 1992, *The Mighty Ducks* premiered. The film starred Emilio Estevez as Gordon Bombay, a crass Minnesota lawyer sentenced to community service that includes coaching a youth hockey team.

Bombay gets the boss of his firm (Gerald Ducksworth) to sponsor the club, changing the team name from District 5 to the Ducks after he promises to get Ducksworth his own jersey. The sponsorship does wonders for the Ducks, who instantly have professional looking equipment and uniforms, while Bombay has actually dedicated himself to coaching after reconnecting with his mentor and family friend, Hans, and recruiting a couple key players.

The season comes with its struggles and Bombay actually loses his job at one point over a player eligibility dispute. But like any good Disney film, the Ducks ultimately win the Minnesota Pee

Wee Championship when Charlie Conway (played by Joshua Jackson) scores on a penalty shot.

The North Stars made a couple cameos in the movie, and Bombay takes his team to a game against the Hartford Whalers in the film. Basil McRae and Mike Modano have a short scene around the middle of the movie, where Bombay's pee wee hockey career playing alongside McRae was somehow enough to discuss a minor league tryout.

> McRae: Hey, Gordo! Gordon Bombay, right?
>
> Bombay: You remember me?
>
> McRae: Sure, from pee wees. (*To Modano*) This guy used to rule in pee wees.
>
> Modano: Oh yeah? I heard you were a farmer.
>
> Bombay: Actually, I became a lawyer. But I'm coaching pee wee now, and this is my team, the Ducks. Ducks, this is Basil McRae and Mike Modano.
>
> Players: We can see that.
>
> Bombay: All right.
>
> McRae: Hey, Ducks! Listen to this guy. He knows what he's talking about. (*Turning to Bombay*) If you ever want a shot, I'll get you a tryout in the minor league clubs.
>
> Bombay: Thanks.
>
> McRae: No problem. Hey, nice seein' ya.
>
> Modano: Take it easy.

According to McRae, he and Modano had to switch lines. "There was no pressure in the cameo in *The Mighty Ducks* because Mike was an awesome player, Hall of Famer, probably one of the best if not the best American born players in the history of the NHL," McRae said in a 2015 interview with Vishal Hussain. "But he was a terrible actor, so there is absolutely no pressure. I was supposed to be North Star No. 2 and Mike supposed to be North Star

No. 1, but after about three takes, they reversed that, and I was North Star No. 1."

"That's false," Modano retorted. "He was the senior. So he got the good speaking role. So he had seniority over me, so they made that call."

Acting roles aside, the movie was a success. It grossed more than $50 million at box offices and was the 31st highest-earning movie of 1992. (If you were wondering, another Disney movie, *Aladdin* was No. 1 at $217 million.) It helped prompt Disney to jump from pee wee hockey to the NHL.

So in December of 1992, the NHL asked Green to alter his plan. Disney wanted to start an expansion franchise in Anaheim, and the Mickey Mouse company was willing to use Disney stars to help market the sport. Green agreed, and as a "thank you" for letting Disney enter the league, the NHL gave the owner full permission to move the team to whichever market gave him the best deal.

Oh, and a quick note on Bombay. He actually ends up turning into a pretty good player in the minor leagues for the unfortunately fictional Minnehaha Waves, a North Stars affiliate. But a career-ending knee injury prevents him from making the NHL and theoretically playing for the Dallas Stars with his acting buddy Modano. Think about that next time you watch *The Mighty Ducks.*

49 Ralph and Razor

Many hockey fans in Texas learned the game from the iconic broadcasting duo "Ralph and Razor." From 1996 to 2015, Ralph Strangis and Daryl "Razor" Reaugh expertly shared the Stars broadcast booth: Strangis in a play-by-play role with Reaugh providing thoughtful color commentary while seemingly reading out of a dictionary of superfluous jargon.

Strangis moved with the team from Minnesota to Dallas. He had served as the color commentator alongside Al Shaver and held the same role alongside Mike Fornes in Dallas when Shaver elected to retire and didn't move to Texas.

Fornes left Dallas after the 1995–96 season, and Strangis became the new play-by-play voice of the Stars. A former NHL goalie, Reaugh's career was cut short by injuries and he had worked as a color analyst for the Hartford Whalers during the 1995–96 season before joining the Stars and Strangis during the 1996–97 season.

Ralph and Razor had instant chemistry in the booth and were often lauded for their broadcast with Strangis providing sharp, insightful play-by-play and Reaugh giving smart and, well, *colorful* commentary. The fact the Stars simulcast games on both television and radio only helped raise their status. If a hockey fan was catching the Stars game on any given night, Ralph and Razor had their ear.

Their run as a duo came to an end after the 2014–15 season, when Strangis decided to step away from the Stars. Reaugh spent one season as the color analyst alongside Dave Strader, then became the full-time play-by-play voice after Strader passed away in 2017.

50 Hockey History in Dallas

Although the NHL didn't come to Texas until 1993, organized hockey in Dallas dates back almost a century. The Gardner Ice Palace opened in Oak Cliff in 1927 and was home to various high school teams and the Dallas Ice Kings. The Ice Kings played against teams from Fort Worth, San Antonio, and Houston in the Southwestern Ice Hockey League.

The Ice Kings captain, Jim Riley, is still the only athlete to have played in both the NHL and Major League Baseball. Riley played for both the Chicago Blackhawks and the Detroit Cougars during the 1926–27 season. This came six years after he played four games at second base for the St. Louis Browns in 1921.

While organized hockey was around for almost two decades, professional hockey didn't come to Dallas until 1941 when the Dallas Texans joined the American Hockey Association. The team made its pro debut on November 6, 1941 against the St. Paul Saints in front of a crowd of 4,273 fans. General admission tickets cost 55 cents, while box and rinkside seats cost anywhere from $1.65 to $2.20.

Tony Licari scored the first goal for the Texans, who lost 4–1 and allowed three power play goals by St. Paul. That was the first and only season for the Texans in the AHA.

World War II led to the cancelation of the league, and the Texans missed the playoffs in their only AHA season. Hockey returned to Dallas when the Texans joined the United States Hockey League, joining the Kansa City Pla-Mors, Omaha Knights, St. Paul, Tulsa Oilers, Fort Worth Rangers, and Minneapolis Millers for the 1945–46 season.

The first USHL season was an up-and-down one for the Texans. In February they lost consecutive games 13–1 to Kansas City and 12–1 to Tulsa. The next two games on the schedule featured a pair of 10–2 wins against the Kansas City and Minneapolis.

In addition to odd scores, the Texans also had a strong rivalry with Fort Worth that dated back to the AHA season.

Before the 1947–48 season, the Texans became the USHL affiliate for the Montreal Canadiens, but it was short lived as travel costs started to mount and the Texans—along with teams from

Fort Worth and Houston—dropped out of the USHL after the 1948–49 season.

There were frequent talks and discussions to start a more southern-based professional hockey league, but it never materialized, and pro hockey wouldn't return to Dallas until 1967 when the St. Louis Braves—a minor league affiliate of the Dallas Black Hawks in the Central Hockey League—were relocated to Dallas and renamed the Dallas Black Hawks.

The Black Hawks were a fixture in Dallas until they folded after the 1981–82 season. During their tenure they won four Adams Cups as the CHL champions and developed a nasty rivalry with the Fort Worth Wings and Texans. (The Fort Worth team changed names back and forth a couple times.)

Ten years later the Dallas Freeze joined the CHL before the 1992–93 season. The Freeze played at Fair Park Coliseum but ultimately couldn't compete in the market when the North Stars moved to Texas one season later.

51 Do the Stars Have a Rival?

The NHL loves to sell rivalries. It's a story of animosity and hatred. It harkens back to the days when fights were actually commonplace in hockey.

"The Battle of Alberta" between the Calgary Flames and Edmonton Oilers comes to mind. Montreal Canadiens vs. Toronto Maple Leafs is always a classic, while the New York battle royale between Rangers and Islanders divides families within the same city. For almost every franchise, there is a signature rival. And if there isn't one, NBC will find a way to shoehorn a team into one for its "Wednesday Night Rivalry" games.

But what about the Stars?

Stuck on a bit of a geographic island in the NHL—at least until Houston lands an NHL team—the Stars don't have that one hated opponent. And for those that come close to rival status, another key element is missing: the other team's fans actually hating the Stars.

The Detroit Red Wings were a frequent opponent in the playoffs in the late 1990s, and Mike Modano playing for the winged wheel certainly felt like a shot at the Stars. But the teams haven't played a playoff series in almost two decades, and Detroit's move to the Eastern Conference effectively neutered any chance at continued animosity.

The Stars have played a recent playoff series with the St. Louis Blues, and it went seven games. That series even had a bit of competitive fire with Blues forward Ryan Reaves blowing a kiss to the Stars bench after a fight with Curtis McKenzie. But St. Louis fans also don't think about the Stars as a rival, even though both team's origins date back to the 1967 expansion.

Calling Stars vs. Blues a rivalry is a disservice to that very real rivalry in St. Louis with the Chicago Blackhawks. And the Blackhawks aren't a rival for the Stars; they just tend to be universally hated in the NHL for their recent successes.

Stars vs. Avalanche had potential to be a great rivalry and the teams met in the playoffs multiple times. Unfortunately, it will never live up to the Detroit-Colorado hatefest from the mid-1990s, and both teams have gone through difficult stretches and drifted from relevance.

Stars fans may hate the Anaheim Ducks but so does most of the NHL. You could make a case for Stars vs. Wild (call it the Norm Green series), but those head-to-head meetings have been more "Minnesota Nice" than nasty.

Moral of the story? The Stars don't have a true rival, but the North Stars did. North Stars vs. Blackhawks was a blood feud based on geography, repetition, and playoff series. It started in 1967 when the North Stars entered the league and infringed upon the Blackhawks' claim as the team of the Midwest. After spending years as the NHL's western outpost in the Original Six era, the Blackhawks had to share a region with the North Stars. And they often shared the ice. In 26 seasons the North Stars and Blackhawks met 169 times. The intensity was often ratcheted up a notch with the teams clashing in six playoff series, including a stretch of four-straight playoff series from 1982 to 1985.

In the first game of the 1982 Playoffs officials handed out 125 penalty minutes. Two games later a brawl in Chicago featured a fan-thrown glass bottle that landed dangerously close to North Stars goalie Gilles Meloche.

The next year—this time in a regular season matchup—Chicago's Jack O'Callahan allegedly bit Minnesota's Ron Friest in the first of two bouts. One month later a bench-clearing brawl halted play for more than an hour as Friest was ejected for bouncing the head of Chicago forward Steve Larmer off the Met Center ice.

In 1986 Dino Ciccarelli and Al Secord got into a first period fight that ended with the North Stars forward swinging his stick and nearly decapitating a referee. On December 28, 1989, a brawl started during warmups and each team was fined $25,000.

Later that season, on April 1, 1990, the teams combined for 243 penalty minutes. Stars defenseman Shane Churla had his hands taped like a boxer and was ejected for that after a fight with Dave Manson.

One year later the teams met in the playoffs with Minnesota winning the series in five games. In Game 5—which the North Stars won 6–0—Chris Chelios attacked Brian Bellows at center ice and scratched Bellows cornea.

The great rivalry was finally put to bed when the North Stars moved to Dallas, coming to a close with a 3–2 Chicago victory on April 13, 1993, which happened to feature a fight between Stu Grimson and Enricco Ciccone.

52 Dallas Stars All-Time Lineup

How do you pick an all-time lineup? It's an interesting question. While some players are obvious choices, filling out the final roster becomes a difficult decision. How do you weigh longevity versus one or two great seasons? What about personality and fan appeal? Does that come into play?

Considering a series of factors, including statistics, longevity, and overall standing in franchise lore, here is the Dallas Stars all-time lineup. The North Stars get their own all-time team in the next chapter.

First line: Jamie Benn—Mike Modano—Jere Lehtinen

This line features two players who have their numbers retired and a third that could join them once he finishes his career. Modano holds virtually all the offensive records in franchise history, while his linemate, Lehtinen, won three Selke trophies and had 514 career points in 15 seasons. Benn, the Stars current captain, won the only scoring title in franchise history.

Second line: Brenden Morrow—Tyler Seguin—Brett Hull

Hull scored the biggest goal in franchise history in 1999 and made a huge impact in just three seasons with 196 points in 218 games with the Stars. Morrow had 528 points in 835 games and served as the captain for seven seasons in Dallas. Seguin has scored at least 70 points in each season since getting traded by the Boston Bruins.

Third line: Loui Eriksson—Joe Nieuwendyk—Jamie Langenbrunner

Nieuwendyk won the Conn Smythe Trophy as the Stars hoisted the cup and was one of the key pieces of the golden years in the late 1990s. Langenbrunner was also a key to that era and scored 10 playoff goals in 1999. Eriksson had 357 points in seven seasons before getting traded for Seguin in 2013.

Fourth line: Steve Ott—Guy Carbonneau—Bill Guerin

Carbonneau was the savvy defensive center who helped define the Stars mentality when they won the Stanley Cup. Ott played both wing and center and was a fan favorite for a decade. Guerin only spent three seasons in Dallas but had 159 points in 216 games.

First pair: Derian Hatcher—Sergei Zubov

The two most important defensive players in franchise history. Trading for Zubov in 1996 put the wheels in motion for Dallas to be a true contender, and his number should be retired at some point. Hatcher was the captain from 1994 to 2003 and an intimidator feared across the league.

Second pair: Richard Matvichuk—Darryl Sydor

Matvichuk was a stalwart on the blue line for more than a decade and was underrated because of the more noticeable defenders on the roster. But that was his strength. When Matvichuk was on the ice, bad things rarely happened. Sydor had 334 points in 714 career games with the Stars and was a dangerous power play specialist.

Third pair: Stephane Robidas—Trevor Daley

Robidas played more than 700 games with the Stars and was a reliable minute-munching defender for more than a decade. Daley was a fixture for a decade and a fan favorite. Unfortunately, he had to leave Dallas to finally get his championships.

Goalies: Ed Belfour and Marty Turco

This was the easiest selection on the list. The Stars don't win the Stanley Cup without Belfour, who signed as a free agent with Dallas before the 1997–98 season. Belfour had a 160–95–44 record and 2.19 goals against average with the Stars before giving way to Turco, who now holds franchise records for wins, shutouts, and games played.

Coach: Ken Hitchcock

In two stints in Dallas, the longtime coach has a championship and more than 300 career victories behind the Stars bench. Overall he's third in NHL history in victories.

53 Minnesota North Stars All-Time Lineup

The Minnesota North Stars are an important part of Dallas Stars history, and while this book focuses primarily on the second half of franchise history, it would be remiss to ignore the 26 seasons spent in Minnesota. So, I present the all-time lineup for the Minnesota North Stars. When picking this team I kept two things in mind: longevity and whether this player was primarily a Dallas Star or a Minnesota North Star. That's why Mike Modano isn't included here; he only played four seasons in Minnesota as opposed to 16 in Texas.

First line: Brian Bellows—Neal Broten—Dino Ciccarelli
A trio with some offensive pop. Broten is the North Stars' all-time leader in points, while Bellows and Ciccarelli share the franchise record with 55 goals in a season. Bellows and Broten each won cups after trades away from the franchise, while Ciccarelli came close with the Detroit Red Wings in 1995.

Second line: Steve Payne—Bobby Smith—Bill Goldsworthy
Smith still holds the franchise record for points with 114 during the 1982–83 season and was part of a pair of trips to the Finals. Payne had 466 points in 613 games with the North Stars, while Goldsworthy was the second player to have his number retired in franchise history.

Third line: J.P. Parise—Tim Young—Al MacAdam
Parise was a bit of a fan favorite and made a difference with his ability to win possession in the corners. Parise played in the same era as Young and Macadam, who both made their mark as two-way players and clutch playoff performers.

Fourth line: Dennis Hextall—Dave Gagner—Danny Grant
Gagner played in both Minnesota and in Dallas, but fans have far more pleasant memories of the center from his time with the North Stars where he had 404 points in 440 games. Hextall filled the stat sheet with points and fights, leading the team in both categories for three straight seasons. Grant won the Calder Memorial Trophy as the NHL's top rookie in 1969.

First pair: Craig Hartsburg—Curt Giles
In a franchise with a history of rushing defenseman, Hartsburg was the first. He had 413 points in 570 games with the North Stars and could have had more if not for injuries. Giles was a featured force in two trips to the Stanley Cup Finals and was a devastating checker.

Second pair: Tom Reid—Gordie Roberts
Reid's NHL career was cut short at just 31 due to a skin ailment. Before that he was a defensive anchor in Minnesota from 1969 to 1978. Roberts had a successful eight year stint in Minnesota with 257 points and a trip to the Finals.

Third pair: Fred Barrett—Lou Nanne
Nanne played both wing and defense in his time in Minnesota, but is better known for his time as a general manager. As a player he was a career North Star with 635 games. Barrett spent 12 seasons in Minnesota and could have played way more games if not for the injuries he sustained with a bruising style on the blue line. Brad Maxwell and Barry Gibbs also got heavy consideration for this third pairing.

Goalies: Gilles Meloche and Cesare Maniago
The first choice is easy. Meloche endured years of terrible teams in Oakland and Cleveland before joining the North Stars in a franchise merger. Expansion in 1967 gave Maniago a chance to prove himself as an NHL starter, and he posted an enviable .906 save percentage for that area.

Coach: Glen Sonmor
Sonmor was a tortured soul and took several leaves of absence during his career due to alcoholism. But when he was on the bench, the North Stars were a better team and he had a 177–161–83 record in 421 career games. He also led the North Stars to the 1981 Stanley Cup Finals.

54 The Frank Selke Trophy

Throughout their history in Texas, the Stars haven't had many individual award winners. And of those individual awards that have been presented to a Dallas Stars, one was a reflection of a team award when Joe Nieuwendyk won the Conn Smythe Trophy as the playoff MVP in 1999. Another was based on points and wasn't voted on a league-wide scale when Jamie Benn won the Art Ross Trophy as the NHL's leading scorer in 2015.

It's not for a lack of candidates. Benn finished third in Hart Memorial Trophy voting for league MVP in 2016, and Mike Modano should have been a perennial MVP candidate during his early years in Texas.

Marty Turco should have won the Vezina Trophy as the NHL's best goalie in 2003 after he led the league in both save percentage and goals against average. But he finished second after Martin Brodeur was handed his first of four Vezina trophies on virtue of wins and being a bigger name.

Through a combination of bad luck, being a so-called "non-traditional" hockey market, and team success overshadowing individual performances, it hasn't been easy for a Dallas Star to snag an individual trophy.

That's what makes Jere Lehtinen's trio of Selke Trophies—awarded annually to "the forward who best excels in the defensive aspects of the game"—even more impressive. "That's how good he was," Craig Ludwig said. "While other players on our great teams didn't win awards, he was so good at what he did that you couldn't help but recognize him for that."

Starting in his second NHL season, the Finnish winger received Selke Trophy votes in 12 straight seasons. He won his first Selke

Trophy in 1998 when he received 60.74 percent of the voting points and had 18 first-place votes. In 1999 he received 70.18 percent of the voting points and had 23 first-place votes.

Because of an injury, Lehtinen missed most of the 1999–2000 regular season and he only played 17 games. But even in that limited showing, Lehtinen still received a first and second-place vote for the Selke Trophy. Those votes came from those who knew who the best defensive forward was in hockey.

After finishing third in voting in 2002, Lehtinen captured his third Selke Trophy in 2003 when he received 76.66 percent of the voting points and 39 first-place votes. It was the largest margin of victory in his career as he totaled 476 votes compared to the runner-up, John Madden of the New Jersey Devils, who had 241.

Lehtinen also finished second in Selke Trophy voting in 2006, losing out to the Carolina Hurricanes center Rob Brind'Amour—a sign of the times that Selke Trophy voters had started to value the center position with more weight when it came to defensive responsibilities. Lehtinen is one of five players to win at least three Selke Trophies and he credits two other members of that club for helping him progress his career.

Bob Gainey won four Selke Trophies during his playing career with the Montreal Canadiens and he was Lehtinen's first NHL coach before stepping down to focus on general manager duties during the 1995–96 season.

Guy Carbonneau won a trio of Selke Trophies during his time with the Canadiens. When he joined the Dallas Stars during Lehtinen's rookie season, he provided a wealth of information for the Finn, who watched the defensively sound center play consistent, reliable hockey into his late 30s in Dallas. "I learned so much from Guy and Bob," Lehtinen said. "They were tough. You needed to be tough in the NHL, and they were great examples."

That's why it was fitting when Gainey and Carbonneau entered Lehtinen's jersey retirement ceremony carrying the Selke Trophy to the stage.

55 Video Clips and Rock Music

Movie clips are now a common occurrence at sporting events. Whether it's a reactionary in-game element (perhaps to a questionable penalty call) or an attempt to fire up the crowd, you are likely going to see a snippet from a movie or television show on the video board during the course of a game.

The Dallas Stars actually started this trend. During their first season in Dallas, the Stars experimented with video clips from movies. They went to Blockbuster, cut clips from the rented VHS tapes, and showed the clips as a tool to entertain.

"I remember at one point we were playing the Ducks, and Michael Eisner was at the game, and there weren't suites at Reunion Arena so he was sitting a row or two away from me," Stars president Jim Lites said. "We played a clip, I can't remember which one, and he turned to me and said, 'Jim that's a great idea. Who at our studio gave you the rights to play that?' Now, I'm thinking we're screwed here, and I turned back to him and said, 'Mike, let me get back to you on that.' I never got back to him, and eventually it became common practice for all sports teams. But that whole trend could have died right there. Who knows what would have happened if he had been pissed off?"

From their first game in Dallas, the Stars have tried to present a somewhat unique in-arena experience for their fans. As a non-traditional hockey market, it was both a necessity and an excuse to experiment. "We didn't have hockey fans right away; we had sports fans that wanted to be entertained," Lites said. "We had to keep that in mind. That's why we adopted rock music and video clips. We were selling the game, but we also had to make sure everyone left Reunion having a good time."

That's why the Stars never had an organ, the goal song has changed several times, and even two decades into the franchise's Texas experience, video board bits and acts have been built around adding atmosphere to the game. "Non-traditional market, non-traditional presentation," said Jeff Kovarsky, who has played several roles with the Stars, most recently as the public address announcer. "The thing that has always excited me about the presentation is the Stars have found a way to make it Dallas centric. You want to make sure when you go into a building it's stuff that you can't get anywhere else. It's not this generic hockey presentation that you could lift and put in any other city. The Stars are able to do things that were Dallas specific."

And for the first eight years of the franchise, the presentation was a little limited in Reunion Arena. "It was an old barn, and once the Stars moved to the AAC, it really evolved," Kovarsky said. "It was like getting a sports car; now you really had the vehicle to impress some people."

Perhaps the best way to gauge the Stars in-arena presentation against the rest of the league is twofold. First, how many other arena DJs have a cult following like Michael "Grubes" Gruber? And how many other teams are generating viral moments the way the Stars have found a way to toe the line with topical humor?

In 2014 the video board was "hacked" by North Korea, wishing a happy holidays from Kim Jong-un. In 2015 goals by the Washington Capitals were redacted on the video board in a shot at the government.

In January of 2017, the Stars announced attendance as 1.5 million, a clear shot at the inauguration attendance and claims by

President Donald Trump. "Some of those things are planned; others are really just quick thinking," Kovarsky said. "As a team and as a group, it's important to react to the game and find a way to add little things. And I think it's done a nice job of adding little things that just add to the overall experience but don't distract from the game."

56 Marketing Hockey to Texans

Shane Churla was the original face of the Dallas Stars. The original enforcer—who still holds the franchise record for penalty minutes—was the Star (pun intended) of the team's first advertising campaign.

With the help of quick cuts and fog, Churla was featured in a promo putting on his hockey equipment in dramatic fashion. After pulling on a Stars jersey, Churla walked through a hallway and punched a stack of boxes, revealing the text "The Cold War is Here!"

Churla instantly became a fan favorite in Dallas. His rough and physical style endeared him to fans, but his placement in the ad campaign was a lucky break for the marketing department. "The reason it's all Shane Churla is because he is the only player that was here," Stars president Jim Lites said. "The week we shot, he was the only player in town. And we even had to use different camera angles because we had an old Minnesota North Star jersey and used different cuts. We didn't have a jersey yet and we only had one player in town, so that's what we did."

That pretty much embodied how the Stars had to market hockey in their first season. When Lites—who left the Detroit Red Wings to be the Stars presiden—arrived in Dallas he was told selling season tickets would be a breeze.

That was entirely false. "They had 15,000 names, but they hadn't even asked for a deposit. So the moment we told people [what] the tickets were gonna cost, they thought it was going to be like high school football, like $3," Lites said. "And the moment we told them it was going to be $65 to sit downstairs, it melted. We had maybe 6,000 or 7,000 [season] tickets when we started."

Clearly this wasn't going to be an easy sell.

The team had to pay Home Sports Entertainment, the precursor to Fox Sports, to show the Stars game on television. As team president Lites made thousands of speeches to local groups trying to sell the product.

At one point Lites gave a speech to the Grapevine Rotary Club in the back of a hardware store. "It's an insurance guy, a dentist, and the hardware store owner hosting," Lites said. "We've got TV dinners, and there are like 14 people there and they're all in their bib overalls and they are nodding [off]. And I slap in this video showing crushing hits. After the speech I got to the car and I had a cell phone, one of those big ones. And I called my wife and I'm thinking, 'Oh my god, what have we done to our kids and career?'"

Luckily the speaking engagements got bigger, and former Dallas Cowboys quarterback Roger Staubach helped introduce hockey to the wealthier community in Dallas. "We've got things like this going on, and then all of a sudden 4,000 people show up for a pick-a-seat event," Lites said. "I looked around and I said, 'You know what, we might be okay.'"

To make sure they were okay, the Stars marketed the tougher side of the game. Fighting and big hits were a big part of the sell, and it worked well with the imagery of Churla preparing for "The Cold War." "We were a fighting bunch," Lites said. "We weren't a high-end skill team, but we were tough. It was Bob Gainey's team, and it was tough. Without that I don't know how many Texans would have bought in back then."

57 "Norm Greed"

As you can guess, Norm Green isn't a very popular man in Minnesota. When Green first arrived in Minnesota he was a hero. He had saved the franchise from relocation to California and was saying all the right things. "I have a chance to take a poorly managed hockey team, one that lost $16 million over four years in a good hockey market, and make it profitable in the first season," Green said at the time. "It's as if I were in heaven."

That wasn't the case, and as we've covered in this book, the North Stars were relocated to Dallas after three seasons. Soon Green became the most hated man in the "State of Hockey."

Fans in Minnesota labeled him as "Norm Greed" and merchandise with that slogan or "Norm Sucks" became a somewhat hot ticket item. T-shirts, hats, buttons, and bumper stickers were popular choices of those hawking items outside the Met Center, and chants of "Norm Sucks!" or "Norm Green Sucks!" were common in the North Stars final games. Well aware of the anger aimed his way, Green avoided the Met Center after announcing his team would be moving. The chants weren't limited just to hockey. During the 1993 National Invitational Tournament, the USC men's basketball team played against Minnesota at the Met Center. Former associate head coach Jack Fertig recalled the incident in his book *Life's a Joke*. Midway through the second half, the fans started chanting, "Norm Green Sucks! Norm Green Sucks!" Not much of a hockey fan, USC Head Coach George Raveling asked some of the fans behind the bench, "Who's Norm Green?"

"He's the SOB that moved the North Stars to Dallas," a fan said.

"Oh, yeah," Raveling said. "He does suck."

The unfortunate fact is that Green tried to save hockey in Minnesota. In the end it was a business, and he had to make a difficult decision. Minneapolis-based television anchor Scott Goldberg properly relayed those thoughts to author Adam Raider, who wrote *Frozen in Time: A Minnesota North Stars History.* "Fans played a role," Goldberg said. "It's a chicken-and-egg thing; either the fans weren't going because the team stopped winning, and the venue was bad. Or the team stopped winning, and the venue was bad because fans weren't going. Either way the North Stars were losing money, and that's not a sustainable model."

The NHL returned to Minnesota in 2000 when the Wild entered the league as an expansion franchise, but it didn't heal any old wounds for hockey fans in Minnesota. Shirts that say "Norm Green Still Sucks" are still available for purchase, and the man himself has no plans to ever return to the state. "I'm scared to go back," Green told the *Dallas Morning News* in 2014. "Honestly, you just don't know how people would react. It would be an invitation for trouble."

58 Tom Hicks Saved the Stars

The NHL lockout that canceled half of the 1994–95 season nearly killed off the Dallas Stars. After a successful season on ice and, more importantly, success financially during the 1993–94 season, the Stars were seemingly in a good place. But on October 1, 1994, the lockout went into effect. "The moment we had the lockout that blew us back," Stars President Jim Lites said. "It set us back with tickets, it put Norm [Green] in jeopardy, and we didn't know if we'd be able to pay the players. That's something we had to figure

Former Stars owner Tom Hicks (seen at left alongside former American Airlines chairman and CEO Don Carty, former Dallas Mavericks owner Ross Perot Jr., and former Dallas mayor Ron Kirk) is often credited with bankrolling the Stars' championship team, as well as building them a state-of-the-art arena in the American Airlines Center.

out with the NHL, and [Gary] Bettman was a new commissioner, so we didn't know what we were dealing with."

The Stars didn't even have enough money to pay back season ticket holders for the games they missed, so it was a mad scramble to figure out how to make everyone whole without bankrupting the franchise. Adding to complications, the Stars were almost swindled by John Spano before Tom Hicks saved the franchise and bought the team in December of 1995. "A neighbor of mine in Highland Park asked if I knew Tom Hicks," Lites said. "I said no. And he said, 'Well you should meet him.' The whole world changed when I walked into Tom Hicks' office."

Hicks opened the conversation by saying, "Well, tell me about this hockey, Jim. I'd like to buy it."

Months later he bought the team.

Hicks truly didn't know anything about hockey. Since Reunion Arena didn't have suites, Hicks had Lites pick out ideal seats and had the president sit behind the owner. Lites would then explain what was happening to Hicks throughout the game. "I sat in the two seats right behind Tom," Lites said. "He would just ask me to sit over his shoulder and he'd want to know why goals would occur. He'd want to know what happened before and who screwed up."

While Hicks didn't know hockey, he was willing to provide the money to make the Stars a success. "Mr. Hicks, he wanted to win," Les Jackson said. "He was a key to that success in the late 1990s and throughout the time he owned the team. We don't win the Stanley Cup without him coming in and footing the bill like he was willing to do. He's a big part of the history of this team."

Before he even closed on the team, Hicks approved the trade for Joe Nieuwendyk—a deal that would require future spending by the owner.

At the end of each season Hicks would sit down with Lites and general manager Bob Gainey and ask the following question: What do you need? "Before Tom Hicks we couldn't even dabble in the free agent market," Lites said, "because there was no lid on spending. But we told Tom Hicks we'd like to add some free agents, and he said, 'Do what you've got to do.'"

59 Tom Gaglardi

Tom Gaglardi is different than the other team owners in Dallas Stars history. While Norm Green and Tom Hicks were both interested in the sport, they were businessmen first. The Stars were more of an asset, and Hicks' desire to win came from both an internal fire of competition and an adopted love of the sport.

Gaglardi was a hockey fan before he was a businessman. He's not the guy in the suit. Gaglardi is the guy who shows up to a prospects tournament in Traverse City in jeans, a Stars golf shirt, and matching "Victory Green" shoes, and is constantly picking the brains of scouts in attendance about his team. "He's the first owner I've worked with that was a hockey fan first and a businessman second," Stars president Jim Lites said. "I've had great relationships with all of our owners, but this was the first owner this team has had that actually understood the game on Day One."

Hicks deserves credit for the Stars success in the late 1990s and they don't win the Stanley Cup without his money. But he started spreading himself too thin, buying the Texas Rangers, and part of the English Premier League soccer club Liverpool. At the same time the United States was going through economic hardship, and Hicks, who had made a majority of his money as a buyout specialist—buying companies with debt and later flipping them for profit—had his bubble burst. He was bankrupt, the Stars were bankrupt, and for the second time in team history, they needed another owner to step in and save the day.

And Gaglardi, who made much of his money in hotels, saw an opportunity to finally own an NHL franchise. Gaglardi was already a part-owner of the Kamloops Blazers in the WHL and had tried to purchase his hometown Vancouver Canucks in 2003. In 2010 he submitted a proposal to buy the Atlanta Thrashers and move them Hamilton, Ontario. So Gaglardi was a motivated buyer, even if the Stars came with their warts.

After the 2010–11 season the Stars had dropped to 28th in attendance, they were losing close to $35 million per season, and the team sucked. That dropped the team to a very affordable $240 million, and Gaglardi pulled the trigger. He was officially introduced as the owner on November 18, 2011.

In the salary cap era, the impact of an owner is somewhat limited; it's not like the late 1990s where Hicks could try to outspend the competition, but Gaglardi has already put his fingerprints on the team.

He re-hired Lites as the team president—a move that directly led to Jim Nill's addition as the team general manager. He also re-branded the team in the new "Victory Green" color scheme. Both attendance and on-ice success have taken a positive turn since he got the keys to the franchise.

In a town known for high-profile owners—Jerry Jones owns the Cowboys and Mark Cuban owns the Mavericks—Gaglardi has found his niche as the billionaire fan. He's extremely hands-on (he gets a ticket report daily), but he lets the hockey department handle the hockey decisions. He is also one of the biggest fans of his own team.

60 Mr. Big Shot

John Spano pulled off one of the greatest con jobs in sports history. On October 10, 1996, it was announced that Spano would purchase the New York Islanders from longtime owner John Pickett for $165 million. He was supposedly worth $230 million and was expected to help save a franchise that had fallen on hard times.

The Islanders fans assumed he was their savior. Even Clark Gillies thanked him during a speech before the Islanders retired the forward's number. Here is the problem: John Spano didn't have the money.

It was a long con built on bravado and fraud and it worked for almost a year. Spano was running the Islanders. He added money to the team payroll and forced Mike Milbury to give up his responsibilities as head coach. Spano even tried to secure a new arena deal while he didn't have any money.

The formal closing came on April 7, 1997. Spano failed to show up with $17 million that was supposed to be wired for closing as a down payment. That should have been a breaking point, but Pickett was motivated to sell and agreed to close with a guarantee he'd get his money eventually. "Some of the times—and I hate to say this—it was a game with myself. 'Will they believe this?'" Spano said in an *ESPN 30 for 30* documentary on his ownership. "I would have told them pigs would fly out my ass if I could get the time to cross the line."

Eventually things started to unravel for Spano. He forged a letter from his banker and then faxed it from his own Dallas fax machine. That information ended up with reporters from *Newsday*. The newspaper started digging deeper and revealed more of Spano's lies.

On July 9, 1997, *Newsday* printed a full-length story on Spano's lies. Two days later he was out as the owner of the Islanders. By October of 1997, he was pleading guilty in court to fraud. It was a horror story for Islanders fans and one that could have been a reality for Stars fans.

Two years earlier Spano nearly bought 50 percent of the Dallas Stars for $42 million he didn't have in 1995. Thanks to some high-profile connections, Spano was able to start negotiations with Stars officials and then-owner Norm Green. He had a letter from the bank stating he was worth more than $100 million, and for a while, it looked like Spano might actually get away with the deal.

On September 15, 1995, Green announced Spano's offer to the media. No one had really heard of Spano. He was a Stars season ticket holder and passionate hockey fan, but his credentials in sports and business were a mystery. The deal was supposed to close within a week of that announcement. It never happened.

Stars president Jim Lites was part of the negotiations at the time and said Spano seemed like a legitimate buyer because of his connections. That included a loose connection to former Dallas Cowboys quarterback Roger Staubach, who was actually influential in helping bring the franchise from Minnesota to Dallas.

Spano said he had the financing in place and a bank commitment to make the purchase. But the Stars had a key question: where was the money?

Minor issues kept coming up, and each time it seemed like they were closer to a sale, another red flag would worry the group negotiating a potential sale for the Stars. "The longer we got to know him, the more bizarre he became," Lites said.

There was a cocktail party at Spano's gaudy $2.5 million home in Park Cities, a well-to-do part of Dallas. The house was beautiful, but there wasn't any furniture.

At one point during the negotiations, Lites was with a group that went out to lunch with Spano. When the check came around,

Spano didn't budge. "I'm used to owners automatically picking up checks, and the check sits there," Lites said. "And it sits there embarrassingly long. And we've got to get back to the offices now, and this guy is kind of looking at the check, and I'm looking at him, and he's looking at me. And finally I had to pick up the tab for lunch. We were all there because of him. And we all traveled there at our own expenses, and this guy didn't pick up a lunch check, which seemed totally bizarre to me."

His excuses for pushing back a sale were also laughable, according to Lites. At one point Spano called saying he couldn't close without the operating agreement for the Kalamazoo Wings, the Stars minor league affiliate at the time. Another time he couldn't close until his partners from South Africa had spent time in the Stars office.

Eventually, Green grew sick of Spano's antics and canceled any potential deal with him, setting the stage for Tom Hicks to eventually buy the team.

It was an upsetting turn of events for Spano, who later said that the denial in Dallas motivated him to fulfill his goal of buying an NHL team. "I took that personally, I took it like it was my new mantra," Spano said. "That was my new bar."

Spano first went after the Florida Panthers, but a new arena deal for the current ownership group nixed that before negotiations could go any further with the con artist. But through his Florida negotiations, Spano was told to look into the buying the Islanders and he jumped at the opportunity.

Looking back on Spano's ability to buy the Islanders, Lites was shocked the NHL didn't call the Stars for insight on the self-proclaimed millionaire. "No one from the Islanders ever called me," Lites said. "I thought it was bizarre. I never got a call from anybody in Long Island or Gary Bettman to ask me about our experiences with Spano."

61 Richard Matvichuk

In the late 1990s the Dallas Stars had their four core defenseman who helped define an era. Sergei Zubov was the flashy one, the wizard with the puck who should be a Hall-Of-Famer. Derian Hatcher was the captain, the physical force that lifted the Stanley Cup first. Darryl Sydor was a hybrid, known for his offense and defense.

Richard Matvichuk was often the forgotten one. He was the defenseman who blended into the background and let the others shine. That was when Matvichuk was at his best. If you didn't notice Matvichuk on the ice, he was doing his job and frustrating the opponent.

Matvichuk was drafted eighth overall in the 1991 NHL Entry Draft by the Minnesota North Stars. He made his NHL debut in 1992–93 as a 19-year-old with Minnesota and then split the next two seasons between Dallas and the minor leagues before grabbing a full-time NHL role before the 1995–96 season. And once he grabbed the role, he was rarely on the ice for a negative moment against the Stars. Matvichuk finished with a positive plus-minus each season from 1995 to 2004 and averaged more than 22 minutes per game.

As a defensive-minded defenseman in the pre-analytics era, Matvichuk's career is poorly defined by stats. His 38 goals and 129 assists in 733 games don't garner much attention. Hits and blocked shots weren't officially counted until 1997 and they weren't well standardized for a couple seasons. By that point Matvichuk was nearing the end of a 14-year stint with the franchise.

Matvichuk's tenure with Dallas came to an end after the 2003–04 season. He finished his career playing for the New Jersey Devils after the lockout and then entered the coaching ranks.

He was an assistant coach and assistant general manager for two seasons with the CHL's Allen Americans before getting his first head coaching job in the ECHL with the Missouri Mavericks. Before the 2016–17 season, he was named the head coach of the Prince George Cougars in the Western Hockey League.

62 Darryl Sydor

One of Darryl Sydor's defining moments—and one that will make him a Dallas Stars fan favorite for life—came in a loss. Less than three minutes into Game 6 of the 2000 Stanley Cup Finals, Sydor got twisted up along the boards after attempting to hit Scott Gomez. His leg got twisted up underneath him, he tore ligaments in his knee, and he severely sprained his ankle.

The referee didn't blow the whistle, and the New Jersey Devils had a de facto power play with Sydor out of the play. Instead of lying still, Sydor worked his way back toward the front of the net. At first he tried to skate, but that was impossible. So the defenseman crawled on his hands and knees to the front of the net. He was going to do whatever it took, willing to block a shot with his disabled body to help his team.

Eventually the officials blew the play dead, and Sydor was helped off the ice with an ovation from the Reunion Arena crowd.

"You will see that shot until hell freezes over and as long as the Stanley Cup is awarded," Gary Thorne said on the ESPN broadcast. "You will see that shot of Darryl Sydor crawling to the front of the net whenever anyone asks what the Stanley Cup is all about."

The Dallas Observer later deemed that moment as DFW's "Best Sports Moment of 2000," and described it this way: "Like other great moments in recent Dallas sports history, the best one of the year was a frozen one: Darryl Sydor, during Game 6 of the Stanley Cup Finals, crawling across the ice to defend his goal after he'd broken his ankle. ESPN analysts shouted in disbelief as Sydor, in obvious and tremendous pain, pulled himself across the ice with his arms, dragging his now-bum leg behind, and began throwing his hands in the air trying to deflect the puck as eventual champs New Jersey tried to score. It personified what makes hockey, and the Dallas Stars, so enthralling. Hockey at its best is a game that is at once more violent than football and more graceful than basketball, a game with an honor code that demands that hockey players not only play hurt, but play in blinding pain. Sydor's exhibition of, pick your cliché—heart, determination, guts, whatever you want to call it—almost made losing the Stanley Cup acceptable because fans knew that moment reflected the Stars' effort and the commitment fans ask of their sports stars."

Sydor was a key part of the Stars defensive core than defined the championship era in the late 1990s. When the Stars started building their eventual championship team in the mid-1990s, Sydor was one of the key pieces they brought into the fold. After five seasons with the Los Angeles Kings, the Stars acquired Sydor on February 17, 1996, in exchange for fan favorite Shane Churla and Doug Zmolek. And with that trade the Stars had their core four defensemen set with Sergei Zubov, Richard Matvichuk, Derian Hatcher, and Sydor.

Sydor received votes for the Norris Trophy as the NHL's top defenseman in his first three full seasons with Dallas, and when Dallas won the Stanley Cup in 1999, he had 12 points (three goals, nine assists) in 23 games. Sydor also holds a rare distinction in franchise history as the Stars have involved him in four different trades.

In 2003 Sydor's first stint in Dallas came to an end as he was traded to the Columbus Blue Jackets for Mike Sillinger (who never played for Dallas) and a second-round draft pick. Three years later he returned to Dallas on July 2, 2006 in a trade with the Tampa Bay Lightning, costing the Stars a fourth-round pick.

Then a 34-year-old, Sydor had 21 points in 74 games that season and was still averaging more than 20 minutes per game. But the Stars didn't re-sign him as a free agent, and he signed with the Pittsburgh Penguins.

On November 16, 2008, the Stars re-acquired Sydor in exchange for Philippe Boucher, and he finished out that season—and ultimately his Stars career—with 13 points in 65 games with Dallas. Sydor finished his Dallas career with 69 goals, 265 assists, and 334 points in 714 games played. His career plus-82 is sixth all-time in team history, while his assists and points are third in franchise history behind Zubov and Craig Hartsburg.

63 Benn vs. Iginla

Jamie Benn has never been afraid to drop the gloves. While the Dallas Stars captain is better known for his offensive prowess, he's also grown a reputation as a bit of a brawler. His fights don't happen often, but when they do, they often include a heavyweight or top-tier player from the other team—the type of bout that grabs your attention and ends up getting countless plays on YouTube as soon as it's posted.

Benn's battle with Jarome Iginla in 2010 certainly fit the bill and it's widely considered one of the best fights since the NHL lockout that cancelled the 2004–05 season.

It was December 23, 2010. The Stars and Calgary Flames were still tied 0–0 early in the first period, and Benn laid a big, but clean, hit on Flames defenseman Mark Giordano in front of the Stars bench.

Iginla, one of the better power forwards of his generation and the Calgary captain, took exception to the hit. Benn accepted the challenge, and the two combatants circled back to center ice at American Airlines Center; this was a fight deserving of center ring treatment.

Both players dropped their gloves, Iginla removed his helmet and elbow pads—a pretty savvy veteran move, as it's easier to swing that way—before they started trading blows. Benn started as the aggressor and took the action to Iginla early. Using his left hand to hold off the then 33-year-old Flames captain, he swung with his right hand and connected, opening up a gash above Iginla's right eye. Iginla countered and controlled what you could classify as Round 2, firing in short jabs with the left before both players started swinging wildly in what we'll call Round 3. In Round 4, essentially the final 15 seconds of the fight, Iginla got a couple parting shots in as Benn was clearly tiring from the 65-second flurry.

Benn's Big Bouts

Jamie Benn's fight with Jarome Iginla is his most memorable, but the Stars captain also has a history of finding other big name opponents.

Dustin Byfuglien—A true heavyweight bout with one of the bigger players in the league on November 2, 2017. The Stars were getting embarrassed in Winnipeg, and the captain stepped up to try and motivate his team.

David Backes—It's a battle that's happened several times, most recently off the opening faceoff on February 26, 2017. The rivalry dates back to Backes' time with the St. Louis Blues. The pair of team leaders have always shown animosity toward each other.

Joe Thornton—Two big-name players gave us a throwback to old time hockey on February 23, 2013. Benn and Thornton each dropped the gloves, unbuckled their helmets, and started throwing.

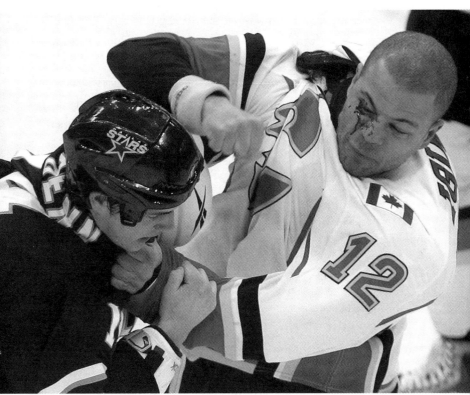

Never one to fear dropping the gloves, Jamie Benn's 2010 scrap with the Calgary Flames' Jarome Iginla is widely considered one of the best on-ice fights in the modern hockey era.

On the judges' scorecards and the voting public at HockeyFights. com, Benn won the bout on a split decision. It also sent a message that then 21-year-old was ready for a leadership role in the future. "When he fought Iginla, that, for me, was when he kind of took that next step to be a leader in this league," Willie Desjardins, the Stars associate head coach in 2010, later remembered. "To stand up with one of the top forwards in the league and someone who has a history of leading his team with those fights, that was a big moment for Jamie and he delivered."

Three years later Benn was named the sixth captain in franchise history and even with the "C" on his jersey he hasn't shied away from a challenge. Benn has had at least two fights in each season since he was named captain, including a bubbling rivalry with David Backes, who he's fought three times. While his rivalry with Backes is always something to watch, Stars fans will gladly remember Benn's bout with Iginla as the captain's best bare-fisted battle.

64 Reunion Arena

Reunion Arena was never supposed to be the long-term home for the Dallas Stars. In fact, when the team moved from Minnesota to Texas, there was a promise from the city to Stars owner Norm Green that an updated arena would be opened sooner rather than later. But while it stood, Reunion Arena was a more than suitable placeholder for the Stars, who reached the playoffs in seven of the eight seasons in their old home.

Construction started in 1978 and was designed with hockey in mind with ideal sightlines and a capacity of 17,001 for the Stars. Owned and operated by the City of Dallas, Reunion Arena sat next to the iconic Reunion Tower, a fixture in the Dallas skyline.

And, most importantly, fans showed up. After years of disappointing attendance at the Met Center in Bloomington, Minnesota—averaging as little as 7,838 fans during the 1990–91 season—Reunion Arena opened with the Stars averaging 16,119 fans during the 1993–94 season. "Reunion Arena was one of the best places to play in the NHL," Mike Modano said. "It really became a home ice advantage. They were loud, and it was our home; it was a place other teams didn't like playing."

Attendance continued to grow with the Stars success with the final two years in Reunion being an average sellout. While the fans showed up, the old arena had its flaws. It wasn't updated and lacked luxury suites: a must-have in today's world for team to generate revenue.

In 2001, the city of Dallas opened the American Airlines Center, a new modern facility for the Stars and Dallas Mavericks. While the main tenants were gone, Reunion remained opened until June 30, 2008, hosting a series of concerts and regional sports events before finally shuttering its doors.

In August of that year the city announced plans to implode the structure. There were hopes that a filmmaker from a big budget film would be interested in handling the explosions and footing the bill. Hollywood never bit on the offer, and in November of 2009, Reunion Arena was officially demolished. The site is now part of a public park and massive green space in the shadow of Reunion Tower.

65 Jokinen Masters the Shootout

The NHL officially killed off ties before the 2005–06 season. As the league tried to rebound from a lockout that cancelled the entire 2004–05 season, the shootout was designed to bring excitement to the sport and appeal to a wider audience.

Fans didn't want to see ties. They wanted to see games decided with displays of skill, and the one-on-one showdown initially became can't miss television for a sport recovering from a massive black eye caused by the labor disputes. The shootout also became an instant boon for the Dallas Stars and rookie forward Jussi Jokinen.

While penalty shots and breakaways have always been a part of the NHL, it wasn't much of a practiced skill before the tiebreaking procedure was introduced in 2005. The entire NHL was entering the format with a blank slate, while Jokinen actually had two years of experience with shootouts after the Finnish Liiga had adopted the shootout before the 2003–04 season.

Jokinen wasn't lethal on shootouts in Finland, but it provided an opportunity for him to test and figure out his moves. "I started to work on my shootout moves a little bit more: the low blocker and the one-handed move," Jokinen said in 2012. "I still spend time over the summer practicing those moves and some new ones."

And that was the combination that left NHL goalies baffled. Jokinen had a quick release and would beat goalies low on the blocker side. If a goalie overplayed the shot or cheated, Jokinen would pull out the one-handed finish that Peter Forsberg first made famous with his postage stamp move that helped Sweden win the Olympic gold medal in 1994. Jokinen started the season perfectly in the skills competition.

On November 5, 2005, he sealed the first shootout in Stars history when his quick wrister beat Colorado Avalanche goalie Peter Budaj on the stick side. "We tried a lot of people in training camp," Stars Coach Dave Tippett said when he originally picked Jokinen to shoot. "We did a lot of things in practice just to try to get an idea of who our shooters would be, and he was a guy that really caught our eye that was very successful early. I think he was 3-for-3 in the preseason, so we put him in and he's been successful."

Mixing his quick shot and paralyzing one-handed finish, Jokinen scored on the first nine shootout attempts of the season. That included a three-game stretch in late January where the Stars went to a shootout in four straight games and won each of them with Jokinen shooting in the second slot each time.

While it was an individual showcase, Jokinen would often get an assist from Stars backup goalie Johan Hedberg, who would give feedback on which route to take on that given night. "What I did lots in my first two years, before every shootout, I talked to whoever our backup goalie was," Jokinen said. "It was usually Johan Hedberg. So I'd talk with him about what I think I'm going to do and his thoughts. And that really helped me."

Hedberg often worked with Jokinen in practice on shootouts and he was impressed, but a perfect 9-for-9 start was never expected. "I knew he had some good moves, but I didn't expect him to be this good," Hedberg said at the time. "I think it shocked everybody. He scored some goals in the preseason that gave him a chance to be in the shootout lineup, and now, everybody knows him. He's the big shootout star."

Jokinen's streak of perfection finally came to an end on March 18, 2006 against the San Jose Sharks. Vesa Toskala was the first goalie to stop Jokinen, who was once again the second shooter. But Dallas prevailed and won the game when Antti Miettinen scored in the seventh round.

Jokinen finished the season with 10 goals on 13 attempts. His goal total and shooting percentage (76.9) were by far the best in the league, and the Stars turned in a 13–1 overall record in shootouts. That team performance in shootouts helped the Stars win the Pacific Division title. The Stars won their division with 112 points that season, while the Sharks finished second with 99 points.

As Dallas picked up 13 extra points in the shootout—which happened to be the final margin in the standings—the Sharks struggled and went 1–9 in one-on-one showdowns.

66 Youngest Captain in NHL History

Officially, Edmonton Oilers captain Connor McDavid is the youngest captain in NHL history. McDavid was 19 years and 266 days old when the Oilers named him their permanent captain in October of 2016. That surpassed the previous record of 19 years and 286 days, which had been held by Colorado Avalanche captain Gabriel Landeskog.

While those are the official NHL records, the Stars actually have claim to the youngest player to ever wear a "C" as the captain in an NHL game when Brian Bellows filled in for Craig Hartsburg on an interim basis during the 1983–84 season. Bellows was only 19 years and 131 days old at the time. His captaincy is officially remembered in Stars history, but since he wasn't the full-time captain, NHL records don't recognize his achievement.

Giving Bellows the "C" at such young age was a sign of the lofty expectations for the left winger. The North Stars made a big trade, sending Don Murdoch, Greg Smith, and a first-round pick (who would be Murray Craven) to the Detroit Red Wings for the second overall pick. To make sure they got Bellows, the North Stars sent Brad Palmer and Dave Donnelly to Boston on the condition that Bruins general manager Harry Sinden wouldn't select Bellows with the first pick.

The trade caught Bellows by surprise and he got an idea something was up the night before the draft. Bellows was at the bar with his father and agent when they saw a couple Bruins executives there. The Boston brass didn't come over and say hello to the prospective No. 1 pick. "That's when we figured out something was up," Bellows later recalled.

Sinden ended up picking defenseman Gord Kluzak (which proved to be a big mistake), and the North Stars were able to pick Bellows, a player that had 213 points in 113 career OHL games with the Kitchener Rangers and was drawing comparisons to Wayne Gretzky.

It's not easy being compared to Gretzky and it's impossible to live up to the hype that comes with it. Throughout NHL history, the number of junior hockey players that have been called "The Next Gretzky" and have ultimately flamed out is a long one. While Bellows had initial struggles with lofty expectations—particularly as an 18-year-old rookie—he turned in a solid 10-year stint with the North Stars and is one of the Top 10 players in franchise history after scoring 342 goals and dishing out 380 assists for 722 points in 753 games between 1982 and 1992. During the 1989–90 season Bellows scored a franchise record 55 goals in one season, a mark that he shares with Dino Ciccarelli.

Bellows' career in Minnesota came to an end when he was traded to the Montreal Canadiens on August 31, 1992 for Russ Courtnall. The trade worked out for both sides. Courtnall had 79 points during the 1992–93 season with Minnesota, second behind Mike Modano's 93 points. Courtnall's 36 goals that season led the team, and he was one of just four players to appear in all 84 games that season.

The next season—the first in Dallas—Courtnall had 80 points, once again good for second on the team. He was also one of just three players to appear in all 84 games that season. On the other end of the trade Bellows won a Stanley Cup with Montreal in 1993. He led the Canadiens with 40 goals the season immediately after the trade and then had 15 points in 18 playoff games for Montreal.

Bellows is still a constant fixture in the Stars record book. His 342 goals ranks second in franchise history, his 380 assists are fourth, and his 722 points are third behind Neal Broten and Mike Modano.

67 "Ambassador of Fun" in the GM Chair

Brett Hull's place in Dallas Stars history starts with his playing days. Hull was the key to a Stanley Cup Championship. He scored the game-winning goal in Buffalo and he provided Stars fans with numerous memorable moments from 1998–2001.

But Hull's post-playing career in Dallas comes with a collection of head-scratching moments. After he retired as player, Hull joined the Stars as a special assistant to Stars President Jim Lites. He was also given the title "Ambassador of Fun."

As the Ambassador of Fun, Hull appeared in ad campaigns promoting ticket sales. In one commercial Hull is walking down the hallway in the Stars corporate offices where he runs into a group of ice girls, a drumline drummer, and a werewolf in a suit. It was a fun, silly role for an ex-player that somehow morphed into Hull being named general manager six months after that commercial first aired.

Hull entered the 2007–08 season as a special advisor to the hockey operations staff. But when the team fired general manager Doug Armstrong on November 13, 2008, Hull was named the interim co-general manager alongside Les Jackson.

While Jackson had more than two decades of managerial experience, Hull didn't fit the mold, and the hire was widely questioned by the hockey community—especially after he looked wildly unprepared throughout his time as an analyst with NBC during the 2006–07 season.

But with Jackson's help, Hull seemingly acquitted himself early on. During the 2007–08 season the co-general managers pulled off one of their bigger moves by trading for Brad Richards. That trade helped the Stars reach the Western Conference Finals, the deepest playoff run since the 2000 team reached the Stanley Cup Finals.

After that playoff push, Stars owner Tom Hicks rewarded Hull and Jackson with three-year contract extensions, removing the interim tag from both titles and fully embracing the dual general manager system.

That's when everything fell apart for the former Ambassador of Fun. The Stars went from the Western Conference Finals to missing the playoffs during the 2008–09 season. The season was largely defined by controversy and frustrations by Sean Avery, a controversial forward that Hull and Jackson signed in the offseason.

After the season came to an end, the dual general manager experiment was killed off, and Joe Nieuwendyk was brought in as the new general manager. Both Hull and Jackson kept jobs within the organization but received demotions. "Brett and Les have done a great job as co-general managers, but after analyzing the situation, it is in the team's best interest to return them to roles that fit their respective strengths," Hicks said at the time. "Brett will assist the club in several business areas and serve as an adviser to me and president Jeff Cogen, while Les will go back to what he does best: overseeing our scouting department."

Hull remained with the Stars front office for two more seasons before leaving the organization in 2011. He is now the executive vice president of hockey operations for the St. Louis Blues.

68 Red, White, and Blue?

When Tom Gaglardi bought the team, he wanted to usher in a new era of Dallas Stars hockey. That meant a return to success on the ice. It also meant a new look for the team.

The end result was the "Victory Green" color scheme. It's one of the more unique looks in today's NHL, a league where more than half the teams have a shade of red or blue as their primary color.

The Stars almost joined that group. Broadcaster Daryl Reaugh advocated for a move to red, white, and blue—like the Texas flag—in a blog post after Gaglardi purchased the team. "With new ownership will come changes—changes for the good we all trust and changes that maybe should include the very colors the franchise flies. Remember when Mark Cuban bought the Mavericks back in 2000, what was one of the first things he did? That's right, he re-imagined the Mavs colors and logo. He rebranded," Reaugh wrote. "So what is Dallas' 'color'? Well, blue seems to be a pretty strong thread. And the flag of Texas would seem to provide a red and a white that complement the blue well. Vibrant. American. Texan."

That idea didn't fly with many Stars fans. Moving away from green would be sacrilegious, and they made their voices heard through social media and communicating with their ticket representatives. But that didn't stop the Stars from at least looking at all options.

In addition to Texas-flag themed red, white, and blue, the Stars also looked at a black and blue color scheme to match the Dallas Mavericks and Dallas Cowboys—a move that would have been similar to the Pittsburgh Penguins adopting black and gold colors for unity with the Pittsburgh Steelers and Pittsburgh Pirates in 1980.

In fact, the Stars actually received mocked up jerseys from Reebok in blue and gold that they greatly considered. "There were other possibilities," Gaglardi said. "Blue was in the mix. Black was in the mix. Blue, red, and white were in the mix. That's pretty much it. There were really no other colors. There was a big push for Texas state colors, and we had a good look at that, and blue was a big consideration because of the sports teams in the market. But that's also one of the reasons we decided it was important to stay with green."

In the end Mike Modano was the difference maker. "You can also thank Mike Modano for the decision we made," Gaglardi said. "We were seriously considering blue. In fact it was this same jersey but blue instead of green with the same logo. Modano got me on the phone and he was adamant; he was not going to allow us to get away from green."

For the most famous player in franchise history, any other color would have looked ridiculous. "[Gaglardi] was talking about blue, he was talking about something else, and there was a few of us that felt really strong about trying to get green back in the jersey in some way shape or form," Modano said. "It's a good color, it's different. Obviously, no one else has it. That's the way it was with the North Stars; the green was unique and different."

69 Watch Practice

Among the professional sports teams in the Dallas-Fort Worth Metroplex, the Dallas Stars are the most accessible to their fans.

Unlike the other three major professional teams in the area, the Stars have practices that are consistently open to the public and free of charge at the team facilities in Frisco.

When not on the road, the Stars typically practice in the late morning or early afternoon. The schedule is made public on the Stars website, and the players are often more than willing to sign autographs or take pictures with fans before leaving the rink.

And for those who don't live near Frisco, the Stars will hold one practice a season at area Dr. Pepper StarCenters across the metroplex.

70 Les Jackson

You'd be hard-pressed to find someone with more first-hand experience with the Dallas Stars than Les Jackson. With the exception of the 1999–2000 season—where he was the assistant general manager for the Atlanta Thrashers—Jackson has been consistently employed by the Stars since 1985.

He first joined the team as an assistant coach before the 1985–86 season and has since served in a laundry list of roles, including scout, director of amateur scouting, director of hockey operations, assistant general manager, general manager, and most recently as a senior advisor to general manager Jim Nill. Jackson discussed his time with the Stars and the North Stars in an interview for this book:

Q: You've essentially been here from the beginning. What sticks out to you about moving hockey from Minnesota to Dallas?
A: It was a time of uncertainty because Minnesota had been our home for eight years up to that point when we moved. But coming here, it was a tough year leading up to it because there was so much uncertainty about where we were even going. And everyone is wondering where we were going and what's happening? But once we got here—and it was my first time ever coming to Dallas—I looked at it and said, "Wow, this is gonna be great." It was a great opportunity for us to start with a clean piece of paper and see how we wanted to make this team.

There were some trials; we had to clean up the practice rink because we didn't have one. I found that Mr. (Norm) Green did a good job of getting us to know the important people in Dallas. One of the first people I met in Dallas was when we had lunch as a group with (former Dallas Cowboys head coach) Tom Landry. To me, that was cool. For the most part the community embraced us, so it was a good move. It was a fun move.

Q: What was it like for your family?
A: They adjusted well; we had a young family at the time. And people here are so nice. The Texas people are just awesome. They are genuine and I love living here.

Q: What about creating hockey fans? Did people understand the sport?
A: It was good that we had Mike Modano. He was a good leader, and I think that people liked the fact that he was an American leader and the face of the organization. At the same time, I think people

liked the pace of the game and the physicality. So they embraced guys like Basil McRae and Shane Churla and Mark Tinordi, then into (Derian) Hatcher, (Richard) Matvichuk, and Craig Ludwig. They embraced those guys as much as they embraced Mike. Then as they went along we added Jere (Lehtinen) and (Brett) Hull, people got more excited. But it came back to the skill of Modano and his identity; he was an integral part to people embracing the team.

Q: How important was early on-ice success? What was that like to watch as the sport grew in Dallas?
A: We were fortunate because Bob (Gainey) was our lead guy and he had come from an organization that had years and decades of success. He was prepared and knew what we needed to do to put the team together. We had the resources to do that. I think the trade when we picked up Mike Keane and Brian Skrudland, and then we added Guy Carbonneau, those older guys that really complimented our skill and our youth…that was a pretty good recipe by Bob. And then the addition of Hitch kept building things.

Then getting Eddie (Belfour). He was the key guy. He was one of our most valuable players. We had a legitimate group of players that could play in all situations, but we really weren't going to be a championship team until we got Eddie.

Q: What was it like working with Bob Gainey?
A: Bob was an awesome guy to work with because whatever role you were in, he let the guys do it. And if you ever had a problem he was one of the guys that could sort through issues and give the guys directions.

And he spent most of the time with the big team and Hitch, so he was hands on that way, but he kind of kept you off balance with the team. For example, some nights we would play and we would win, and he didn't think we played good, so he always kept you on your toes. While there were games where we would lose and he'd think it was a really good game. So he kept the guys guessing in a good way. I don't think there is one guy that worked in our team that had any doubt about Bob's ability and his leadership and his plan. He was awesome to work with.

Q: What was it like to watch Hitch's evolution as a coach?
A: Yeah, I have a long history with Hitch. I met him when he was back coaching midget hockey in Alberta, so I followed his career for a long time. But I never really had any doubt of his ability or that he was gonna end up in the NHL. I think when he came here, the support he had from Bob and with Rick (Wilson) and his staff… Rick and Bob were his mentors and the guys he entrusted everything with.

And Hitch is a good coach. I don't think guys ever realize what he's trying to do in the process, and he's not that much fun. But a good leadership with a group of guys can sell his message to the rest of the group.

Q: It's not easy to fire yourself, which is what Bob did when he stepped back as a head coach to focus on his job as a GM. What do you remember about that?
A: I think he looked at it where he wanted to put everyone in the right chairs, and he saw that he was better suited for management. We had a good coach on the way. I think it really was: let Hitch take it at that time, or sometime soon, or probably lose him to another team. And he loved Hitch's style. He developed a relationship with him where he trusted and knew what he did. It was just a move that put guys in the right places, and ultimately was the right move.

Q: This team had a tendency to bring in former Canadiens, including Carbonneau and Keane. What did they bring to the team?

A: They had won. Even when you look back at young kids and draft and try to acquire them, you look and try and see what's their history of winning? And those two particular guys could play key junctures of the game, and they could handle particular issues in the locker room and what was going on with the team. They were really an extension of the coaches. When they spoke, their messages carried some weight.

Q: Another trade around that time was for Joe Nieuwendyk, and it was a deal that worked for both sides. But did you have any idea that Jarome Iginla would be as good as he turned out?

A: At that time the only thing you can go on is that he was a top player in junior, and usually if they have the character and work ethic you think that will carry over into a good pro. That was really all we had to go on, but for Calgary to pick him up in that trade, it was a wise choice by them. And for us, the timing of it was right. Joe really helped put our team on the map when you talk about stabilizing success and putting our franchise on the map. Both teams won there. We would have loved to keep Jarome. But that's just the way it works.

Q: How much were trades like the one for Nieuwendyk and Sergei Zubov used as selling points to free agents like Ed Belfour and Brett Hull?

A: I think we were really fortunate to have Mr. Hicks as the owner. We couldn't have done any of that without his support and financial resources. He was real open to winning. When we presented him with the ideas he embraced it.

And Eddie, I said it before, but he really was the backbone of that championship. With how great some of those other players were, you needed a goalie like that to win. And I think he saw what we were trying to do, felt he could be that piece, and became the backbone of the team. We talk about a lot of other things, but without that guy, we don't have a chance.

Q: We've talked about those teams in the 1990s. More recently you've worked with Jim Nill. What's that been like?
A: Jim is a lot like Bob. He's real organized, he knows what he wants in players, he lets the guys do their work. And the unique thing about Jim is you don't know if you just won or lost; he's the same guy.

You're also never afraid to drop an idea or plan to him because he's going to respect and consider all options. He's always thinking and working on the team. In a lot of ways, that makes him even more like Bob.

Q: You've been involved in finding players throughout your career. How much has that evolved?
A: Working with Jim may be my seventh, eighth, or ninth general manager. Each general manager has their own way of doing things for who they want for players. So you have to adjust and work through that. For example, we've had times where the GM wasn't interested in European players, so that was how the scouting staff had to function. Then we had GMs who just wanted big guys and nothing else, so we had to focus on that.

Once thing I've noticed over the past in the last eight or nine years, there isn't any limitations on players. It's an open book; go find players anywhere and see what you can find. And you look at our team now: (Esa) Lindell is there and if (Julius) Honka gets there, and if (Miro) Heiskanen is ready soon, with (John) Klingberg, we'll have pretty much an all-European defense, and that's not a bad thing. I will say one thing that's stayed the same is what's always really mattered is the passion and the character of the player.

Q: You mention passion and character. Is that something that you saw in some later draft picks like Jamie Benn and John Klingberg that panned out?
A: Jamie played in the BC junior league, and a lot of teams didn't get to see him. And the level is like Minnesota high school. It's not quite the junior level, so you go to some of those games and you aren't seeing a real evaluation of the player. So we had to take him as an individual and look at him that way, and we saw that character.

With Klinger we only had two scouts who had seen him, so it was really just trusting the scouts on John Klingberg. The motto for us has always been draft for every round. If you get one in the first, great, and if not keep working. Jamie and Klinger are two great examples of that. Also if we hadn't hit with Klingberg and Benn, would we be having this conversation?

71 1991 Stanley Cup Finals

While the Minnesota North Stars never won the Stanley Cup, the trophy was presented in Bloomington to the Pittsburgh Penguins on May 25, 1991.

And Game 6 of the 1991 Stanley Cup Finals was more of a coronation than a contest for Pittsburgh as the Penguins won 8–0 and dominated the game from opening faceoff and were led by Conn Smythe winner Mario Lemieux, who had scored one of the more iconic goals in playoff history back in Game 2 of the series.

1991 Stanley Cup Finals

Game 1: North Stars 5, Penguins 4
Game 2: Penguins 4, North Stars 1
Game 3: North Stars 3, Penguins 1
Game 4: Penguins 5, North Stars 3
Game 5: Penguins 6, North Stars 4
Game 6: Penguins 8, North Stars 0

It was a sour ending to a Cinderella story for Minnesota, who by all accounts shouldn't have reached the final series of the season. The North Stars were a below average team during the regular season. They had the 15th best record in the 20-team NHL and only had a 27–39–14 record. During the regular season, the North Stars had six stretches where they went at least four straight games without a win, including one of those streaks in the final two weeks of the season.

So heading into the playoffs there wasn't much hope for the North Stars, especially when they were set for a matchup with the regular season champion Chicago Blackhawks in the Norris Division semifinal.

But Minnesota stole Game 1 on the road in overtime. Brian Propp scored at 4:14 of the overtime session, giving the upset-minded North Stars an early lead in the series. Chicago seemed to squash those aspirations with wins in Game 2 and 3, as the Blackhawks offense racked up 11 goals in two games and took a 2–1 series lead.

Then the Blackhawks offense went cold.

In Game 4, Minnesota limited Chicago to 17 shots in a 3–1 victory to tie the series. In Game 5, North Stars goalie Jon Casey only had to make 25 saves in a 6–0 shutout, while the Minnesota offense scored six goals against a pair of future Hall of Fame goalies in Ed Belfour and Dominik Hasek.

In Game 6, the North Stars completed the upset. This time Casey made 27 saves in a 3–1 victory. Brian Bellows scored twice—including once on the power play—sending the North Stars to the Norris Division Finals against the St. Louis Blues.

The Blues had been the second-best team during the regular season with 105 points, and even with the North Stars' upset against the Blackhawks, St. Louis was expected to ease its way past Minnesota.

Once again the North Stars stole Game 1, this time clinging to a 2–1 victory as Casey made 31 saves. St. Louis, like Chicago in Round 1, seemingly reset world order to proper balance with a 5–2 victory in Game 2. This time the North Stars offense took over and scored 13 combined goals in Games 3 and 4.

Curt Giles, Stew Gavin, Bellows, and Neil Wilkinson all scored first period goals in a 5–1 victory in Game 3, forcing the Blues to make a goalie change from Vincent Riendeau to Pat Jablonski. The goalie change didn't make much of a difference in Game 4, and Minnesota stormed out to an 8–4 win. Mike Modano and Bellows each had a pair of goals in the win, and the North Stars now had a 3–2 series lead.

St. Louis extended the series with a 4–2 win in Game 5, but the Blues couldn't extend the series in Game 6 as the North Stars won 3–2 on pair of third period goals by Smith.

In the Conference Finals, the North Stars helped put an end to the Edmonton Oilers dynasty. Led by Wayne Gretzky, the Oilers had won four Stanley Cups in five seasons between 1983 and 1988. After the 1988 season, Gretzky was shockingly traded to the Los Angeles Kings, a move that didn't defuse the dynasty.

Two seasons later the Oilers were champions again, this time hoisting the Stanley Cup with Mark Messier as the captain and Bill Ranford leading the way as the Conn Smythe Trophy winner in net.

Heading into Round 3, this for sure was when the North Stars run would come to an end. It was one thing to beat back-to-back divisional opponents, but the defending champion Oilers would certainly be too much, right?

Wrong.

After facing a bit of adversity in their series against Chicago and St. Louis, Minnesota dispatched Edmonton in five games. With the series tied 1–1 after Game 2, the North Stars outscored the Oilers 15–6 in the final three games, clinching a spot in the Finals with a 3–2 victory in Game 5 after Smith scored the game-winning goal in the third period.

There was hope the North Stars' miracle run would continue against the Penguins, and they opened the Stanley Cup Finals with a 5–4 victory on the road with Smith (who else?) once again scoring the game-winning goal.

Game 1 turned into a wakeup call for Pittsburgh, and Game 2 turned into one of the defining moments in their franchise history. Paul Coffey returned to the lineup after missing most of the game with a broken jaw, providing an emotional boost for his team, while Lemieux scored a goal that still lives in playoff highlight packages. Lemieux danced through a pair of defenders, deked Casey out of position, and slid the puck into the empty net as the highlight of a 4–1 victory.

Returning back to Bloomington, the North Stars actually won Game 3 by a 3–1 score and moved within two games of their first Stanley Cup. It was a win that should have come with an asterisk as Lemieux, who was battling a back injury all season, was a late scratch.

With their captain back in the lineup, Pittsburgh won Game 4 by 5–3. For the North Stars a blown opportunity in the third period would come back to haunt them. Trailing 4–3 at the time the North Stars were given a five-minute major power play in the third period with 6:57 remaining. The North Stars didn't get a single shot on net during the lengthy opportunity, and the series went back to Pennsylvania tied at 2–2.

Back in Pittsburgh the Penguins started fast and led 4–0 in the first period. Minnesota eventually cut the lead to 5–4, thanks to a pair of short-handed goals but couldn't complete the comeback after Troy Loney scored a late goal for Pittsburgh. That set the stage for Game 6, where the Stanley Cup made its first—and to this day, the only—appearance on the ice in the "State of Hockey."

72 1981 Stanley Cup Finals

The Dallas Stars reached the Stanley Cup Finals in back-to-back seasons in 1998 and 1999. Both of those trips have been immortalized in the rafters at American Airlines Center, including the 1999 Stanley Cup Championship banner.

But 1999 wasn't the franchise's first trip to the final series of the season. Twice before they moved to Texas, the North Stars reached the ultimate series, including a 1981 run that featured one of the top rookie scorers in NHL playoff history.

During that playoff run, Dino Ciccarelli set an NHL rookie record with 21 points in 19 games. Ciccarelli's 14 goals are still a record today, while his 21 points were later matched by Philadelphia Flyers rookie Ville Leino in 2010 and Pittsburgh Penguins rookie Jake Guentzel in 2017.

It would have been a bit of a Cinderella story if the North Stars had been able to beat the New York Islanders. Minnesota was a good, but not great team during the 1980–81 season. The North Stars finished third in the Adams Division behind the Buffalo Sabres and Boston Bruins with a 35–28–17 record.

The North Stars entered the playoffs as the ninth seed in the 16-team bracket and swept the eighth-seeded Boston Bruins in a mild upset. Minnesota opened the series with a 5–4 overtime win in Boston Garden. Steve Payne completed a hat trick just 3:34 into overtime, giving the North Stars their first ever win in Boston—the team had actually gone winless in their first 35 trips to Boston over 14 seasons.

That overtime victory instilled confidence heading into Game 2, where the North Stars scored three goals in each period on their way to a 9–6 victory, taking a commanding 2–0 lead back

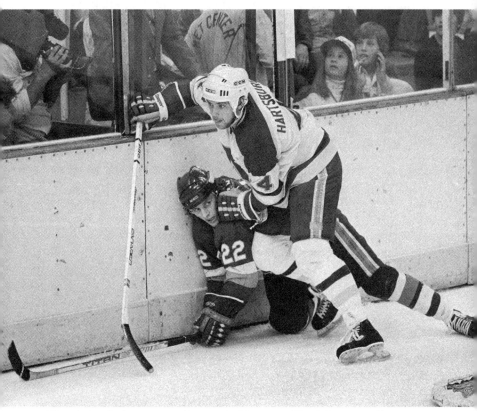

Though they had never won the cup, the Minnesota North Stars actually went to the Finals twice, including in 1981 where they had their Cinderella run stopped by the New York Islanders.

1981 Stanley Cup Finals
Game 1: Islanders 6, North Stars 3
Game 2: Islanders 6, North Stars 3
Game 3: Islanders 7, North Stars 5
Game 4: North Stars 4, Islanders 2
Game 5: Islanders 5, North Stars 1

to Minneapolis. In Game 3, the North Stars completed the sweep with a 6–3 victory, Payne led the way with two goals an assist as Minnesota advanced to the quarterfinals against the Buffalo Sabres.

The series against Buffalo, now a best-of-seven series, also went rather quickly with Minnesota winning in five games. Once again the North Stars opened a series with overtime, this time winning Game 1 in Buffalo when Payne delivered again and scored the game-winning goal 22 seconds into overtime.

The North Stars also won Games 2 and 3 before Buffalo won Game 4 in overtime 5–4. In Game 5, the North Stars completed the series victory with a 4–3 win and advanced to the semifinals against the Calgary Flames. Like it had in the first two rounds, Minnesota was able to steal Game 1. The Flames won Game 2, knotting the series up at 1–1 before it shifted back to Minnesota.

That's when the North Stars took control of the series, led by Bobby Smith. He had two goals and two assists in a 6–4 Game 3 victory. Two nights later Smith had a goal and three assists as the North Stars won 7–4 in Game 4 and took a 3–1 series lead.

Calgary extended the series with 3–1 victory at home in Game 5, but Minnesota never trailed in Game 6 and reached the Stanley Cup Finals with a 5–3 victory at home. The dynastic Islanders ended up being too much for Minnesota in the Finals. On their way to their second of four-straight Stanley Cups, New York was 11–2 heading into the final series with Minnesota and had the NHL's best record in the regular season.

New York dominated the first three games of the series and took a commanding 3–0 series lead before Minnesota extended the series and won the first Stanley Cup Finals game in franchise history 4–2 in Game 4.

Payne and Smith each scored in the third period for Minnesota, breaking a 2–2 tie that forced Game 5. In Game 5 a deep and experienced Islanders lineup was the difference early. New York jumped out to a 3–0 lead in the first period and ended up hoisting the cup with a 5–1 victory.

73 2007 NHL All-Star Game

In 2007 the NHL All-Star Game came to Texas for the first time as the Western Conference defeated the Eastern Conference 12–9 at American Airlines Center on January 24, 2007.

Dallas Stars goalie Marty Turco played the third period and got the win. He was also a star on the broadcast. Turco was mic'd up during the third period and spent most of the period interjecting into the conversation with Versus commentators Mike "Doc" Emrick and Eddie Olczyk. While Turco gave some actual insight during the broadcast, his comedic quips made it a more memorable show for Versus (which was later rebranded as NBC Sports).

Early in the third period Emrick asked if Turco was able to hear all of the commentary from the booth.

"Yeah, I can hear you loud and clear," Turco said.

"We're not bothering you?" Emrick said.

"Well, I don't have a choice right now."

Later in the broadcast, after Zdeno Chara had scored his second goal, Emrick pointed out that no defender had scored a hat

Jeff K Drops from the Rafters

As part of the opening of the 2007 NHL All-Star Game Jeff Kovarsky, better known as Jeff K, made a dramatic entrance from the ceiling at American Airlines Center. On a floating platform with turntables, Jeff K slowly entered the arena with flames shooting from the platform. The moment was jaw-dropping in the arena and was also part of the on-television intro. Jeff K shared his recollection of that moment for this book:

Jeff K: "So the NHL comes in 2007 for the All-Star Game, and our game presentation kind of takes a back seat as the league comes into run the show. But they wanted to use local talent, so I was told to meet with the bigwigs with the NHL and pitch what I wanted to do musically for the All-Star Game.

"So I sat down with the representative, and I had all these lists made up of what I wanted to do for the skills competition, for the rookie game, and the actual game, and even goal songs. And they were very impressed, but then they said, "What we'd like to do is we'd like to shoot an opening sequence that somehow includes you and flames and maybe we'll lower you on a stage," and in the back of my mind, I'm thinking I have no idea what they're talking about. But I said okay, I'm in.

"So turns out what they wanted was just that. So we had a state, and we had to rehearse this several times. I had to walk up to the catwalk of the American Airlines Center, the very top above the scoreboard.

"So I had to get on the catwalk and I had to have a harness, a full-body harness, that was covered in a Stars jersey. There was a hole cut in the back where it clipped into a security wire where it connected to the stage. But the stage hung below the catwalk by about 20 feet. So in order to get down there, they had to drop a rope ladder from the catwalk, and I had to climb up and over on to this rope ladder and ease myself onto the stage. On the stage was a table with two turntables and a mixer, two slabs of vinyl, and I was supposed to scratch and mix something; they didn't know what it was.

"I told them, what if I did kind of a hip-hop remix of "We Will Rock You" by Queen. They said that was a great idea, so I went back in the studio with one of my DJ buddies, and we worked on this Queen's "We Will Rock You" with some funky beats. And a crowd chanting, "Make some noise" so it was really, really cool.

"So the thing was I was going to mime to that because there was no way the needle would have stayed on the table as I'm going down. So what I had to do was put that file in the click effects and have my assistant music director fire the song at the right moment. So we had to rehearse this. I get on down to the stage, the stage would start lowering, and then I would hear the song start the beats—boom, boom, clap—then I would know to go.

"Well, half the time we practiced it just looked horrible. I would start scratching too early, or he would fire it off too early, it just looked horrible. So then came the actual All-Star Weekend, or the week since it was during the week.

"The first night was like the Fan Fest, so let's maybe try it on the first night as a practice for the game and let's see how it goes. So I climbed down, and we have an arena full of people, and I'm waiting and I'm waiting, and nothing's happening. I'm lowering and nothing's happening, and finally a song starts and its Third Eye Blind's "Semi-Charmed Life."

"So I just started scratching like that and it looked horrible, and I was embarrassed. And these were the days of the Dallas Stars message boards and before social media, so the message boards had a field day with this. 'Jeff looks like an idiot,' and 'What the heck does he think he's doing?'

"So we got it corrected and here we are at the night of the All-Star Game. I climb up on the catwalk, it's a packed house, and now the stage is an extra 15 feet lower than it was before. So the rope ladder, which was 10 steps, is now like a 30-step thing. So I'm swaying on the rope as I go down. I get clipped in, the pyro guy is ready, and I start lowering.

"And it starts lowering and the PA goes, 'Now ladies and gentlemen, It's Jeff K!' and I'm thinking, 'Please start, please start.' And the song starts and I start scratching and the flames are going and we get down to the bottom, and then my job was to welcome everybody out to the All-Star Game. In the arena it looked cool, and everybody on the message boards shut up and said it looked cool. And now I have that video to show my grandkids someday."

trick in the All-Star Game. "That's great Doc, that's awesome, love to hear that," Turco said.

When Martin Havlat scored with 1:02 remaining to give the West an 11–8 lead, Emrick told Turco that he liked his chances. Ever cognizant of the situation, Turco responded. "Oh yeah, I love it," Turco said. "Now all I got to do is let one more in and I get the win. Don't tell my teammates though."

Twenty-seven seconds later the East scored to cut the lead to 11–9, and Turco officially got the win. Dion Phaneuf scored in an empty net with 12 seconds remaining to make it 12–9, while Danny Briere was named the game's MVP in the loss after registering five points.

Turco was joined in the game by teammate Philippe Boucher, who actually started after Anaheim Ducks defenders Rob Niedermayer had to miss the game with an injury.

There had been hope that a third Star, Mike Modano, would be able to play in the game. But injuries had limited him to just 10 games before the midpoint of the season, and his hip ailment was still lingering. "That's very disappointing, not to be able play in that game," Modano said in 2007. "That's the hard part because you look forward to that game here and that one time you can play at home in front of everybody."

While it hadn't been finalized, it was believed that NHL commissioner Gary Bettman was willing to make an exception to get Modano into the game if he were healthy. After all, this was the face of hockey in Texas, and there is past precedent of "Commissioners Selections" being used to get hometown players into the game.

On a league-wide scale, the 2007 All-Star Game is known for a couple key points. It was the first All-Star Game for Alexander Ovechkin and Sidney Crosby, who were already becoming the new faces of the NHL and it laid the groundwork for the arguably the most fun All-Star moment in NHL history.

Stars goalie Marty Turco makes a stop during the 2007 NHL All-Star Game, which was played in Texas for the first time.

All-Star Games are supposed to be for the fans, and in 2016 the fans took back the All-Star Game. By traditional terms John Scott isn't an All-Star caliber player. The longtime enforcer had just 11 points in 286 career NHL games and was a fringe roster player much of his career. But in 2016 fans decided they wanted Scott, who was a member of the Arizona Coyotes at the time. He quickly became the vote leader in the Pacific Division.

Around the time it became clear Scott would be voted into the game he was demoted to the minors and actually traded to the Montreal Canadiens, theoretically making him ineligible to play in the All-Star Game. Eventually the NHL yielded and Scott captained the Pacific Division team to the championship on the 3-on-3 tournament (a format the NHL had adopted that season) and was voted the MVP. It was a feel-good story that has already inspired both a book (by Scott) and a movie.

But before John Scott, there was Rory Fitzpatrick and the 2007 NHL All-Star Game. Fitzpatrick was a depth defender with the Vancouver Canucks. He had spent much more time in the AHL than the NHL in his career, but a fan movement started during the 2007 season to get him to Dallas. T-shirts were made, YouTube videos were posted, and Fitzpatrick reached as high as second in votes among Western Conference defenders, which would have made him a starter.

Eventually the "Vote for Rory" campaign came up just short, and Fitzpatrick finished third, thus missing a chance to start in Dallas. But Fitzpatrick's loss planted an idea that hockey fans fully capitalized on almost a decade later.

74 Trevor Daley

If a player has a significant impact on a franchise and leaves before the end of their career, they are often honored with a video tribute in their first game back in the original city. For Trevor Daley, the Dallas Stars had to wait almost three years to finally honor the defenseman when he returned to American Airlines Center.

The Stars traded Daley and Ryan Garbutt to the Chicago Blackhawks on July 10, 2015, in exchange for Patrick Sharp and Stephen Johns. Before Chicago visited Dallas that season, Daley was traded to the Pittsburgh Penguins on December 14.

The next season Daley was injured when Pittsburgh visited Dallas, meaning the tribute video would be put on hold at least one more season. On October 10, 2017, then playing with the Detroit Red Wings, Daley finally got his video tribute. "It's special. I had some good years here and met a lot of great people. No matter where you go, where you end up and see those faces, it's special. It's pretty cool," Daley said that day.

Daley may be one of the most underrated defenseman in franchise history. In 11 seasons with the Stars, he appeared in 756 games and had 231 points. He ranks eighth all time in games played in franchise history and among defenseman he ranks in the Top 10 in nearly every major category.

Daley eventually won back-to-back Stanley Cups with the Penguins in 2016 and 2017. While it wasn't with the Stars, it was a silver lining for many hockey fans in Texas to see the defender finally win a championship.

75 Kari Lehtonen

Kari Lehtonen deserves more credit for his time with the Dallas Stars. In more than nine seasons with the team, Lehtonen ranks third all time in games played, wins, and minutes played behind Marty Turco and Cesar Maniago. And Lehtonen's career save percentage with Dallas (at .912 at the time of this book) is the highest career mark in franchise history.

The problem is Lehtonen's career covered one of the most difficult stretches in franchise history. After spending the first six seasons of his NHL career with the Atlanta Thrashers, Lehtonen was traded to Dallas late in the 2009–10 season and was labeled as the heir apparent to Turco, who left the Stars as a free agent after that season.

Over the next five seasons, Lehtonen was one of the busiest goalies in the NHL. He played 294 games from 2010 to 2015, starting 291 of them, and had a .915 save percentage on a team that only made the playoffs once during that stretch. Lehtonen was a good goalie on a bad team. Had he been on a better team, he could have been considered one of the best goalies in the NHL between 2010 and 2013.

Lehtonen's numbers in his only playoff series with Dallas—a six-game loss to the Anaheim Ducks in 2014—and the lack of a competent backup for over a decade led to the Stars experimenting with a 1A-1B situation with Antti Niemi, who had won a Stanley Cup earlier in his career with the Chicago Blackhawks.

The system worked well enough in year one; each goalie won 25 games, and the Stars had the best regular-season record in the Western Conference. But neither goalie could hold down the starting job in the playoffs, and the Stars were ousted in the second round by the St. Louis Blues. The final season of the Lehtonen-Niemi pairing was one of the worst seasons in team history. The Stars went from the top seed in the West to a lottery pick team, and the goalies—right or wrong—took most of the blame. Niemi was bought out and left the team after that season, while Lehtonen was kept around as the new backup goalie to Ben Bishop.

Lehtonen made a graceful transition to the backup role. And early in the 2017–18 season, he passed Mikka Kiprusoff, an idol in Finnish goaltending, for the most games played in NHL history by a Finnish goalie. He also picked up his 300th career win and ranks in the top 30 in NHL history for all-time victories. "The last three years have been different, and it's taken some adjustments, but I'm happy with where I am," Lehtonen said in December of 2017. "I want to be a part of a team that wins. I want to take pride in the fact I can help us do well in any role. You can find happiness in different ways. Right now, I cherish every game I get to play. So that's happiness to me."

Lehtonen won't make any all-time teams because of the presence of Ed Belfour and Turco in franchise history, but he's earned Stars fans' admiration for both his longevity and career accomplishments after having the prime of his career coincide with the one of the more difficult stretches in franchise history.

As his career has progressed Lehtonen has become more cognizant and taken a further look back at his career. He looks at the trade to Dallas as the move that saved his career, especially after he had struggled with injuries and was frankly out of a shape in his final two seasons in Atlanta. "Honestly, I was young and dumb and I really didn't think about it at the time, but a few years later, I looked back and realized that was a close call and it could have gone either way," Lehtonen said of his career possibly flaming out early. "So looking back, it was important for me to come here. I really did need to change some things, and things did go the right way at the right time."

76 "Never Leave a Hockey Game"

There weren't many highlights in Dallas during the 1995–96 season. The Stars went 26–42–14 and finished last in the Central Division and had the second-worst showing in the Western Conference. The Stars were in the bottom five for goal scoring, and fans endured four winless streaks that lasted five games or longer.

But something special happened at Reunion Arena on October 14, 1995, in a 6–5 victory against the Boston Bruins. Trailing 5–3 with less than a minute remaining, the Stars scored three goals in the final 48 seconds to steal a victory from the Bruins.

Richard Matvichuk started the comeback. Bruins defenseman Don Sweeney tried to flip the puck out of the zone, but Matvichuk used every inch of his 6'2" frame and then some as he leapt to catch the puck and keep position at the point. He then took a quick shot that was initially deflected by Kevin Hatcher and turned into a juicy rebound that Hatcher put home with 48.8 seconds left to cut the lead to 5–4.

The events over the ensuing 20 seconds made the comeback even more improbable. Hatcher iced the puck with 28.1 seconds remaining, and Mike Modano actually lost the ensuing defensive zone faceoff against Adam Oates. But a point shot by Sweeney was blocked, and the Stars quickly transitioned up the ice. Modano beat Craig Billington on the stick side with 15.2 seconds left to tie the game at 5–5.

With the game tied and overtime a mere formality, coach Bob Gainey actually took a conservative approach after Modano's goal. The checking line centered by Guy Carbonneau took the center-ice faceoff in a move designed to guarantee overtime.

Bruins-Stars Scoring Summary

1st Period
01:38—BOS—Cam Neely, Adam Oates, and Shawn McEachern
13:45—DALPP—Kevin Hatche, Mike Modano, and Nikolai Borschevsky
17:11—BOS—Cam Neely, Ray Bourque, and Adam Oates

2nd Period
06:04—BOS—Todd Elik, Kevin Stevens, and Don Sweeney
14:55—DAL—Dave Gagner, Grant Marshall, and Mike Donnelly
16:36—BOSSH—Steve Heinze and Ted Donato

3rd Period
01:16—DAL—Guy Carbonneau, Todd Harvey, and Doug Zmolek
05:44—BOS—Todd Elik, Sandy Moger, and Ray Bourque
19:11—DAL—Kevin Hatcher and Richard Matvichuk
19:44—DAL—Mike Modano, Derian Hatcher, and Greg Adams
19:55—DAL—Guy Carbonneau and Mike Kennedy

Instead, Carbonneau scored the game-winning goal with 4.4 seconds remaining. Carbonneau won the faceoff, and winger Todd Harvey dumped the puck into the Bruins zone. Mike Kennedy won the race for the puck in the corner and he threw a puck to the net where it banked off Carbonneau and past Billington.

Former Stars play-by-play announcer Mike Fornes summed it up perfectly on the air: "We're not gonna make it to overtime. The Stars score again. Storming the ice and pushing one by Billington to take a 6–5 lead. Never leave a hockey game."

It was just the second time in NHL history that a team had trailed by two goals in the final minute and won before overtime.

77 Growing the Game

For an expansion or relocated NHL franchise to succeed, it has to check off a couple key boxes for long-term success: there needs to be some success on the ice, there needs to be interest in the sport from local corporations and sponsors, and youth hockey needs to grow. The Dallas Stars helped set this model when they moved from Minnesota to Texas in 1993.

When the Stars moved to Dallas, they purchased the only full-time rink in the area and had to upgrade it to a suitable NHL practice facility. It boiled down to this: as much as the Stars wanted to sell the game, there wasn't a realistic option for young kids to learn to skate or to try and play the game.

That's why the Stars started to build and operate rinks in the late 1990s. In 2017 ground was broken on the eighth Dr. Pepper StarCenter in Mansfield, joining facilities in Euless, Farmers Branch, Frisco, Irving, McKinney, Plano, and Richardson.

The coaching and instruction also improved over the years. Many ex-Stars have retired and remained in their area, several volunteering as coaches for youth hockey teams. USA Hockey has also held youth national championships in Frisco and Plano. Trying hockey is easy for youngsters with Mike Modano's Little Rookies program, which also extends to Austin and Houston.

Something must be working because since the start of the 2013–14 NHL season six players born in the Dallas area have made their NHL debut, including Jon Rheault, Chris Brown, Seth Jones, Stefan Noesen, Nicolas Kerdiles, and Blake Coleman. The other three NHLers from Texas—Brian Leetch, Tyler Myers, and Mike Christie—were all born in Texas but didn't grow up in the state.

Hockey's growth in Texas was also highlighted when the Stars made their pitch to host the 2018 NHL Draft. While it was mainly a way to celebrate the Stars 25th season in Texas, it was also used as a showcase and opportunity to grow the game, sending a message that hockey players do indeed come from Texas.

78 The Stretcher Drop

This was one of the lowlights in Dallas Stars history, and thankfully it didn't end up much worse. On February 26, 1994, Mike Modano was knocked out in the third period of a 3–1 win against the New York Rangers.

Modano carried the puck into the offensive zone and was leveled on a blindside headshot by Rangers captain Mark Messier. The blow, which came from Messier's shoulder, knocked Modano's helmet off, and he hit the ice hard.

No penalty was called on the play, and after the game, Stars team doctor Dr. John Brook said Modano suffered a concussion and had a cut on the back of the head. He was out for about 10 minutes and was wheeled off the ice on a stretcher.

And the stretcher journey didn't go as planned. As captured on television cameras during the broadcast, while Modano was being loaded into an ambulance, the stretcher was knocked off balance and dropped with the player strapped in. After the game Brooks said he didn't think the stretcher drop made things worse for Modano.

In today's NHL game, it likely would have been a penalty, and Messier would have been suspended. But at the time it was a hit that was legal and widely accepted in the NHL. In fact Stars coach Bob Gainey had no issues with Messier's actions. "I didn't think it was a dirty hit. He got his shoulder right on the jaw," Gainey said. "I don't know if it was so much a hit as Mike turned and skated right into him."

Messier, who would lead the Rangers to a Stanley Cup that season, was genuinely concerned for Modano after the game. "I saw him biting his mouth guard, and that's a bad sign," Messier said at the time. "You don't want to see a guy swallow his tongue."

Modano would return to the ice six days later and had an assist against the Vancouver Canucks on March 4, 1994. He finished that season with a career-best 50 goals and 93 points.

79 Barons and Golden Seals

As of 2017 the Cleveland Barons were still the last major professional sports team in the United States to cease operations. After two ill-fated seasons in Cleveland, the NHL closed up shop in Ohio in 1978 and didn't return until the Columbus Blue Jackets joined the NHL as an expansion franchise in 2000.

It's a fun piece of trivia; feel free to use it to stump your friends that didn't buy this book.

In that same category of fun trivia, the Stars have a shared history with that doomed franchise in Ohio. In 1967 the NHL doubled in size from six to 12 teams, welcoming the California Seals, Los Angeles Kings, Minnesota North Stars, Philadelphia Flyers, Pittsburgh Penguins, and St. Louis Blues alongside the Original Six franchises.

Four of those teams are still in the NHL today, Minnesota moved to Dallas, and the Seals struggled to become more than a fashion footnote in NHL history with different colored skates. The franchise started as the California Seals, but midway through the inaugural season, they were rebranded as the Oakland Seals and had that name up until 1970, when the name was once again changed to the California Golden Seals.

No matter the name, the Seals struggled on the ice. In nine seasons there were seven different head coaches, the team averaged just 20 wins per season, and never finished above .500. After the 1975–76 season, minority owners George and Gordon Gund convinced majority owner Melvin Swig to move the team to Cleveland after an arena deal couldn't be secured to move the team from Oakland to San Francisco.

It didn't get much better in Cleveland. In their first season, the Barons went 25–42–13. The next season they were even worse at 22–45–13. Fans also weren't showing up. "We had the big, cavernous building in the middle of a farmer's field and we couldn't draw flies," Gary Sabourin told the *Guardian*. "It wasn't a very good experience."

On top of that, the team was bleeding money. At one point the players weren't getting paid and threatened a potential strike before a game. At another low point, the NHL actually considered a midseason dispersal draft to liquidate the Barons assets and drop a franchise in the middle of the season.

Swig wanted out and sold his majority ownership to the Gunds, who tried every possible angle to keep the team in their home city. They just couldn't make it work. "So that wasn't funny. Especially because it was the city we grew up in. We felt a great deal of love for it; it was very hard," Gordon Gund said. "We were sad because we couldn't make it work there and we were taking away a professional sports team from the city. We were going to have to unwind it, but it turned out the best solution was to merge it."

So the Gunds opened up conversations with the NHL and the North Stars about merging. Both franchises were losing money, and this could be the needed lifeline for Minnesota. "We didn't know if the league would approve what we said we needed to do until we had to do it," Gordon Gund said. "A lot of people weren't sure they wanted to merge the teams until they understood the facts, which was just have one team fold instead of two and what would that look like for the league."

On June 14, 1978, the teams officially merged.

The merger provided a nice boost for the North Stars on the ice, who had only won 18 games the season before combining with the Barons. The goaltending got better with the addition of Gilles Meloche, while forwards Dennis Maruk and Al MacAdam added some scoring punch and helped the North Stars improve by 10 wins the following season.

Three years after the merger, the North Stars reached the Stanley Cup Finals for the first time with help from a couple former Barons as Meloche won eight playoff games, and MacAdam had 19 points in the playoffs.

A decade after that Stanley Cup appearance—which the North Stars lost to the dynastic New York Islanders—the NHL technically unmerged the franchises. The Gunds wanted to bring a franchise back to the San Francisco Bay Area, and by unmerging the franchises, the San Jose Sharks were born. So, in a way, the Stars also have a shared history with the Sharks.

80 Fabian Brunnstrom

Heading into the 2008–09 season, the Dallas Stars were looking for their next offensive stalwart. Mike Modano was entering the twilight of his career, and so was Jere Lehtinen. The Stars were a franchise preparing for a transition from the old guard, and there was an opportunity for a younger player to emerge as the next go-to offensive weapon.

In his first NHL game, Fabian Brunnstrom looked like that player. An undrafted Swede, Brunnstrom was a highly sought-after free agent during the 2007–08 season. The Vancouver Canucks, Detroit Red Wings, Montreal Canadiens, and Toronto Maple Leafs were all reportedly close to a deal with the forward before he signed with the Stars on May 8, 2008.

Brunnstrom was a healthy scratch in the Stars' first two games, but he got the nod for Game 3 against the Nashville Predators on October 15, 2008.

Brunnstrom delivered with a hat trick, scoring twice in the second period and completing the task in the third period. He became the third player in NHL history to score three times in their NHL debut, joining former Montreal Canadien Alex Smart, who did it in 1943, and Real Cloutier, who did it for the Quebec Nordiques in 1979. Since Brunnstrom, two other players have joined the opening-night hat-trick club.

The hype machine took off from there. Brunnstrom scored again two games later and finished his rookie season with 29 points in 55 games. His numbers likely would have been better, but he struggled with injuries and seemingly couldn't adapt to the physicality in North America.

The following season Brunnstrom's stock continued to drop. In 44 NHL games during the 2009–10 season, he had just two goals and 11 points. Eventually he was waived, unclaimed, and assigned to the Texas Stars.

That would be the end of Brunnstrom's brief and, for a moment, promising career with the Dallas Stars. He started the 2010–11 season in the AHL with Texas and was traded to the Toronto Maple Leafs in the middle of the season for little-known prospect named Mikhail Stefanovich.

Brunnstrom—who played five games with the Detroit Red Wings before pulling the plug on his North American career—became a bit of the poster child for the Stars from 2008 to 2013. Despite starting the 2008–09 season with so much hope, Dallas missed the playoffs in five straight seasons, the longest drought in team history.

81 The Texas Stars

In 2009, the Dallas Stars made a logical decision to bring their AHL affiliate closer to home. And it's a move that's paid off.

Since their inaugural season in Cedar Park, just three hours south of Dallas, the Texas Stars have established themselves a perennial playoff contender, won a championship, and helped grow both hockey and the Stars' reach in Central Texas.

For the first 16 years in Dallas, the Stars' top minor league affiliate was always at least a plane flight away. Prospects were housed in Michigan, Utah, and Iowa before the Stars started to lay the groundwork for a closer AHL affiliate in 2008, when they ended their affiliation with the Iowa Stars.

After spending one season with prospects spread across four AHL teams, the Stars were granted a provisional AHL franchise on April 28, 2009 contingent upon the Stars owner Tom Hicks buying an existent AHL franchise. Two weeks later Hicks formerly purchased the Iowa Chops—which had changed its name from Iowa Stars—and moved the team to Cedar Park and the brand new Cedar Park Center for the 2009–10 season.

The Texas Stars had instant success. During their inaugural season, the Texas Stars had a 46–27–3–4 record and finished second in the Western Conference. For the playoffs a dominant team got even better. Future Dallas Stars captain Jamie Benn, then an NHL rookie, joined the AHL team for the playoffs despite not having played a single regular season game for Texas.

Benn became the final piece that pushed the Texas Stars to the Calder Cup Finals and had 26 points (14 goals, 12 assists) in 24 AHL playoff games. In the second round against the Chicago Wolves, Benn scored the game-winning goal of overtime in Game 7, giving Texas a 6–5 victory. In the Western Conference Finals, he had six goals in seven games, including the insurance goal in a 4–2 Game 7 victory.

In the Calder Cup Finals against the Hershey Bears, it looked like the Texas Stars would win a championship in their first AHL season. Texas won Games 1 and 2 on the road in Hershey and returned back to Cedar Park with three straight home games to potentially complete a championship season. Unfortunately, the Texas Stars ran out of magic. The Hershey Bears won four straight games and hoisted the Calder Cup with a 4–0 victory in Game 6 back in Pennsylvania.

Four years later the Texas Stars got the job done and won the Calder Cup.

After a strong 2012–13 season and a disappointing second round playoff exit, the 2013–14 season felt like a year-long coronation for the Texas Stars. With 106 points, they had the AHL's best record. Travis Morin was the named the league MVP, Curtis McKenzie was named the AHL rookie of the year, and the Texas Stars outscored their opponents 274–197 in the regular season.

Heading into the AHL Playoffs, it felt like a foregone conclusion that the Texas Stars would be playing for the Calder Cup. The only question was who they would meet out of the Eastern Conference when they were there. Texas opened the playoffs by sweeping the Oklahoma City Barons in three games, then made relatively quick work of the Grand Rapids Griffins in a six-game series in the second round.

The Western Conference Finals against the Toronto Marlies turned into the biggest test of the postseason for Texas. In a 2–3–2 format, Texas came to back Cedar Park with a 3–2 lead in the series and a chance to close out Toronto. In Game 6 Marlies goalie Drew MacIntyre stole the game with 36 saves in a 3–1 victory.

And it looked like that trend would continue in Game 7. Toronto scored on its first shot of the game and led 2–0 just 23 seconds into the second period. The Stars clawed back and outshot Toronto 20–10 in the second period, and finally tied the game on goals by Mike Hedden and Dustin Jeffrey late in the period. Then the Texas Stars offense exploded in the third period.

Brett Ritchie and Matej Stransky scored goals in a 17-second span early in the third period, giving Texas a 4–2 lead. Eight minutes later Justin Dowling gave Texas a 5–2 advantage, and Jeffrey scored on an empty net to seal Texas' trip to the Calder Cup Finals.

In the final, Texas met the St. John's IceCaps, a team that had finished fourth in the AHL's Eastern Conference and taken advantage of a playoff bracket defined by upsets—the top three seeds all fell in the first round.

Texas opened the series with a 6–3 victory in Game 1, with then Stars prospect Scott Glennie leading the way with two goals and an assist. The IceCaps took Game 2 as Michael Hutchinson stole game with 49 saves on 50 shots in a 2–1 victory.

Hutchinson did everything he could as the series reverted back to St. John's. In Game 3, Hutchinson made 34 saves before Morin scored the game-winning goal in a 2–1 overtime victory. Game 4 had a similar ending as Morin once again scored the game-winning goal in overtime—this time in a 4–3 victory.

The series needed one more overtime game, and this time the Texas Stars were able to celebrate their first championship when Patrik Nemeth scored on a backhand at 14:30 of overtime to give Texas a 4–3 victory in Game 5. Morin was named the playoff MVP with 22 points (nine goals, 13 assists) in 21 games.

Four years later Texas made another run to the championship series. A long shot after an average season, Texas met Toronto in the Calder Cup Final but fell in Game 7 as its unlikely run came up short.

82 Drink Modano's Beer

Looking for a cold beverage to enjoy while watching the Dallas Stars? America's all-time leading goal scorer has got you covered with Mike Modano's 561 Kolsch, a Kolsch-style beer made by Rabbit Hole Brewing.

The name is a nod to the number of goals Mike Modano scored in his NHL career. It's a clean and crisp drink with a smooth finish. It also has a slightly spicy hint of hops. It's a light beer that is suitable for both the locker room after a beer league game or at the bar, where you can find it on tap at various locations across North Texas.

Beer aficionados have also given strong reviews of the brew. The Beverage Tasting Institute gave the drink a Gold Medal rating (93 out of 100) in 2015 with the following review: "Gold color. Aromas of raisin bread toast and honeyed citrus with a supple, lively, finely carbonated, dry-yet-fruity medium body and a tingling, stimulating, medium-length arugula, light pepper, and minerals finish. A delicious, toasty, fruity kolsch with a snappy hop finish and super sessionability."

So how did Modano go from hockey to craft beer? The founders of Rabbit Hole were connected with Mondano through a mutual friend before the company was even in the planning stages. One of their homebrews, a Bohemian Pilsner, found its way to Modano who enjoyed the drink.

Modano asked about the brewery, but there wasn't any commercial enterprise at the time. Once Rabbit Hole was in the formal planning stages, they connected with Modano again about a partnership opportunity, and the Modano 561 was born.

Modano—who has an ownership stake in the company—worked with the brewers to create something with European flavor. Modano's favorite brews included Spaten Lager and Stella Artois, so the Rabbit Hole brewers created something along those lines, but with its own twist. Rabbit Hole also did a nice job with the can, which says "Icing is no longer an infraction," and comes with simple instructions for building an at-home hockey puck:

- Empty can
- Place can on the ground
- Crush the can
- Enjoy your new puck

83 Fight Night

Thanks to a combination of speed and awareness, fighting doesn't have the same place in hockey that it once did. The game is faster and players, who only had an NHL roster spot thanks to their fists, have been effectively phased out. Concussion awareness and side effects have also played a role. Essentially, the old bravado and fight code that existed through the 1990s has slowly been removed from the sport.

With that in mind, it's unlikely the Stars will ever have another game like the ones on December 31, 1993 and March 13, 1998.

Stars vs. Hawks—December 31, 1993
In the Dallas Stars' first season they paid homage to the Minnesota North Stars vs. Chicago Blackhawks rivalry from the 1980s.

The first four games that season had been somewhat tame. The teams had only combined for two fights and, while there were many holdovers from the North Stars era, there weren't many signs of an all-out brawl breaking out.

That changed at the opening faceoff as both teams started their heavyweights. Seven seconds into the game, Shane Churla and Jocelyn Lemieux were fighting, and both players continued to swing wildly while being restrained by the linesmen. On the very next faceoff, Jim McKenzie and Darin Kimble fought. This time the officials let the players tire themselves out, finally jumping into intervene after McKenzie dropped Kimble with a right hook.

That fight settled things for a bit. The remaining 19 minutes of the first period and all of the second period were played without a fight, but the third period was one of the most violent in franchise history.

At 14:24 of the third period, a high stick reignited the teams, and a line brawl broke out between the Stars' Mark Tinordi, Derian Hatcher, and Mike Craig and the Blackhawks' Chris Chelios, Dirk Graham, and Steve Smith. Three minutes later Russ Courtnall fought Chicago's Christian Ruuttu. Courtnall was a decisive winner in that fight, landing several shots before the linesmen separated the players.

With 37 seconds remaining in the game McKenzie had his second fight of the game, this time against Cam Russell. That was the seventh fight of the game, the most the Stars have ever had in a single game since the franchise moved to Texas.

Stars vs. Mighty Ducks—March 13, 1998

Five years later the Stars had another late-season line brawl that fans remember well. This one was at home against the Mighty Ducks of Anaheim as the teams combined for 187 penalty minutes.

The Stars were a good team that season. They were already a lock for the playoffs, while the Ducks were struggling and all but out of the postseason with a couple weeks to play.

With less than five minutes remaining in the third period, Stars defenseman Craig Ludwig leveled Mighty Ducks forward Teemu Selanne with an elbow to the head. Ludwig was ejected for the hit, and an expected fracas broke out, leading to ejections for a trio of Ducks that went after Ludwig: Jason Marshall, Dave Karpa, and Peter Leboutillier.

One minute later there was a line brawl after a faceoff. In the first shift after Ludwig's ejection, Craig Muni fought Warren Rychel, and Darryl Sydor fought Brent Severyn. Sean Pronger, Greg Adams, Guy Carbonneau all received roughing penalties and were sent to a packed penalty box. On the very next faceoff, Jason Botterill fought Steve Ruchin. Ruslan Salei fought Grant Marshall, and Dmitri Mironov fought Pat Verbeek.

All of the fights overshadowed what was a standout game for Joe Nieuwendyk, who scored four goals in a 6–3 win.

84 Mark Parrish Hat Trick

Mark Parrish had a more-than-desirable NHL career. The right winger played parts of 12 NHL seasons with seven different franchises and had 387 points in 722 career games. He played for the United States in the 2006 Olympics and captained the Minnesota Wild during the 2007–08 season.

He also had one of the more shocking hat tricks in Stars history. That's because after that 2007–08 season with Minnesota, it looked like Parrish's NHL career might be over.

The Wild bought out the final three years of Parrish's contact that summer, and he couldn't find an NHL job. Looking to extend his career, the then 31-year-old Parrish signed a 25-game professional tryout contract with the AHL's Bridgeport Sound Tigers, an affiliate of the New York Islanders.

Parrish only played three games with Bridgeport, tallying a goal and an assist before the Stars signed him to a one-year, two-way contract on November 3, 2008. Four days later Parrish made his NHL debut when the Dallas Stars beat the Anaheim Ducks 5–2 in California.

Parrish led the way with a natural hat trick. "I was hoping to get off to a good start, but I certainly wasn't expecting that," Parrish said after the game. "Some nice bounces kind of came my way, and there were some great plays by my linemates."

Parrish scored his first goal at 10:44 of the first period, capitalizing on a pass from Sean Avery and Philippe Boucher on the power play to give Dallas a 2–0 lead. In the second period, he struck again on the power play, this time giving Dallas a 3–1 lead 1:13 into the middle stanza when he scored on a rebound after initial chances by Brad Richards and Mike Ribeiro.

He completed the hat trick four minutes later when the Ducks defenseman Scott Niedermayer—one of the better skating defenseman in NHL history—inexplicably lost his balance and turned the puck over at the Anaheim blue line.

Parrish picked up the loose puck, took a couple strides, and beat Jean-Sebastien Giguere with a wrist shot to complete the hat trick. "I'm still trying to figure out how the third one went in. I don't know who was more surprised, myself or Giguere, that thing went by him," Parrish said after the game.

It was a stellar debut for Parrish, but it wasn't a sign of things to come for him in Dallas. While he proved he was still a viable option, age was catching up with Parrish, and he only played 44 games that season and recorded just eight goals and 13 points.

After the season came to an end he wasn't re-signed by the Stars and found himself in a similar situation—in the AHL on a minor-league contract. Parrish once again was able to secure an NHL contract in the middle of the season and signed with the Tampa Bay Lightning, but he wasn't able to replicate the one-game wonder showing he had with the Stars in 2008.

85 Boucher Plays Big for Parents

Philippe Boucher could have missed the Dallas Stars game against the Los Angeles Kings on November 24, 2006. Boucher's father, Jean-Claude, was battling pancreatic cancer back in Quebec. His mother, Jacqueline, recently had bypass surgery. Boucher was scheduled to fly to Quebec the next day to be with his parents, and Stars coach Dave Tippett had given the defender permission to skip the game and fly to Quebec early.

He opted to stay with his teammates and scored one the first hat tricks of his career in a 5–3 victory. "With everything going on in his life right now, I asked him if he even wanted to play tonight, but he told me he wanted to play, and I'm glad he did," Tippett said.

Boucher said staying on the ice was a welcome distraction and dedicated the performance to his parents. "Playing 60 minutes of hockey is an escape for me," Boucher said after the game. "I'm going to go back and give [one of the pucks] to [my father]."

It was the only hat trick of Boucher's 16-year career and he scored all three goals on the power play. "There was traffic on all three goals," Boucher said. "It was just crank and shoot. Our guys did a great job screening the goalie."

Overall it was a game dominated by the power play. Of the eight combined goals, seven were scored on the power play. The final tally was an empty netter by Jere Lehtinen with 26 second remaining.

Boucher opened the scoring and gave Dallas a 1–0 lead on his first point blast early in the period. Roughly eight minutes later, Sergei Zubov doubled the Stars lead with a power play goal of his own. Boucher then scored his second goal 26 seconds later, giving the Stars a 3–0 lead before the first intermission.

In the second period, Kings forward Dustin Brown tried to emulate Boucher and scored back-to-back power play goals to cut the lead to 3–2. But Boucher responded and completed the hat trick with another point shot, giving the Stars a 4–2 lead. "Power plays were the difference in the game," Kings coach Marc Crawford said at the time. "I was not surprised with [the Stars']power play.

Philippe Boucher waves to the crowd after completing a hat trick against the Los Angeles Kings in 2006. While he contemplated flying back to be with ailing parents, Boucher opted to stay and play the game, putting up one of the best performances of his career in a 5–3 victory.

Their offense comes from their point men, and tonight Boucher found holes on three of his shots."

Los Angeles cut the lead to 4–3 in the third period on another power play tally, this one by Alexander Frolov, before Lehtinen iced the game with his empty-net goal.

That season ended up being the one of the best of Boucher's career. He finished the 2006–07 season with a career-high 19 goals and 32 assists. He also averaged close to 23 minutes per game and for the only time in his career he received votes for the Norris Trophy as the NHL's best defender.

Later that season Boucher was selected as an injury replacement for the NHL All-Star Game in Dallas. It was the only All-Star selection of his career, and he considered passing on the honor to visit his ailing father, but that wasn't an option. "My dad said I was going to play, that it was a big honor," Boucher said at the time. "So that's what I am going to do."

86 Stefan's Slipup

Patrik Stefan was supposed to be star in the NHL after entering the NHL with much fanfare. Some even considered him the best prospect since Jaromir Jagr. But his career didn't match the hype and ultimately an embarrassing moment with the Dallas Stars in 2007 defined his career.

Stefan's pre-draft hype started during the 1998–99 season with the Long Beach Ice Dogs in the IHL. As a teenager he had 35 points in 33 games but missed most of the season thanks to a concussion that also forced him to miss the 1999 World Junior Championships.

Despite the small sample size, Stefan had his supporters in the scouting community, while his coach in Long Beach, John Van Boxmeer, considered the Czech center a cross between Sergei Federov and Mike Modano.

Van Boxmeer wasn't the only person to buy into the hype, and the expansion Atlanta Thrashers took Stefan with the first overall pick—and the first pick in franchise history—in the 1999 NHL Entry Draft after trading up in a series of deals that allowed the Vancouver Canucks to draft twins Henrik and Daniel Sedin with the No. 2 and No. 3 picks. "We really felt it was so important for our franchise to not only select first, but to pick the player that we really wanted," Thrashers general manager Don Waddell said at the time. "We're real excited about adding Patrik to the team that we selected yesterday…this process has begun, and in time we'll be a competing team, and Patrik will be a big part of that."

He wasn't.

The Thrashers finished their 13-year stay in Atlanta without a single playoff victory before relocating to Winnipeg. Stefan was traded with Jaroslav Modry to Dallas on June 24, 2006, in exchange for Niko Kapanen and a seventh-round draft pick.

Stefan only played 41 games for Dallas that season and had 11 points. He really should have had 12.

With the Stars leading 5–4 and the Edmonton Oilers' net empty on January 4, 2007, Stefan forced a turnover at the blue line and skated toward the empty net with 15 seconds remaining. Somehow he missed, lost his footing, and fell on the right side of the Oilers' net.

It was bad. And then it got worse.

Edmonton gathered the puck, sent a long stretch pass the other way, and Ales Hemsky scored on a forehand-to-backhand move with 2.1 seconds remaining to tie the game at 5–5 for Oilers and force overtime.

Despite Stefan's gaffe the Stars ultimately won the game 6–5 in the shootout, but that minor detail—along with Stefan's goal earlier in the game to start a comeback—has taken a back seat to the blown empty net by one of the biggest draft busts in NHL history.

It also marked the virtual end to Stefan's NHL career. After the 2006–07 season, the Stars didn't re-sign the center, and after a three-game stint in Switzerland, he retired.

More than a decade later, Stefan has learned to cope with the gaffe and he's used it as teaching point for his two sons. "My kids ask me about that now," Stefan told the *Detroit Free Press* in 2016. "My first thing about it is, bad things happen, unlucky, whatever it is. How are you going to respond after that? Good or bad? I tell the kids you can have a bad shift, bad game. There's always next shift, next game. I didn't kill somebody. It's a game. Mistakes happen."

87 Gagner Gets Caught in the Snow

It's fitting that this story took place on April Fool's Day because it felt like a cruel joke to Dallas Stars fans watching the Detroit Red Wings 3–2 win at Reunion Arena on April 1, 1995. With 3.4 seconds remaining, Dave Gagner was awarded a penalty shot after an infraction called against Detroit defenseman Bob Rouse for intentionally pushing the net off its moorings.

It was an ideal situation for the Stars. Gagner had scored at least 30 goals and registered 60 points in six straight seasons. If the game was on the line, Gagner wasn't a bad choice to deliver.

Problem is he never got the shot off.

As Gagner carried the puck in, it jumped off his stick between the hash marks, he lost control, and the Red Wings won the game without goalie Chris Osgood even having to make a save.

After the game Stars coach Bob Gainey said, "I haven't see that in the NHL before." Gagner, understandably, was frustrated after the game. "It's the most embarrassing thing that can happen to a guy," he said. "I just have to deal with it and go on."

Gagner refused to make excuses after the game, but bad ice conditions and a bit of mischief by Osgood played a big part in his misfortune.

It was a hot day in April. The ice was choppy and slushy, and the Red Wings goalie saw an opportunity to bend the rules. While the call was being sorted by officials, Osgood made two trips to the hash marks, each time dragging his stick to collect as much slush as possible and deposit it right at each hash mark.

The Stars players saw exactly what Osgood was up to. "Osgood pushed the snow, scattered in around the front of the slot," Stars defenseman Paul Cavallini said. "The puck hit that area when Dave carried it in."

While it wasn't the most ethical move by the Detroit goalie, it wasn't technically against the rules.

88 Lucky Lotto

The 2016–17 season was one of the most disappointing campaigns in franchise history. One season removed from a trip to the second round of the playoffs and posting the best record in the Western Conference, the Stars dropped from 109 points to 79. The high-profile offense disappeared—partially due to injuries—and any resemblance of defensive structure went out the window under a coaching staff that wouldn't return for the 2017–18 season.

After a frustrating season, the Stars were finally winners in the NHL Draft Lottery on April 29, 2017. Dallas entered the lottery with the eighth best odds of getting the No. 1 pick, a slim 5.8 percent, but had accepted they'd likely be picking in that range. And with how the Stars luck went the past season, it felt like a foregone conclusion that Dallas had a better chance of moving back in the draft than moving up.

But things started to change during the lottery as results were announced in descending order. When the Philadelphia Flyers were skipped at spot No. 13, Stars general manager Jim Nill was almost certain Dallas would be picking at No. 8. "When a team behind you moves up like that, the odds are telling you that you aren't going to get one of those top three picks," Nill said. "You kind of have to accept that."

But as the announcements progressed, the Stars were also skipped, meaning that one of the ping pong balls had bounced their way and Rich Peverley, who represented the Stars at the lottery, was about to get more facetime on NBC Sports Network. "That was a moment where you start to realize that it's going to bounce your way a bit," Peverley said. "It was Jim's idea to send me to the lottery. It was a pretty cool experience already, and then you get to be part of that moment where your team is going to get a top three pick."

The New Jersey Devils were the big winner of the night and grabbed the top selection, but the Stars were still one of the biggest winners as they jumped to No. 3. They would be making their highest pick since the franchise moved from Minnesota to Dallas in 1993. For the record, the North Stars had three No. 1 picks including Bobby Smith in 1978, Brian Lawton in 1983, and Mike Modano in 1988.

It created a rare opportunity for director of amateur scouting Joe McDonnell who runs the Stars draft. "We actually had a chance to draft the best player on our board. That's something I'm not used to doing," McDonnell said. "You have a chance to actually look at the top tier of players, and it's a reality you may get one of those players. Oftentimes when you approach the draft, you do your due diligence on the top players, but know deep down there is no chance to draft them."

That's how the Stars ended up drafting defender Miro Heiskanen with the No. 3 pick after the New Jersey Devils picked Nico Hischier and the Philadelphia Flyers drafted Nolan Patrick. McDonnell said the Stars could have taken Heiskanen with the No. 1 pick if they had it, and the value of drafting the then-17-year-old Finn was too much for Nill to seriously entertain the many trade offers he got for the pick. "It was tempting, but with the value we assigned there, it was just something we couldn't pass up," Nill said.

The Stars are hoping Heiskanen can reverse a trend. Top picks haven't had much luck in Dallas. Before Heiskanen was picked in 2017, defender Richard Jackman was the highest pick in the Dallas era when he was selected fifth overall in 1996. He only played 38 games with Dallas before being traded to the Boston Bruins in 2001. Right wing Scott Glennie was taken with the eighth selection in 2009 and only played one game with Dallas during the 2011–12 season and was never able to escape from the AHL.

89 The Wrong Lundqvist

In the 2000 NHL Entry Draft, the Dallas Stars had the right family; they just picked the wrong brother. In the third round, Dallas picked Joel Lundqvist with the 68th overall pick. Joel Lundqvist was a solid two-way center; he could kill penalties and he turned into a serviceable NHL player that skated in 134 games with the Stars.

It wasn't a bad pick, especially when you consider the two preceding draft picks never played an NHL game. And in most cases a third-round pick that played 100-plus games would be a minor footnote in franchise history, but this draft pick had a twin brother, and that really spins the wheel of what ifs for Stars fans.

The New York Rangers turned Henrik Lundqvist into the steal of the 2000 draft when they drafted him in the seventh round with the 205th overall pick. With hindsight being 20-20, the future Hall of Fame goalie should have gone first overall. Entering the 2017–18 season, Henrik Lundqvist was 10th in NHL history with 405 wins and 17th with 61 career shutouts, all with the Rangers.

That's tough for Stars fans to swallow when you think that as an 18-year-old prospect Henrik Lundqvist wanted to be drafted by the Stars. After Joel was taken in the third round, Henrik sat and waited. Twenty-one goalies had already been picked at that time, but he was hopeful the Stars would pick him in the sixth round with the 192nd selection. "I mean, all my buddies had been taken and were kind of looking at me. We were all sitting in the same row. Nobody knew exactly how to act or what to say. It was kind of like, 'Come on, Hank.' It was not a great feeling," Henrik Lundqvist told the *New York Post* in 2014. "Then, after the fifth

The Dallas Stars' 2000 Draft

Steve Ott—first round, 25th overall—Played nine seasons for the Stars and became a fan favorite as an antagonist. In 566 games, he had 220 points and 1,170 penalty minutes.

Dan Ellis—second round, 60th overall—Only appeared in 15 games for Dallas, starting 11 and had a 6–6–0 record. A career NHL backup goalie who had his best moments in Nashville.

Joel Lundqvist—third round, 68th overall—Spent three seasons with the Stars and had 26 points in 134 games.

Alexei Tereshchenko—third round, 91st overall—Never left Russia. He was still playing for Moscow Dynamo in the KHL during the 2017–18 season.

Vadim Khomistky—fourth round, 123rd overall—Khomistiky did play 16 games in the AHL with the Iowa Stars but quickly returned to Russia and like Tereshchenko, he was still playing in the KHL during the 2017–18 season.

Ruslan Bernikov—fifth round, 139th overall—Another Russian who never came to North American, he retired in 2011 after playing for Torpedo Nizhny Novgorod.

Artyom Chernov—fifth round, 162nd overall—The theme continues with Dallas drafting another Russian, and another one that never stepped foot in Texas.

Ladislav Vlcek—sixth round, 192nd overall—A Czech this time, but another player that never left his home country. Vleck retired in 2011 after playing one game with Kladno in the Czech league.

Marco Tuokko—seventh round, 219th overall—Had a lengthy career in Finland and retired in 2014.

Antti Miettinen—seventh round, 224th overall—The second most successful pick for Dallas in this draft. Miettinen played for Dallas from 2003 to 2008 and ended up with 539 career NHL games.

round, someone from Dallas said since they'd taken my brother, they were going to take me in the sixth round."

So when they were about to announce the Stars pick, Henrik was ready. "I was really excited," he said. "I starting moving up to the edge of my seat, thinking I would hear my name. I remember hearing, 'Dallas selects…'"

Ladislav Vlcek.

"It seemed like such a long time before they said his name," Henrik said. "I didn't know what to do."

Eventually, the Rangers ended Henrik Lundqvist's misery and picked him in the seventh round with the 205th pick.

Six years later the Lundqvist brothers became the third set of twins to play against each other in an NHL game on December 14, 2006. The Rangers and Henrik won the game 5–2 as he made 43 saves and Joel was held without a shot. "He was lucky," Joel Lundqvist said after that game. "But he had a really good game. So I'm happy for him, but it was too bad for our team today."

And Ladislav Vlcek, the player Dallas drafted instead of Henrik Lundqvist, never left the Czech Republic.

90 Visit the Hockey Hall of Fame

The Hockey Hall of Fame is a must-see for any hockey fan, and for a Dallas Stars fan making the trip to Toronto, here is a quick checklist for a complete trip:

- Visit the builders section. John Mariucci, Walter Bush, and Herb Brooks were all inducted as builders. All three played a key role in Minnesota North Stars history, and without their contributions, the North Stars may not have ever survived long enough to make it to Dallas.

- Find the 12 North Stars and Stars players. As of this writing, a dozen players have reached the Hockey Hall of Fame after playing with the franchise at some point in their career. They include Harry Howell (class of 1979), Gump Worsley (1980), Leo Boivin (1986), Mike Gartner (2001), Larry Murphy (2004), Brett Hull (2009), Dino Ciccarelli (2010), Ed Belfour (2011), Joe Nieuwendyk (2011), Mike Modano (2014), Eric Lindros (2016), and Sergei Makarov (2016).

- Find the Stanley Cup and figure out which one it is. Little known fact, there are actually *three* Stanley Cups. There is the presentation cup, presented to the winner each year; the original 1892 bowl, which was retired in 1970; and the replica cup that was made in 1993 as a stand in for when the presentation cup isn't in the Hockey Hall of Fame. You can tell which cup it is by looking at the 1984 Edmonton Oilers. On that entry Basil Pocklington's name is covered with x's on the presentation cup, while it's completely missing from the replica.

- Find the Selke Trophy. As far as individual trophies go, this one has the greatest connection to Dallas. Jere Lehtinen won it three times, while two other Stars (Bob Gainey and Guy Carbonneau) each won it before their time in Texas.

91 Jordie Benn

Jordie Benn didn't make the NHL because of his younger brother. That's a common misconception and a false narrative that was often thrown around during his six seasons with the Stars. And it's a narrative that unfortunately detracts from the incredible path the defenseman took to an NHL career.

Benn wasn't drafted after a successful Junior A career in the British Columbia Hockey League and he signed an ECHL contract with the Victoria Salmon Kings during the 2008–09 season. After one season in Victoria, Benn signed with the Central Hockey League's Allen Americans for the 2009–10 season. In his one season in the CHL—a league that later merged with the ECHL—Benn had 18 points in 45 regular season games. He was a defensive stabilizer on a team that reached the Ray Miron President's Cup Finals.

The next season Benn signed an AHL contract with the Texas Stars. He appeared in 62 AHL games that season, and on July 2, 2011, he signed a one-year, two-way contract with Dallas. Over the next two seasons, Benn split time between the NHL and AHL, eventually securing a full-time role with Dallas during the 2013–14 season. By reaching the NHL, Benn and his brother joined a group of 47 siblings to play on the same team in NHL history.

During his time in Dallas, Benn played a reliable and simple defensive game while his younger brother was more of a goal scorer and point producer. Benn could have left in free agency after the 2015–16 season but opted to sign a three-year contract with Dallas that would keep him and his brother on the same team through at least the end of the 2018–19 season.

But the family connection was split up when the Stars traded Jordie Benn to the Montreal Canadiens for Greg Pateryn and a fourth-round draft pick on February 27, 2017. It was a move that Stars general manager Jim Nill said he had to make to prevent losing Benn in the upcoming expansion draft.

Benn was with his brother at the time of the trade, as they were roommates. "I think [my brother] was more shocked than I was," Jordie Benn said. "He was just like, 'Well, let's start packing up; let's get ready.' I think I was packed and out of the house in an hour. It was a quick turnaround, and now I'm [with the Canadiens]."

"It was pretty hectic. He was out of here pretty quick," Benn's younger brother said. "He was just packing his bag and receiving phone calls. I just wished him good luck and was kind of joking around with him. I think we play them in a month, so I told him I'll see him at center ice when the puck drops."

While it was a shocking trade, the Benn brothers had their share of memories from five seasons together in Texas. The highlight likely came on a short-handed goal against the Ottawa Senators on November 24, 2015.

While killing a penalty Jordie picked up the puck in his own zone and saw his brother streaking down the ice. Jordie made a picturesque looping pass to his brother, who finished off a breakaway with a forehand to backhand move. It was, as Stars color commentator Daryl Reaugh put it so eloquently, "Double Bennetration."

"It was fun while it lasted. Over a span of four or five years here, it was great," the younger Benn said.

Even after he was traded, Jordie Benn was part of Stars lore. When the Montreal Canadiens and Dallas Stars were both trying to sign free agent forward Alexander Radulov, the Benn brothers posted a picture of themselves playing bubble hockey in their respective jerseys. If you believe the tweet, the winner of that bubble hockey game would soon have the Russian forward as a teammate.

Oh, and if you were wondering, Jordie's younger brother is named is Jamie.

92 15 Goals in One Game

The Winnipeg Jets had been the class of the World Hockey Association. In the seven-year existence of the WHA, the Jets won three Avco Cups, including back-to-back championships, before the NHL-WHA merger at the start of the 1978–79 season.

The merger essentially saved top-level hockey in four markets that joined the NHL (Winnipeg, Quebec City, Hartford, and Edmonton), but also laid the groundwork for the highest-scoring game in North Stars history.

Current owners didn't want the four new teams to succeed when they entered the NHL. The WHA had aggressively recruited NHL players to the upstart league in 1971, including Bobby Hull. In exhibition competitions the WHA teams actually had a 34–22–7 record against NHL clubs.

So if those WHA teams were going to enter the NHL, they were going to struggle on the ice and arrive in form of expansion rather than a true merger. It was one of the more confusing expansion drafts in NHL history. Each NHL team could reclaim the WHA players they held rights to prior, while the incoming teams could protect up to four players (two skaters, two goalies) that would count as their priority selections. After that, current NHL teams could protect 15 skaters and two goalies in the expansion draft.

That didn't leave a very desirable crop of players. The incoming teams were essentially picking fourth liners in the expansion draft, and in the upcoming entry draft, the four former WHA teams were placed at the end of the draft order. Somehow the Edmonton Oilers were able to hold onto Wayne Gretzky in the merger thanks to his personal services contract to Peter Pocklington, but that's a story for another book.

The Jets were among the hardest hit teams by the expansion process. After winning back-to-back WHA titles, the Jets posted a 20–49–11 record in their first NHL season. The following season was even worse, and Winnipeg failed to win 10 games during a 9–57–14 showing during 1980–81 season.

It was a rough start for Winnipeg, but the North Stars dealt them a new low early in the 1981–82 season when Minnesota ran away with a 15–2 victory at the Met Center on November 11, 1982.

It wasn't a blowout from the start. The North Stars only led 2–1 after the first period. "I told my team after one period, 'Let's take the game over,'" North Stars coach Glen Sonmor said after the game. "I guess we did."

In the second period, the North Stars scored eight goals on 27 shots. They then added five more goals for good measure in the third period. "Collectively, we were bad, very bad defensively," Jets coach Tom Watt said after the game.

Bobby Smith had four goals and three assists for Minnesota, which fired 51 shots at Jets goalie Doug Soetaert. In an interesting twist, Soetaert's son, Dennis Soetaert, is now the assistant equipment manager for the Dallas Stars.

The 15 goals are still a franchise record for the Stars and one short of the NHL record after the Montreal Canadiens scored 16 goals in a 16–3 victory against the Quebec Bulldogs on March 3, 1920.

The 2016 Hall of Fame Class

There are six Dallas Stars enshrined in the Hockey Hall of Fame in Toronto. Four of them are fairly obvious. Most fans would likely guess that Brett Hull, Ed Belfour, Joe Nieuwendyk, and Mike Modano are on that list.

The other two might surprise you. Not that they're in the Hall of Fame, but it's easy to gloss over the fact that they ever played for the Stars.

Sergei Makarov and Eric Lindros.

Both players had short-lived stints in Dallas and the Stars ended up being their final NHL team. Interestingly enough, both players were inducted into the Hall of Fame in the same class in 2016. Makarov was a staple on Soviet Union's famed national team, the Red Army, and won eight IIHF World Championships and two Olympic gold medals between 1978 and 1990. He was also an 11-time champion with CSKA Moscow in the Soviet league and was part of the famed KLM Line with Igor Larionov and Vladimir Krutov.

In 2008, Makarov was named to the IIHF Centennial Team, which was voted on by a panel of 56 experts and compiled by *The Hockey News*. Makarov was called one of the greatest international players in hockey history.

Eventually Makarov moved to the NHL as Soviet-North American relations improved in the late 1980s. He joined the Calgary Flames for the 1989–90 season and as a 31-year-old "rookie" he won the Calder Memorial Trophy after scoring 86 points (24 goals and 62 assists) in 80 games.

His performance led to the creation of the "Makarov Rule" that states a player must now be under 26 to be considered for Rookie of the Year honors. Had that rule been in place at the time, Mike Modano—who had 75 points that season—would have likely been the NHL's Calder Memorial Trophy winner in 1990.

Makarov spent four seasons with Calgary and was considered one of the pioneers of possessional hockey. While the NHL was still very much a dump-and-chase league at that time, Makarov never abandoned his Red Army mind-set and would carry the puck into the offensive zone. He was built like a tank, and it was nearly impossible to take the puck off his stick.

Makarov then spent two seasons with the San Jose Sharks before spending the 1995–96 season as an assistant coach with the Russian national team.

Before the 1996–97 season Makarov, then 38, joined the Stars and it didn't go well. He only played four games with Dallas and he clashed with Stars coach Ken Hitchcock. In 2010, Makarov told the Russian newspaper *Sport Express* that he was amused when Hitchcock started drawing diagrams and showing him how to find open space on the ice.

The relationship eventually reached an impasse, and Makarov claimed that Hitchcock complained to Stars general manager Bob Gainey that younger players were paying attention to the Russian and not the head coach. While that may be true, Makarov also didn't have much of an impact in his four games with Dallas.

A decade later Lindros finished his career in Dallas with slightly more success than Makarov. Unfortunately, Lindros was a shell of his former self.

When fully healthy, Lindros was one of the most dominant players in NHL history with the Philadelphia Flyers. He could shoot, skate, and score like a smaller player, while his size at six foot four and close to 250 pounds turned him into a physical force.

One way or another Lindros was going to impact a game, and if he didn't score an opponent was physically going to be battered by the centerpiece of the feared "Legion of Doom" line with John LeClair and Mikael Renberg.

But Lindros was never the same after he was caught with his head down at the blue line and leveled by New Jersey Devils defenseman Scott Stevens in the 2000 Eastern Conference Finals. The hit—which was clean by NHL standards at the time—added to Lindros' long line of concussions and ended his tenure in Philadelphia. After stints with the New York Rangers and Toronto Maple Leafs, he joined the Stars before the 2006–07 season and had 26 points in 49 regular season games.

Lindros was a timid player during his time in Dallas; he shied away from contact and he didn't enjoy himself. He told *Sports Illustrated* in a 2017 interview that he would often spend practices looking up at the clock, just hoping it would move faster.

His career ultimately came to an end with a Game 7 loss to the Vancouver Canucks in the first round. It was a conflicting time for Lindros, who wanted the season to keep going for his teammates, but he just wanted his career to come to a close. "I couldn't believe it came to that," Lindros told *Sports Illustrated*. "I knew it was my last game. I wasn't having fun."

And that's how a second Hall of Fame career officially came to an end in Dallas. It was an unfortunate career ending for a player that deserved better. Today Lindros has dedicated himself to raising concussion awareness and protecting future players.

94 Guy Lafleur Was a North Star?

Guy Lafleur is considered one of the greatest players in NHL history. "The Flower" was named one of the NHL's greatest players during the Centennial Season with 560 goals and 793 assists in 1,126 NHL games, most of them with the Montreal Canadiens.

So it might surprise you to find out that Lafleur was actually a member of the North Stars for a day in 1991, three years after he had been elected to the Hockey Hall of Fame. It's a weird set of circumstances that includes an NHL legend coming out of retirement, an expansion draft, and two franchises unmerging.

Our story starts in 1990. Owners George and Gordon Gund had hoped to move the North Stars to the San Francisco Bay Area. The NHL and the other owners denied the request. Moving a franchise wouldn't create any new revenue for the rest of the owners. They were interested in an expansion team that would come with a somewhat lucrative expansion fee.

So the NHL worked out a deal and granted the Gunds an expansion franchise in San Jose. In return they had to sell the North Stars to a league-approved owner. One of the conditions of the deal was that the Sharks would get to draft players from the North Stars organization, and then both teams would take part in a so-called expansion draft.

Essentially it was an unmerging of two franchises. In 1978, the Gunds had merged the struggling Cleveland Barons—previously the California Golden Seals—with the North Stars and combined the rosters of the two franchises. Thirteen years later, when the Sharks entered the league, they were entitled to half the North Stars roster in an unmerging process that was called the dispersal draft.

In the dispersal draft, the North Stars got to protect 14 players and two goalies, while San Jose picked 14 players and two goalies of the remaining pool of players. Still with me? Good. Because we're entering the confusing part.

The North Stars and Sharks then each took part in an expansion draft and selected 10 players to fill out the remainder of their rosters. With the final pick of the draft, the North Stars selected Lafleur from the Quebec Nordiques.

Lafleur had originally retired from the NHL in 1985 and was inducted into the Hockey Hall of Fame in 1988. But he made a comeback after his induction and played three more NHL seasons, including the final two with the Nordiques. Lafleur had made it clear he was going to retire. He had reportedly turned down a contract offer from the Los Angeles Kings after the 1990–91 season and he was planning on taking a front office job in Quebec at the start of the 1991–92 season.

With full knowledge of the situation the North Stars still picked Lafleur in the expansion draft, holding a slim hope that he would potentially reconsider retirement and play in Minnesota. While Lafleur remained retired, the Stars actually had to trade the Hall of Famer back to Quebec.

Since his retirement papers hadn't been filed at the time of the expansion draft, the NHL's anti-tampering laws prevented Lafleur from taking a job with a team that didn't own his playing rights. To fix the snafu, the North Stars and Nordiques worked out a trade. Lafleur's rights were sent back to Quebec, allowing him to start his front office job, while Minnesota received the rights to Alan Haworth, who had already decided to finish his career in Europe.

The trade happened May 31, 1991, one day after the expansion draft, meaning the Hall of Famer was technically part of Stars history for a day.

95 Modano in Detroit

Mike Modano's final game in Dallas didn't come as a member of the Stars. After the 2009–10 season, the Stars elected not to offer Modano, then 40, another contract ending a 20-year year run with the franchise.

That summer Mondano had a couple options. He considered retirement, he considered signing with the Minnesota Wild, and ultimately he signed a one-year contract with the Detroit Red Wings.

It was a bit of a homecoming for Modano, who grew up in Livonia, Michigan. But it also created some weird optics. Modano wearing red and white was an oddity after two decades in green, and his signature No. 9 was already hanging in the rafters in Detroit. (It belonged to some guy named Gordie Howe.)

It was even weirder when Modano returned to Dallas on October 14, 2010 to play against the Stars. Modano played a limited role in that contest as the Stars won 4–1. He had 20 shifts against his former team for a little more than 15 minutes of ice time, but didn't have a shot on net.

Modano was honored with a standing ovation from the fans during the first intermission, a reception he wasn't expecting after a messy split with the franchise four months earlier. After signing with Detroit, Modano had said that his then-wife Willa Ford really wanted him to sign with the Red Wings as way to stick it to the Stars. With that in the back of his mind, Modano wouldn't have been surprised by a somewhat icy reception.

In the end Modano's season in Detroit turned into a minor footnote in a 21-season career. He only played 40 games that season and had just 15 points. He missed most of the season with a lacerated wrist after he was cut by Columbus Blue Jackets forward R.J. Umberger in a freak accident.

By the end of the season, Modano was a depth forward for Detroit and he only appeared in two playoff games as he officially played his final NHL game on May 10, 2011 in Game 6 of a second round playoff series against the San Jose Sharks.

96 Jagr Comes to Dallas

Jaromir Jagr has had one of the most remarkable careers in NHL history. Simply being the NHL's second all-time leading scorer with 1,921 points at the time of this book would be enough.

Winning the Art Ross Trophy five times, the Hart Memorial Trophy in 1998–99, the Lester B. Pearson Trophy (now the Ted Lindsay Award) three times, a pair of Stanley Cups, and an Olympic gold medal only add to his legacy. On top of all that, Jagr somehow defeated aging in his NHL career.

During the 2016–17 season Jagr signed with the Calgary Flames, his ninth NHL team, and competed in his 24th NHL season as a 46-year-old. He'd have played 28 NHL seasons, but he spent three seasons in the KHL and the NHL lockout cancelled the entire 2004–05 season.

Jagr was a star for most of his career and for half of a season he was a member of the Dallas Stars. At the spry age of 40, Jagr was still one of bigger commodities in free agency in 2012. After mulling over offers from several teams, Jagr ultimately signed with Dallas on a one-year, $4.55 million contract. "Jaromir Jagr is, without a doubt, one of the best players in the history of this league and he demonstrated last season that he remains incredibly skilled,

The Dallas Stars have had a number of legendary players on the team—even if just for brief spells—like Jaromir Jagr, who played with the team for half a season.

productive, and valuable," Stars general manager Joe Nieuwendyk said at the time. "We see him fitting into our top two lines and contributing heavily to our offensive attack. We're very excited about adding a player of Jaromir's caliber to our club."

Unfortunately Jagr's time in Dallas was short. Another NHL lockout knocked out the first three months of the season, cutting an 82-game schedule to 48 games, and teams only played within their conference.

Once the season started on January 19, 2013, the Dallas Stars weren't very good. Dallas would finish that season with a 22–22–4 record, and the Stars were sellers by the modified trade deadline. At the deadline they traded Jagr to the Boston Bruins for a conditional second-round pick (left winger Lane MacDermid) and center prospect Cody Payne.

The second-round pick became a first-round pick when the Bruins reached the Stanley Cup Finals that year, and the Stars used that selection on Jason Dickinson.

While it was short-lived, Jagr made an impact in his time in Dallas. He had 26 points and 14 goals in 34 games with the Stars, which was second-most on the team behind Jamie Benn at the time of the trade.

During his time with the Stars, Jagr recorded his 1,000th career assist on March 29, 2013, against the Minnesota Wild, getting the secondary assist on a 5-on-3 power play tally by Benn and becoming the 12th player in NHL history to reach that mark.

Jagr's career started three years before the Stars moved to Dallas, so he never expected to get that milestone marker in Texas. "When I started, I didn't think about it because Dallas wasn't in the league," Jagr said at the time. "I never thought about any assists and points; I was happy to be able to play here [in the NHL early on]. When I came here, I didn't think I'd have a chance to play here. The league was too strong and too tough for me."

97 The Idaho Steelheads

Do you know which professional hockey team has the longest playoff streak in North America? For a while it was an easy answer. The Detroit Red Wings reached the playoffs for 25 straight seasons, and that was a big point of pride for the franchise before they finally fell short during the 2016–17 season.

And with that shortcoming, the Idaho Steelheads took over the title as the professional hockey's most frequent playoff contributor. The 2018 Playoffs were the 21st straight appearance for the Steelheads, and they've yet to miss the postseason in franchise history.

For most of their history, the Steelheads have worked hand-in-hand with the Dallas Stars. Dallas first affiliated with Idaho during the 2003–04 season, and they have been linked together every season since the 2005–06 campaign. There would have been an affiliation during the 2004–05 season, but the NHL season was ultimately cancelled by a work stoppage.

Overall it's the ECHL's third-oldest affiliation. The Wheeling Nailers (Pittsburgh Penguins) and South Carolina Stingrays (Washington Capitals) have been affiliated with their NHL parent clubs since the 1998–99 season.

While there are other ECHL franchises closer to Dallas—including one in the greater DFW area—the Steelheads' history of success has formed a strong bond between the organizations. "We do our best to develop and uphold our end of that relationship, and they do a fantastic job as well," Steelheads coach and general manager Neil Graham said. "It's important to develop talent and know guys are progressing, but they also know there's a level of winning tradition here in Idaho. And they've played a big part in helping us continue that."

There are a couple key facets to that relationship. Each year the Stars have the Steelheads head coach attend prospect development camp, the prospects tournament in Traverse City, and Texas Stars training camp. That way Graham and his staff are well versed in proper terminology, and so prospects playing in the ECHL are playing a similar system to NHL and AHL clubs.

The Stars have also made Graham's life easier as a general manager. Throughout the history of the partnership, Texas Stars general manager Scott White has gone out of his way to sign AHL two-way contracts with players that would be valuable additions in Idaho.

On top of that, the Steelheads coaches are always keeping the Stars management staff in the loop and they have constant communication. "It's been outstanding," Graham said. "Dallas treats us very well. The communication is always forthcoming; there is as much heads up as you can. When you're in a developmental system, there is going to be some quick turnarounds. But since the communication is so strong between Dallas, Texas, and us, [it] makes those last-minute things that much easier."

So if you're looking for a weekend getaway centered around hockey, you should take a trip to Boise and watch the Steelheads. Your trip starts with a stay at the Grove Hotel, which is actually connected to CenturyLink Arena and has suites and meeting rooms overlooking the ice. "You can take the elevator from your hotel room right down to the concourse, I think they kind of set you up for a great hockey weekend," Graham said. "There are lots of restaurants and pubs near the downtown area within walking distance, and if you get out and talk to the people, you can just hear how much they love hockey."

While hockey would be your focus, there are several secondary activities to fill the day while waiting for an evening puck drop.

Craft breweries and wineries are common in Boise, while outdoor recreational activities are available year round, including hiking, fishing, mountain biking, and whitewater rafting. "What better way to spend a hockey weekend," Graham said. "Get outdoors, enjoy nature while rafting or biking, and then come inside for a great hockey atmosphere."

98 North Stars End Flyers Streak

For three months during the 1979–80 season, the Philadelphia Flyers were unbeatable. Starting with a 4–3 win against the Toronto Maple Leafs on October 14, 1979, the Flyers pieced together one of the most impressive streaks in NHL history and went 35 straight games—almost half a season—without a loss.

That streak finally came to an end at the hands of the Minnesota North Stars in early 1980.

It was January 7, 1980 when the Flyers visited the North Stars, and with a chance to beat a team that was 25–0–10 in its last 35 games, the atmosphere was electric. "I remember playing in playoff games there at the Met that didn't have the atmosphere that game had," Craig Hartsburg told the *Minneapolis Star Tribune*. "I think every player who played in that game will remember it."

A then-franchise record 15,962 fans filled the building and watched as Minnesota overcame an early goal and embarrassed Philadelphia with a 7–1 victory.

Mike Eaves, Greg Smith, and Steve Payne scored for Minnesota in the first period after an opening goal by Philadelphia's Bill Barber. Hartsburg and Mike Polich scored in a span of 21 seconds in the second period to make it 5–1, and Ron Zanussi and Bobby Smith added goals in the third period to complete the rally.

The game ended in typical Flyers fashion. This was the Broad Street Bullies era, and if they were going to finally lose a game, they weren't going home without a pound of flesh. As the game ended both benches cleared, and then North Stars Coach Glen Sonmor had to be restrained as he argued with a linesman. According to multiple accounts of the game, the crowd started chanting "Go Home Flyers, Go Home Flyers."

99 One-Game Wonders

Since 1967 more than 600 players have appeared in at least one game for the franchise. Much of this book has been spent discussing those players with lengthy careers in Dallas or those who have made a major impact on the history of franchise. But what about those players that only played in one NHL game with the Stars? What's their story?

Heading into the 2018–19 season, 37 players have had one-game cameos with the Stars. Some still have a chance to play a second, while others have become all but lost in franchise history. Here are some of the more interesting one-game wonders in Stars history.

Ernest "Chuck" Arnasson
Arnasson played one game for the North Stars during the 1978–79 season. He also played 400 additional NHL games with the Colorado Rockies, Kansas City Scouts, Pittsburgh Penguins, Montreal Canadiens, Atlanta Flames, Cleveland Barons, and

Washington Capitals. In addition to the eight NHL teams he played for, Arnasson also skated for four minor league hockey teams, including the Dallas Blackhawks of the CHL. While Arnasson only played one game, he was involved in three trades featuring the franchise. On March 12, 1979, he was traded to Washington for future considerations. One month later he was traded back to the North Stars for cash, and later that summer Minnesota traded him to the Vancouver Canucks for more cash.

John Barrett

Barrett found the scoresheet in his only NHL game with the North Stars, which also happened to be the final game of his 488-game NHL career. Looking for defensive depth late in the 1987–88 season the North Stars acquired Barrett—who had missed most of the season with an injury—from the Capitals for cash considerations on February 22, 1988. One week later Barrett played in an 8–3 loss to the Penguins. Barrett had an assist on Dave Archibald's goal late in the second period. He was also minus-3 and took a cross-checking penalty in the third period. A couple months later Barrett formally retired from the NHL due to complications from repeated breaks in his kneecap.

Don Biggs

An eighth-round pick by the North Stars in 1983, Biggs was called up and played one game as a 19-year-old with Minnesota late in the 1984–85 season after finishing his junior career with the Oshawa Generals. Biggs was traded away the following season and later played 11 NHL games with the Philadelphia Flyers during the 1989–90 season. While Stars fans may not remember Biggs' NHL debut, they may have seen his work on the silver screen where Biggs skated as Patrick Swayze's body double in the 1986 movie *Youngblood*.

Robert Brown

Brown signed with the Dallas Stars as an organizational depth forward before the 1993–94 season. He started the season with Kalamazoo in the IHL and was called up for a game against the Detroit Red Wings on November 27, 1993. It didn't go well for Brown or the Stars: Dallas lost 10–4 that night. Brown ended up finishing his NHL career with 543 games split between five franchises.

Jay Caufield

Caufield had a similar one-game experience with the franchise to Brown. He was called up to Minnesota from Kalamazoo for a game in Detroit on March 3, 1988. It also didn't go well: the North Stars lost 6–3 that night. Caufield ended up playing 208 games in his NHL career—most of them with Pittsburgh—before finishing his career back in the Stars system with Kalamazoo during the 1993–94 season.

Jack Campbell

Of the Stars' one-and-done goalies, Campbell was the busiest in a 6–3 loss to the Anaheim Ducks on October 20, 2013. Campbell faced 47 shots in the loss and made 41 saves, the highest amount of any of the five goalies that appeared in just one NHL game for the Stars. Campbell, a once highly touted first-round pick, had an unceremonious end in Dallas and was traded to the Los Angeles Kings in 2016.

Mike Chernoff

Chernoff's lone NHL game came with the North Stars during their second season in the NHL. The left winger was a late season call up from the CHL's Memphis South Stars during the 1968–69 campaign. Chernoff never got another NHL opportunity, but he did play 39 games in the WHL for the Vancouver Blazers before retiring in 1975.

Colin Chisholm

Chisholm was recalled from the AHL's Springfield Indians and played for the North Stars in a 3–2 loss to the Calgary Flames on February 14, 1987. It was the only NHL game of his career. Chisholm was a third-round draft pick in 1981 by the Buffalo Sabres but never signed with Buffalo and played four years at the University of Alberta before signing with the North Stars. His hockey career came to an end in 1988 due to a medical condition.

Tom Colley

A fourth-round pick by Minnesota in 1973, Colley skated in his only NHL game during the 1974–75 season. He was minus-3 but did have one shot on net.

Kelly Fairchild

Fairchild's name could probably win you a bar bet among fellow Stars fans. There were 32 skaters who played for Dallas during their championship season. Can you name the one that only played in one game? Fairchild was signed as a minor league veteran and depth player before the 1998–99 season and skated in his only game with the Stars on March 17, 1999, a 2–1 overtime loss to the Washington Capitals.

Scott Glennie

Glennie goes down as one of the biggest draft busts in Stars history. He was the eighth overall pick in 2009 and was an offensive monster in the WHL with the Brandon Wheat Kings. He turned pro during the 2011–12 season with the AHL's Texas Stars. With Dallas out of the playoff picture, they called Glennie up for the final game of the NHL season on April 7, 2012. Glennie had 13 shifts and was called for holding in the second period—that was the extent of his NHL career.

Udo Kiessling

Kiessling's lone game with the North Stars was a historical one. It was his only North American professional game, and appearing in a 3–2 win against the St. Louis Blues on March 13, 1982, made him the first German-trained player to ever compete in the NHL. He returned to Germany soon after his NHL debut and was inducted into the International Ice Hockey Hall of Fame in 2000.

Steve Martinson

Martinson was known more for his fists than his skill and in 49 career NHL games he had 244 penalty minutes. So it shouldn't be a surprise that in his one game with the North Stars, on March 1, 1992, Martinson fought Toronto's Todd Gill in the third period. Martinson is still working in hockey in DFW as the head coach and general manager of the Allen Americans, where he has won four championships.

Jarrod Skalde

You can't blame Skalde if he's forgotten his one-game stint with the Dallas Stars on February 4, 1998 against the Philadelphia Flyers. Skalde was a career journeyman, and the 1997–98 season was filled with numerous team changes for the center. He started the season with the San Jose Sharks, was claimed on waivers by Chicago, and then re-claimed back a month later by San Jose. The Stars then claimed Skalde on waiver from San Jose, had him play one game, then waived him, where he was claimed again by Chicago. To complete a full circle, Skalde was claimed again by San Jose before the end of the season. That was five waiver claims in less than three months.

The rest of the one-and-dones:
Joseph Contini, Peter Douris, Ken Duggan, Denis Guryanov, Peter Hayek, Archie Henderson, Kevin Kaminski, Glenn Laird, Perttu Lindgren, Kim MacDougall, John Markell, Mark McNeill, Brendan Ranford, Scott Sandelin, Reid Simpson, Kirk Tomlinson, Sean Toomey, Patrick Traverse, Bob Whitlock, Mark Wotton, Steve Janaszek, Brent Krahn, Jean-Louis Levasseur, Jordan Willis.

100 The Mooterus

The Dallas Stars beat the Washington Capitals 4–2 on October 17, 2003. Philippe Boucher and Bill Guerin each scored in the third period to break a 2–2 tie, and Marty Turco made 23 saves as the Stars improved to 3–2 in the young season.

It was also the debut of the short-lived "Mooterus" as a new alternate jersey. It was a questionable design that may have forced some early anatomy lessons for younger Stars fans yet to take high school health classes.

For the first time, red was introduced into the team color scheme. It wasn't being used in any other marketing materials or further branding, but in this alternate jersey red sleeves were a focal point alongside green and gold.

That itself might have caused some blowback among jersey aficionados, but it was a minor talking point after the new alternate logo was unveiled. The new logo was a constellation of individual stars aligned into a shape of a bull. It was assumed that it was a similar shape to the constellation of Taurus, but the jersey product wasn't even close to the shape that astronomers observed in the heavens.

Instead the jersey more closely reflected high-school health class designs of the female reproductive system. Obviously that's not what the Stars organization had in mind when they first introduced the jersey to the world at the Texas State Fair the night before the game against the Capitals. "It's a fusion of Texas icons and the spirit of the Dallas Stars," said Stars team president Jim Lites when the jersey was released. "We wanted to pay tribute to the State of Texas now that we're starting our second decade here."

Even the players were grouped into promoting the uniform. "It's stylish," Turco was quoted as saying by the Stars website. "It has a great western feel to it, and I think when accompanied with the whole uniform and player it will look really good. It is one of a kind. I think this jersey will be a trendsetter."

Brenden Morrow was also quoted as saying the jersey would help attract new hockey fans, and Stars officials were hoping that it would help better brand the Stars as a state-wide team.

Instead the Mooterus became the butt of several jokes. Instead of becoming an iconic look—like the 1997 alternate that soon became the full-time uniform and became immortalized with a Stanley Cup championship—the Mooterus quickly became a 23-game footnote in Stars history.

The Stars wore the new uniform for 15 games during the 2003–04 season, which was actually enforced by an NHL rule stating teams had to wear a new jersey at least 15 times in its debut season.

The Mooterus survived the lockout and was in the rotation during the 2005–06 season but only made eight appearances and disappeared after an April 3, 2006, overtime loss to the San Jose Sharks. "Good riddance," Stars owner Tom Hicks joked around that time. "The funny thing is that you can't find anyone around here who will take credit for designing it. Nobody's left."

The Stars actually had a winning record in the jersey, going 13–7–3 during that 23-game streak. It was also a financial success; the team made more than $400,000 from jersey sales. But it wasn't enough to make up for the fashion choices, which simply tried to combine too many concepts into one. It was designed by an outside group and wasn't market tested well before being introduced.

Lites, who sang the jersey's praises at its introduction, actually distanced himself from the design. The design first came to fruition while he was working with the then-named Phoenix Coyotes. Since it was put out to pasture, the Mooterus has lived on in "worst of" lists. Whenever a media outlet is listing or ranking the worst jerseys in NHL history, the Mooterus often ends up near the top of the list.

Acknowledgments

I always loved to read.

In fact I "read" my first book before I even knew how to actually read. When I was a two-year-old, I started reciting the words to the first four or five pages of *The Polar Express* when my parents read it to me as a bedtime story.

I wasn't actually reading, I was simply memorizing phrases, but I still like to count that children's book by Chris Van Allsburg as the first book I ever read.

As I got older, I started devouring sports books. I had a light clipped to the head of my bed and after I went to bed each night I would wait for my parents to turn off the hallway light before I would flip the switch and read a couple chapters.

Reading turned into a passion for writing, and writing a book became a goal. It was a grandiose thought in my head—pulling a book off a shelf with my name on the binding—that somehow turned into a reality on March 9, 2017 when I got an email from Bill Ames at Triumph Books.

I was already well-versed on the current edition of the Dallas Stars. I'm entering my third full season covering the NHL team and I've covered hockey in Texas since 2012. But this was a chance to really dive into team history, to dig through the archives, dig up the tape from old games, sit down for hour-long interviews with Stars of the past, and just relive hockey history.

For a hockey nut, it was a dream come true, even if I grew up in New Jersey and actually rooted against the Stars as an 11-year-old kid during the 2000 Stanley Cup Finals.

I didn't know what I would uncover when I started working on this book. I had an idea of what it would look like, but many of the chapters in this book evolved after an interview or learning something new that simply had to be included.

That started with the first interview, where Craig Ludwig relived his time with the Stars and ended up picking up our bar tab (frankly, I couldn't keep up) after making it clear that there had to be a chapter about "The Tent."

Jim Lites and Les Jackson each sat down for more than an hour to relive their lengthy time with the franchise, while others, including Mike Modano, Shane Churla, Marty Turco, Jere Lehtinen, Jim Nill, Ken Hitchcock, Bob Gainey, and numerous others agreed to either in-person, phone, or email interviews for this project.

A special thanks to the fine people at Triumph, including Bill Ames for that initial email and my editor, Jeff Fedotin, who made sure this was a success.

To my parents, Dave and Pam Shapiro; thank you for reading to me right away. Thank you for taking the time each night to read me a book before bed as a small child, and thank you for helping drive my passion as a reader and a writer.

Most importantly, thank you to my wife Christina. Without you none of this would have been possible.

And to our first child…you were still six months from being born when I finished up the book. I hope you'll humor me and read your dad's book someday.

Sources

Publications:
Chicago Tribune
Dallas Morning News
New York Post
The Hockey News
Detroit Free Press
The Hockey Writers
ESPN
The Star Tribune
New York Times
Sports Illustrated
NHL.com
Washington Post
Wrong Side of the Red Line
Vice Sports
USA Today
Slate
Los Angeles Times
Dallas Observer
Defending Big D
The Guardian
In Goal Magazine
Post Media
ECHL.com
TheAHL.com
CBS Sports
The Province
Oak Cliff Advocate
SportsNet

Dallas Stars Media Guides
NHL Guide and Record Book
HockeyReference.com
Fort Worth Star-Telegram
Pittsburgh Post-Gazette

Books:
Life's a Joke by Jack Fertig
The Pictorial History of Hockey by Joseph Romain
Herb Brooks: The Inside Story of a Hockey Mastermind by John Gilbert
Frozen in Time: A Minnesota North Stars History by Adam Raider

Videos/movies:
Dallas Stars 1999 Stanley Cup Championship DVD
ESPN 30 for 30 Films: Big Shot
The Mighty Ducks
Behind the B, NESN